Working Together?

Grounded Perspectives on Interagency Collaboration

UNDERSTANDING EDUCATION AND POLICY
William T. Pink and George W. Noblit
Series editors

Working Together?

Grounded Perspectives on Interagency Collaboration

edited by

Amee Adkins
Illinois State University

Catherine Awsumb
University of Pittsburgh

George W. Noblit
University of North Carolina

Penny L. Richards
University of California-Santa Barbara

HAMPTON PRESS, INC.
CRESSKILL, NEW JERSEY

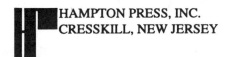

Printed in the United State of America

Library of Congress Cataloging-in-Publication Data

Working together : grounded perspectives on interagency collaboration
/ edited by Amee Adkins . . . [et al.].
    p. cm. -- (Understanding education and policy)
   Includes bibliographical references and index.
   ISBN 1-57273-104-4. -- ISBN 1-57273-105-2 (pbk.)
2. School children--Services for--United States. 3. Family
services--United States. 4. School social service--United States.
I. Adkins, Amee. II. Series.
HV41.W689   1998
362.7'0973--dc21   98-45950
                                                            CIP

Hampton Press, Inc.
23 Broadway
Cresskill, NJ 07626

Contents

Preface

This volume is appropriately the result of a form of interagency collaboration. In the Fall of 1992, the Division of Student Services and Development Services of the North Carolina Department of Public Instruction (NCDPI) began joint planning for the research that is reported herein in conjunction with a research team from the University of North Carolina at Chapel Hill. The goal was to produce information that would document the current state of interagency collaboration, client experiences with services, and best practices from existing collaborative initiatives.

The research itself would have been impossible without the concerted efforts of both the staff of NCDPI and the research team at UNC-CH. From the NCDPI offices we thank Dee Brewer, Ann Bryan, Carolyn Cobb, Jackie Colbert, Bobbye Draughon, Johnnie Grissom, Pat Hill, Henry Johnson, Olivia Oxendine, John Stokes, Suzanne Triplett, and Judy White. Marty Blank of the Institute of Educational Leadership in Washington, DC gave both encouragement and advice.

The UNC-CH research team spent weeks in the field and even more time analyzing data and writing. For their efforts we thank Jackie Blount, Laura Desimone, Wanda Hendrick, Kathy Hytten, Rhonda Baynes Jeffries, Deloris Jerman-Garrison, Brian McCadden, Jean Patterson, Maike Philipsen, and Sue Manley. Also, we wish to thank Dr. Richard C. Phillips for supporting us and helping us make this a priority.

We also acknowledge Julie Rheder and John Niblock of the North Carolina Child Advocacy Institute, as well as Fordham Britt, Joy Evans, Anne Fayers, and Betty Murphy for their efforts with the client narratives interviews. Sharon Marlowe did the subject index better than we ever could. We thank her for her diligence and unfailing good spirit. Finally, we would like to acknowledge the staff and boards of directors for the five collaboratives represented in the third part of this book: Caldwell County Communities in Schools, Cleveland County Communities in Schools, Cumberland County Coalition for Awareness, Resources and Education of Substances, UPLIFT, INC. in Guilford County, and the Wake County Children's Initiative.

Series Preface

Books in this series, Understanding Education and Policy, will present a variety of perspectives to better understand the aims, practices, content and contexts of schooling, and the meaning of these analyses for educational policy. Our primary intent is to redirect the language used, the voices included in the conversation, and the range of issues addressed in the current debate concerning schools and policy. In doing this, books in the series will explore the differential conceptions and experiences that surface when analysis includes racial, class, gender, ethnic and other key differences. Such a perspective will span the social sciences (anthropology, history, philosophy, psychology, sociology etc.), and research paradigms.

Books in the series will be grounded, in the contextualized lives of the major actors in school (Students, teachers, administrators, parents, policy makers etc.) and address major theoretical issues. The challenge to authors is to fully explore life-in-schools, through the multiple lenses of various actors and within the anticipated that such a range of empirically sound and theoretically challenging work will contribute to a fundamental and needed rethinking of the content, process and context for school reform.

The current structure of human services has been built piecemeal over the past 100 years. The result is that services are fragmented and the needs of clients are secondary to the bureaucratic imperatives of the existing services structures. As funding has decreased and calls for efficiency have increased, there have been myriad calls for more coordinated and integrated services. Interagency collaboration has been touted as a way to increase efficiency and effectiveness of services. Remarkably, however, there have been very few studies that have critically addressed these claims. *Working Together?* represents a new phase of research on human and educational services that critically examines the claims of promoters of interagency collaboration. This set of grounded studies is sobering in its critique but moves beyond critique to demonstrate the possibilities for interagency collaboration. It is an excellent example of how this book series can help alter our understanding of how best to serve children.

Authors

Amee Adkins, Illinois State University

Catherine Awsumb, University of Pittsburgh

George Noblit, University of North Carolina at Chapel Hill

Jean Patterson, University of North Carolina at Chapel Hill

* * * * *

Jackie Blount, Iowa State University

Dee Brewer, North Carolina Department of Public Instruction

Laura Desimone, American Institutes of Research

Wanda Hendrick, University of Texas-San Antonio

Kathy Hytten, Southern Illinois University

Rhonda Jeffries, University of South Carolina

Deloris Jerman-Garrison, University of North Carolina at Chapel Hill

Sue Manley, University of North Carolina at Chapel Hill

Brian McCadden, Rhode Island College

Mary Nix, State University College at Buffalo

Maike Philipsen, Virginia Commonwealth University

Penny Richards, University of California-Santa Barbara

1

Working Together?
An Introduction

George W. Noblit
Penny L. Richards
Amee Adkins

Our current system for delivering services to families and children grew in fits and starts over the last century. It is, of course, a misnomer to even refer to our services as a "system." Rather, we have a patchwork quilt of agencies, each created by separate legislation to meet a perceived need at a particular point in history. As successful as these agencies are in meeting their legislative mandates, it is now apparent that these agencies are unable to meet the needs of children and families today. At least part of the problem is that legislated agencies have matured into organizations with logics (patterns of thinking and ways of seeing) and constraints of their own that impede effective service delivery (Lipsky, 1980). Each defines the needs of clients in terms of the services the agencies are mandated to provide, rather than what the client requires to resolve effectively the problems being experienced.

One solution to this expensive dilemma is to promote interagency collaboration focused on the needs of the client. Interagency collaboration, however, if history is any witness, is difficult to achieve (Weiss, 1981). It clearly takes more than simple mandates and good will. It requires careful study of the nature of service delivery in various agencies and an appreciation of the difficulties, as well as possibilities, that interagency collaboration involves. It requires equally careful study and consideration of the different strengths and needs of individual communities as well as the individual clients the agencies are expected to serve. This book enables such a practical agenda, but with a twist. Instead of offering a series of "how-tos", our goal is to provide templates that allow people to compare their experiences and situations. The templates are both detailed case descriptions and summary lessons drawn from our research. Considering these allows people to develop a better understanding of their own situation and an appreciation of the problems and prospects of interagency collaboration. With such understanding and appreciation, it is possible to develop a strategy for interagency collaboration that is responsive to current realities and that transforms the patchwork quilt of services into an effective system.

Most qualitative research is intended to develop a "grounded theory" (Glaser & Strauss, 1967) that interprets and explains what is going on. Although our studies offer a number of grounded theories, they also reveal a gap between rhetoric promoting interagency collaboration and the realities of interagency collaboration in practice. This has prompted us to focus our writing less on theorizing and more on the practical lessons suggested by our studies. These conclude each part and the book itself, and may be read independently of the research that precedes. However, we would argue that the best understanding comes from reading both the cases and the lessons.

In qualitative research, generalizability is not posited by the researchers, but rather left to the reader (Patton, 1990). Readers may compare their experiences and situations with our accounts and decide what, if any, findings are applicable to them. In this book, we have taken the engagement of the reader seriously. The reader is invited to: (a) read and compare the cases with their experience, situation, and knowledge; (b) embark on similar qualitative studies to better understand their own situation; (c) use the part summaries and the final chapters to guide a careful deliberation of current efforts and plans; and (d) conclude which of the grounded perspectives are applicable to their own situations. We thus invite the reader to both generalize from our studies and to critique that which follows.

Six counties, 12 families, and 5 existing collaboratives in North Carolina were sufficiently gracious and courageous to allow teams of field researchers to study the current practice of interagency collaboration and to see what fostered collaboration and what got in its way. It took courage to open oneself and one's agency to detailed scrutiny, especially when the explicit goal was to reveal both exemplary practice and less than exemplary efforts to collaborate. As much courage as this took, it was in service of the larger goal of improving collaboration and services to children and families. The courage and grace of these counties must be kept in mind as we consider the lessons these counties taught us, for the news is not always good. What is good is the commitment of these professionals and counties to improve how children and families are served. This book is an attempt to weigh the masses of data we collected on: (a) current practices of collaboration and service delivery in counties reputed to have some collaborative mechanisms in place; (b) client experiences with agencies; and (c) existing successful collaboratives. Each of the three studies employed case study methods (Merriam,1988; Yin, 1989), providing a range of perspectives grounded in agency, client, and organizational experiences. As with all grounded studies, our results reveal a *multiperspectival reality* (Douglas, 1976; Patton, 1990). These perspectives taken together teach a number of lessons. We offer them as part of the ongoing debate on interagency collaboration. Our studies ask everyone to interrogate their current efforts and future plans with one goal: working together.

LEARNING THE LESSONS

The Divisions of Student Services and Development Services of the North Carolina Department of Public Instruction (NCDPI) initiated this study in the Fall of 1992 to discern what could be done to improve interagency collaboration by looking at current practice, client experiences, and successful collaboratives. The goal of the first study was simply to document current practice so as to know the "state of the art" of collaboration in North Carolina, in common parlance, "warts and all." Six counties that varied in income, region, and population density agreed to participate. In each of these counties, the researchers, doctoral students at the University of North Carolina at Chapel Hill, traced fictional cases, or case vignettes, from their point of entry in one agency through the full provision of services. Each case vignette was written as a composite of school-age children based on the experience of the educators who helped design the study. Further, each case vignette was written to prompt interagency involvement, and thus the researchers followed the case as it went through agencies and across agencies. There were six case vignettes, one each for county agencies of Social Services, Mental Health, Health, and Juvenile Services and two case vignettes for the schools (see Part 1, pp. 13-16). At each step, the researchers interviewed the professionals involved to determine how the case would be treated, why it would be treated in the way suggested, and where it likely would go from there. As a result, the researchers were able to discover when interagency collaboration was and was not taking place, and what seemed to facilitate and/or hinder it. The researchers spent 10 person days on site and then developed detailed reports of each county that serve as the database for part I of this book. The editors of this volume then revised the cases for this volume, editing for redundancy across case studies and distilling salient themes within them.

The second study focused on client experiences with services. Here our concern was to give voice to those being served by services in four of the six counties included in the first study. Given concerns with confidentiality, the women were selected and interviewed by local advocates of the North Carolina Child Advocacy Institute. We provided the training for the interviewers and transcribed the interviews, analyzed the data, and wrote the narratives presented in part II. By design, the clients varied in whether they were approaching self-sufficiency, maintaining themselves via services, or becoming increasingly dependent on services. By chance, they were all women.

The third study was of existing collaboratives. The focus here was on understanding what could be learned from their best efforts. The NCDPI selected five exemplary collaboratives for cases studies. Phone interviews and document review was followed by one day on site for each collaborative. The cases and their lessons are detailed in part III.

Part IV contains two chapters. Chapter 17 presents a summary list of lessons learned from all the studies taken together that point to how difficult collaboration is to achieve and the issues that need to be addressed in assessing current efforts and planning for future initiatives. The final chapter is an epilogue by Deloris Brewer of the NCDPI. It reveals what schools may do to promote collaboration with other public service agencies while waiting for larger legislative initiatives.

LEARNING FROM THE LITERATURE

The literature on collaboration prepared the research team to understand its research in several ways. Because interagency collaboration has many meanings in practice, interviewees were asked to define it for us, and the variety of responses mirrored the literature's wide range. Similarly, there is no agreed-on structure or process that marks collaboration, so the researchers were looking for any formal or informal arrangement or mechanism which seemed to bring together agency personnel in any way. When the county studies revealed great difficulty but continued interest in attaining or sustaining collaborative linkages, that claim was supported by researchers who have cautioned for decades that building collaboration is indeed difficult. Finally, that same lesson from the literature made successful arrangements more apparent as the remarkable achievements they are.

It is easy to become either outraged or demoralized when considering the state of services for children and families, yet it is also true that we know very little about how best to organize for interagency collaboration. What is heartening about the findings is that service providers are trying to figure out how to proceed most effectively. The fact that these efforts may not be all that one may wish is instructive. Clearly, collaboration is not easy to achieve in practice, regardless of the rhetoric in favor of it. We offer grounded perspectives so that policymakers and practitioners may better know the issues that need to be addressed, the practices that can be built upon, and the obstacles to be overcome as they proceed. It should be used as a basis for planning for the future, working together to better serve children and families.

The concept of interagency collaboration, under various names, has been around for some time, and this has generated a literature worthy of consideration. The literature is widely scattered across a range of fields and professions and often addresses the issues from the perspective associated with the author's particular field or profession. This is not to devalue the literature, but rather simply to put it in context. The review that follows is, as a result, selective, drawing on works that are relevant to these studies.

What is called *interagency collaboration* has a variety of names in the literature: agency cooperation, services integration, integrated services, interagency services, and so on. All are defined by the same components: a structure of linkages between agencies, processes of exchange and cooperation, and, as the intended results, improved efficiency and effectiveness to a given population. The precise nature and relative importance of these structures, processes, and results, however, vary from definition to definition: some emphasizing administrative linkages, others linkages among "front-line" providers; some exchanging through shared information systems, others through face-to-face meetings; some measuring success by the achievement of collaboration itself, others by the greater satisfaction of the clientele. In approaching the literature, therefore, definition is the first step.

Terminology has changed from the early 1970s to the present (earlier works, with some exceptions, were omitted from this review because they deal with agencies, technologies, and policies that are inconsistent with current conditions): *Integrated services/services integration* were the more prevalent terms in the 1970s, whereas *Interagency cooperation/collaboration* came to be favored in the 1980s and continue to dominate, although by no means consistently. The literature offers no distinction among the various terms, and in fact several writers comment on the overlapping vocabulary (Martin, Chakerian, Imershein, & Frumkin, 1983; Nordyke, 1982; Weiss, 1981). It appears that services integration is applied more to top-down government programs (especially through the former Department of Health, Education, and Welfare (HEW)), whereas interagency collaboration is attached to a wider variety of informal or localized efforts; however, this slight difference in emphasis is also an artifact of the political and economic climates in which the terms were coined (Agranoff, 1985).

STRUCTURES

Models of structures that characterize collaboration among agencies abound. Gans and Horton (1975) distill three general structures from their early study of 30 projects: *voluntary*, in which an agency itself seeks collaboration with others; *mediated*, in which a separate body is established to aid the development of collaborative efforts; and *directed*, in which that separate body has the authority to mandate linkages between agencies. Martin et al. (1983) instead worked from Heintz's (1976) one descriptive criterion (the line of administrative authority) to name four points on a spectrum: *fully integrated, consolidated, confederated,* and *independent.* In a more prescriptive vein, Leideman, Reveal, Rosewater, Stephens, and Wolf (1991) proposed a design for broad-scale reorientation of service systems in their document for the Pew Charitable Trusts. Edelman and Radin (1991) explored models of service planning and delivery from the past 30 years, including settlement houses, little city halls, and youth bureaus, to discover their adaptability to present needs.

Stepping down in scale, some authors instead write about specific elements of the overall collaboration structure: Lewis, Schwartz, and Ianacone (1988) surveyed educators and administrators to find that a liaison position between public schools and juvenile justice was desirable, but seldom created. Handicapped preschoolers are found to benefit from a centralized referral system (program coordinator) in the work of Lynch, Mercury, DiCola, and Widley (1988). HEW's Service Integration Targets of Opportunity (SITO) projects were studied by Mittenthal (1976) from a systems perspective, and they appear to be a potpourri of projects that most frequently feature a system agent (case manager, broker, advocate) and a data unit (to maintain client, resource, and management information).

Other work focuses on the effects of given collaborative structures. McNeely, Feyerherm, and Johnson (1986) investigated the drop in job satisfaction among human services workers through a restructuring and find that men become more depressed than women in such a shuffle, but satisfaction returns to and surpasses earlier levels as the new program matures over a few years. McGrath (1988) offered a Welsh case study in how collaborative projects may in fact produce structures that inhibit exchange and conflict resolution. Berliner (1979) describe the *structural obstacles* to collaboration between institution-based (hospital, prison, group home) services and community-based agency services. These articles serve as reminders that structures can impede as well as promote collaboration, and that structural changes can be traumatic indeed. Clearly, in 1975, whatever the scale, the variety of structures proposed or observed in the literature would seem to indicate that there is no one best services integration model.

PROCESSES

Advice for practitioners on steps toward attaining collaboration is abundant: Must-do lists, suggestions, calendars, warnings of common pitfalls, and smooth flow charts all but promise to bring an end to the "gaps and overlaps" that are assumed (in much of the collaboration literature) to be the obvious consequences of the more autonomous present arrangement. This advice falls into two categories. One is based on a specific experience, whereas the other is based on general study of the collaboration problem. The first category of process advice most often takes the form of the case study. Nordyke (1982), for example, referred to the case of an Oregon county's interagency task force for handicapped preschoolers to list the goals, activities, considerations, and problems of collaboration, and offered suggestions for initiating and maintaining an interagency group based on that county's experiences. Recent interagency initiatives in New Jersey are the basis of a particularly fine instance of this genre, such as Beatrice's (1990) "A Practitioner's Guide" to strategies at the state level. Others who analyzed case studies and drew similar conclusions (discussed later) include Daniels and Bosch (1978), Hooyman (1976), Iles and Auluck (1990), Roberts-DeGennaro (1988), and Vander-Schie, Wagenfeld, and Worgess (1987).

Other advice is offered on more general grounds, whether logical or theoretical. Guthrie and Guthrie (1991) provided an overview of the interagency issues, with several lists for practitioners: how-to steps, common pitfalls, necessary conditions, and so on. Four conditions and four preconditions are recommended by Wimpfheimer, Bloom, and Kramer (1990), including, for example, "everyone's a winner" in the first category and "creativity" in the second. An early and influential article by Benson (1975) also proposes four conditions necessary to establishing collaboration: domain consensus, ideological consensus, positive evaluation, and work coordination.

Although each of these lists and charts prescribe different steps and stages of approach to collaboration, they have many common elements. Most writers emphasize the importance of not being overambitious. Slow development that starts small is generally recognized as the route most likely to succeed. Along with this caution comes the admonition to plan, plan, plan. Front-end care is seen, in experience and conventional wisdom, as being preferable to having to redress avoidable problems later. Self-evaluation steps were frequently included throughout the process, as are group building, goal setting and resetting, and information sharing. Some described the process as a one-time series of changes, others as a continuous and dynamic effort against the natural tendencies of agencies and administrators to compartmentalize and stake claims. Much of the advice offered verges on common sense, but its various permutations indicate that no such list can be taken as sacred.

EVALUATION

A few reviewed articles, related to those just discussed, approached the problem of evaluating collaboration. Two extremes are exemplified in Flynn and Harbin (1987) and Flaherty, Barry, and Swift (1978). The first proposed a paradigm for evaluating collaboration on five dimensions (climate, resources, policies, people, and process) and at four stages (formation, conceptualization, development, and implementation), and described the use of this paradigm with implications for special education. The second listed the advantages and disadvantages of using existing records (phone logs, correspondence, minutes) to evaluate a collaboration project from the authors' experiment with the method in a small project's office. Both the ambitious, theoretical framework of the former and the concrete, methodological report of the latter may be useful to the practitioner or researcher seeking a way to study interagency collaboration at any scale. Only recently, however, has much thought been given to outcomes and how they might be assessed (Bruner, 1991).

OBJECTIVES

Perhaps surprisingly, few of the early authors who study collaboration write in a positive, complex way about the goals of interagency collaboration. As mentioned earlier, the vast majority of structure and process articles repeated the "gaps and overlaps" assumption about the current system's shortcomings, and followed this with a note that collaboration would clearly bring improved "effectiveness and efficiency," but these were rarely addressed directly in the early literature. More recently, Beatrice (1990) wrote a case study that addresses the objectives of interagency collaboration in more detail and originality than most, with a list of 12 reasons to try coordinating services. Among his reasons, "to avoid reinventing the wheel" (p. 50), "to get more and diverse input into program design and implementation" (p. 49), and to identify and solve problems in a program reflect on the experience (and apparent success) of the statewide cases he studied. Goldman (1982) based his expectations of collaboration between health and mental health services on a historical understanding of the circumstances of their separation, foreseeing benefits to patients (access to care), the public (efficient use of funds), and the mental health sector (access to health's ample funding).

On the other hand, there is a considerable literature that questions, in whole or in part, the idea of collaboration itself as a good, or achievable, goal. Weiss (1981) presented a devastating critique: first enumerating the conceptual, professional, bureaucratic, and political realities of interagency collaboration, revealing these to present significant obstacles to such reforms, then finding that there is little good evidence that collaboration is either more efficient or more effective than uncoordinated systems. Finally, Weiss accounted for the persistent efforts toward "coordination" as the result of the concept's broad symbolic, rather than substantial, appeal. Zald (1969) argued that the complexity of social services reflects layers of social and technological change, and is thus deeply rooted, presenting organizational, political, professional, and economic costs to would-be integration plans. Case researchers have also noted that collaboration is extremely difficult to achieve: The influential study by Gans and Horton (1975) lead them to conclude that "integration of services is not extensive even in the projects recommended as being successful projects" (p. 5).

RECENT REDIRECTIONS

In the late 1980s, the tenor of the literature on interagency collaboration begins to change. There is a renewed optimism about interagency collaboration. Schorr (1988) framed the issue as a redefinition of the capacity of public services: "doing good, not harm" (p. xxiv). Schorr also argued that breaking the cycle of disadvantage was "within our reach," and "that we know what needs to be done and how to do it" (p. xix). Her reviews of research led to a conclusion that has relevance to the research reported here:

> In short, programs that succeed in helping the children and families in the shadows are intensive, comprehensive, and flexible. They also share an extra dimension, more difficult to capture: Their climate is created by skilled, committed professionals who establish respectful and trusting relationships and respond to the individual needs of those they serve. The nature of their services, the terms on which they are offered, the relationships with families, the essence of the programs themselves—all take their shape from the needs of those they serve rather than from the precepts, demands, and boundaries set by professionalism and bureaucracies. (p. 259)

Her argument that we know enough to proceed effectively reflects a maturing of the research on human services and on interagency collaboration.

The recent literature also argues that the current plight of children and families is such that the system must be redesigned, and sufficient research exists for the design of successful collaborative systems. Melaville and Blank (1991) identified five factors that affect the implementation of interagency collaboration projects: climate at time of initiation, processes to create trust and manage conflict, the people included, policies that help or hinder, and availability of resources. Their research and the literature on effective collaborative efforts help them develop a series of implementation guidelines for practitioners: involving all key players, choosing a realistic strategy, establishing a shared vision, agreeing to disagree, making promises that you can keep, keeping your eye on the goal, building ownership at all levels, avoiding "red herrings," institutionalizing change, and publicizing your success. Bruner (1991) tried to foster conceptual clarity regarding interagency collaboration by defining collaboration, discussing state roles and strategies, the role of the private sector, possible negative consequences of collaboration, and how collaboration may help to improve child outcomes. Edelman and Radin (1991) directly discussed the changes in view of collaboration since the 1960s. They argued that most collaborative initiatives failed because of inadequate funding and shifting priorities, not because of any internal problem with the idea. They also reviewed what has been learned about interagency collaboration and offered a perspective for the 1990s. They argued for the importance of modesty and humility, awareness of limited resources, the need for diversity and collaboration, the limiting effects of complexity, and the need to build synergy. With such a view, they signaled a more historically informed optimism for interagency collaboration.

Melaville and Blank (1993) observed a growing momentum for interagency collaboration and have created a guidebook to help communities develop a plan that will work for a given locality. They proposed a five-stage process and offered suggestions for getting together, building trust and ownership, developing a strategic plan, taking action, and implementing strategies reflecting profamily principles. Each stage of the process is broken down into milestones that allow local communities to locate and track their development.

LESSONS FOR PRACTICE

The literature, as a whole, expresses four guiding lessons about interagency collaboration. First, collaboration is difficult to accomplish. Successful collaboration demands careful planning at the outset and constant tending as new issues, goals, and questions arise; it cannot be simply jump started and then left to maintain itself. Second, the literature cautions there is no one best way to accomplish interagency collaboration. Circumstances, resources, and objectives specific to individual attempts must be taken into account in any project design. Third, the literature on collaboration is now sufficient to proceed, yet there remains much to learn from practical attempts. New knowledge will be needed as interagency collaboration proceeds. Fourth, the inconsistency with which "collaboration" is defined is an issue in any effort to organize for increased interagency collaboration. Collaborators should seek a shared understanding and clarity in their terms, objectives, and means. Each of these four practical lessons were encountered during the course of the field research and analysis. That is, the six counties, 12 families and five existing collaboratives offered evidence that to neglect these four aspects poses serious threats to attempts to implement interagency collaboration.

PART I
Mapping Current Practice:
Case Studies of Service
Delivery

George W. Noblit

The case studies in part I present the current practice of interagency collaboration among human services agencies in six counties in North Carolina. They are the result of a systematic study of how a range of public agencies work together in serving families and children. These counties were selected because they were reputed to have some level of collaboration already in existence; the mixed accomplishments in each county thus represent a challenge to anyone seriously interested in interagency collaboration. The scope of this challenge is revealed in the case studies that follow. The following questions guided the case studies: Do agencies that serve the same children and families work together or in isolation? How similar are their mandates and philosophies? How do various rules, regulations, and working practices help or hinder these agencies in jointly meeting the needs of their clients?

CASE STUDIES OF CURRENT PRACTICE

The six case studies that follow present a detailed description of interagency collaboration and its limits as experienced in six North Carolina counties. The data was collected in a single week in January 1993 by tracking the same six

11

fictional case vignettes of multiple-needs children through the public agencies of each of the six counties. In order to document the many patterns of interaction that make up interagency collaboration, the case vignettes specified different points of entry into the social services system: two began in the schools and one each began in the county agencies of social services, mental health, health, and juvenile services.

The case studies lay the groundwork for the rest of the book in two ways. First, they enable people interested in fostering interagency collaboration to begin from practice rather than theory. The actual conditions for collaboration described in the case studies can feed policy decisions and collaborative initiatives. Second, they reveal specific enablers and barriers to increased interagency collaboration that may need to be addressed. The study was designed to capture a realistic picture of collaboration as it actually exists. By tracking these cases through the system the researchers were able not only to describe what would happen to each hypothetical client, but also to identify more generally what opportunities there are for interagency collaboration and what factors make it easier or harder for agencies to work together on each of the cases. It should be noted, however, that in dealing with hypothetical cases interviewees are likely to present a "best-case scenario" of how the case would be handled in their county. The current extent of interagency collaboration may therefore be overstated in the case studies.

DEFINING COLLABORATION

Because the purpose of the case studies in part I was to describe the actual practice of collaboration rather than to impose a theoretical framework, collaboration was defined very loosely at the outset. Indeed, one of the research tasks was to discover how practitioners defined collaboration. The collaborative practices described range from informal phone calls between acquaintances at different agencies to highly structured interagency task forces. Collaboration is any mechanism, no matter how casual, through which personnel from different agencies work together to address the needs of at-risk children and their families. Efforts to encourage increased interagency collaboration must take into account this wide range of practices.

DESCRIBING THE DIVERSITY OF THE STATE

The six counties studied were selected by NCDPI to accommodate the diversity of North Carolina. They vary with regard to size, geography, urbanization, racial mix, and economic resources. Although these six counties cannot be said to represent the entire state in the sense of scientific sampling, they do present a good cross section of the conditions that exist for interagency collaboration across the state. The wide range of issues these counties faced in handling the same fictional clients indicates that a "cookie-cutter" approach to increasing collaboration will not work as well as one that builds on the specifics of circumstances and resources in particular locations.

In order to provide a rich, multidimensional description of current collaborative practice, the study was limited to these six counties and to the five agencies that served as points of entry (POEs) for the fictional client cases. Information falling outside of this scope was not pursued. Within that defined focus, the researchers attempted to provide a comprehensive account of how these particular cases would be handled and the opportunities and obstacles for interagency collaboration which would be encountered.

CLIENT VIGNETTES

Justin—Age: 5, Grade: K

Justin, age 5, entered kindergarten at the beginning of the school year. His mother enrolled him in this school because it was closest to the shelter where she, Justin, and his younger sister, Julia, age 2-1/2, are living. Justin's mom is trying to make a new life for herself and her two children. A recovering alcoholic, she left an abusive home situation a few months earlier to enter a shelter for abused women. Both children have witnessed the physical abuse of their mother several times and have been physically abused themselves.

Justin's mother is concerned about his lack of readiness for kindergarten; his speech and language development are very slow, making it difficult for him to follow directions or express his needs. The kindergarten teacher assessed Justin and found him to be functioning below kindergarten level. He is unable to follow simple directions, identify or print any letters, or count to 10. The school-based committee made Justin a focus of concern for speech and language special education through the school system. While waiting for the special-education assessment, he is given extra assistance to enable him to follow directions and function in a group setting.

Soon after his arrival, the teacher discovered that Justin quickly became frustrated and has difficulty managing his anger. He has been placed on behavior contract and earns extra stars for good behavior. On many occasions, Justin needs a safe place to express his emotions; his teacher and counselor often hold him while he cries or expresses his rage. It sometimes takes as long as 45 minutes before Justin is ready to resume activities with the rest of his class. At the school's recommendation, Justin began seeing a counselor at the Mental Health clinic.

Point of Entry: Mental Health

Cal—Age: 15, Grade: 10

Cal is a 15-year-old who has been convicted of selling drugs and was carrying a weapon at the time of his arrest. Local law enforcement officers believe that he is a member of a local gang who have been involved in several local robberies. Returning from training school, he is going back to live with his mother, stepfather, four brothers and sisters, and three cousins. His stepfather is described as an unemployed, disabled alcoholic. Cal's father, whom he idolizes, is generally absent, offers no financial support, and is suspected of using drugs.

His mother works the night shift as a nurse's aide to support the family, leaving Cal to watch the children. She wants to enroll in night school but cannot find a day-shift job. Transportation to her work and to agency services is costly and inconvenient because the family has no vehicle.

Cal is described as very bright, very emotionally needy, and a nonstop talker. He has a good vocabulary, scored at the 11th- and 12th-grade levels on achievement tests, but has only a few high school credits. He is now ready to return to the regular high school in his local community.

Point of Entry: Juvenile Services

Jerome—Age: 14, Grade: 7

Jerome is a teenager who has failed two grades in elementary school. He is the oldest of three children in the family. Angela, age 10, helps Jerome care for Dwayne, age 2. There is no male in the household, and all three children have different fathers. The head of the family is Ms. Johnson, who is unemployed and an alcoholic.

Jerome is responsible for preparing breakfast for Angela, Dwayne, and himself and getting himself and Angela off to school in the mornings. Because of these responsibilities, Jerome often misses the school bus and, therefore, is frequently absent from school. Ms. Johnson has been uncooperative with the school in improving Jerome's attendance. In the afternoons, Angela cares for the baby and cleans the house. Jerome does laundry and prepares the family's evening meal.

Jerome is small for his age and comes to school in dirty clothes and smells of wood smoke in the winter. He frequently has sores and injuries that become infected if unattended by the school nurse, who comes to the school twice a month. Jerome's math skills are about 3 years behind grade level, and his reading is 4 years behind grade level. He also uses poor English and does not use the word "her" at all. Psychological evaluations show that Jerome is borderline learning disabled, and he is frequently inattentive in class and consistently disturbs others by talking. On several occasions in early morning, Jerome has been caught stealing the lunch of teachers whose classrooms were nearby.

Point of Entry: Social Services

Tina—Age: 12, Grade: 3

Tina was born with spina bifida and is confined to a wheelchair. She has severe attacks of anger, striking out at anyone who is nearby when she is upset. Her problem of being "emotionally conflicted" has only recently been diagnosed by a school psychologist, but she has had no counseling to date. Educational evaluations show her to be borderline educable mentally handicapped. Tina likes to be sent out of the classroom to sit in the office during the day.

Tina's father is an alcoholic and has a history of physically abusing her and her mother. Tina exhibits hostility and can't get along with anyone at school. She is able to learn, but her emotional state prevents her concentration. Each episode of failure in the classroom deepens her lack of self-confidence and frustration.

She was retained in three grades because of her poor reading skills. Her mother, who works hard and struggles to make a living, does not have the time to become involved in her daughter's life. She has come to a few teacher conferences and broke down in tears over Tina problems. She feels helpless to take charge of the situation.

Point of Entry: School

Tommy—Age: 10, Grade: 4

Tommy gets very little to eat outside of the free lunch program at school and appears malnourished. He is sick more than half the time, with poor attendance, and his grades are barely passing.

Tommy is pale and thin, with the additional problem of a disfiguring skin rash on his face. This is probably due to an allergy, but he receives no treatment for it. His parents, with a family of four to support, work at minimum-wage jobs. Both only completed the ninth grade. They do not have the resources to help Tommy and are too proud to ask for outside assistance. Everybody knows them as good, church-going parents who love their children. The minister is encouraging Tommy to participate in the Youth Choir at the church.

Tommy comes to school in winter without adequate clothing, keeps a continual cold, and can hardly stay awake in class. He is quiet and well-behaved, and seems to enjoy playing with the other children. He continually says, "I can't do this" as he tries to do his assigned class work. Tommy can read at grade level but is continually under pressure to complete his work because writing is difficult for him. Because he is so quiet and frequently absent, he has few friends. In fact, he is bullied by some students in his class who take advantage of him because of his small size and poor health. His teachers have tried to help by referring him to the school nurse and social worker and feel they cannot teach him until he comes to class well on a regular basis.

Point of Entry: School

Maureen—Age: 16, Grade: 11

Maureen is a lovable student. She keeps up well in her school work, and is always available to help fellow students who are having problems. She makes valuable contributions in her 11th-grade classes at the local high school. Maureen has been a cheerleader for 2 years, had the lead role in the school play last year, is active in student government, and sings in the choir of her church, where she teaches a Sunday school class at the primary level.

Maureen's family is working class. She will be the first member of her family to go to college, and a substantial scholarship seems assured. However, her parents have not agreed to let her attend college or accept the scholarship. Everyone begins to notice that Maureen is different in undefinable ways. She seems lost in thought in her classes and almost never volunteers an answer. If she is called on, she always has to ask the teacher to repeat the question. Her eyes are often puffy, and she seems to have been crying. Her teachers hold her in high enough esteem that they make an effort to understand what is happening to her, but they are at a loss to explain it.

Her art teacher, Ms. D., who has always been one of Maureen's favorites, fears that perhaps her parents are thinking of a divorce or that there is some illness in the family that she doesn't know about. One day she keeps Maureen after class, closes the door, and asks if everything is okay with her family. Maureen assures Ms. D. that everything is fine and is surprised that the teacher would ask.

Ms. D. presses her and states that she just isn't the same as she used to be. Maureen again assures Ms. D. that everything is fine, but begins to cry. After securing Ms. D.'s promise that she won't tell anyone, Maureen begins to tell her story.

Maureen states that she has been dating a young man from a nearby college. On one of their dates, they went to the drive-in. As soon as Jim, (the young man) turned off the engine, he was "all over" Maureen. According to Maureen, Jim would not take "no" for an answer.

Maureen suspects that she may now be pregnant. However, she is more worried about Jim's frequent, past sexual experiences with boys and about telling her parents she might be pregnant. Her parents have told her that if she gets pregnant before marriage, she will be "kicked out" of the house. When Ms. D. asks Maureen if she has seen Jim recently, she says that Jim never returned to college for the fall. She has heard that he has pneumonia. Ms. D. persuades Maureen to go to the local Health Department.

Point of Entry: Health Department

THE RESEARCH PROCESS

Once the client vignettes had been written to simulate a range of potential collaborative situations and the sites had been selected to represent the diversity of the state, 12 field researchers were selected and trained. The researchers had prior training and experience in case study research and qualitative interviewing. They also received two days of project-specific training covering such issues as the specific objectives of the research; the data-collection process; interviewing, observation, and document-analysis techniques; data analysis; and writing.

Researchers went out to the six counties in pairs during the week of January 4-8, 1993. They began following each case at the appropriate point of entry and continued tracking it though all referrals and resources mentioned by interviewees. The objective was to be true to the decision-making logic and case-management strategy of the particular agency in the particular county. Some cases were handled entirely within the first agency visited; others required as many as 12 separate interviews. A total of 119 agency personnel were interviewed. Each interview began by having the interviewee read the client vignette and then proceeded according to a semistructured interview guide designed to capture the full case flow and extent of interagency collaboration. This guide specified essential information being sought and suggested ways for the researcher to elicit it, providing sets of probes to help get the detail needed. Researchers also collected documents relevant to the hypothetical clients, including eligibility paperwork, policy statements, program brochures, and the like.

After completing data collection, the researchers began reading and coding their field notes and the documents they had collected. During the coding they focused on identifying key themes and issues, agency decision points, and specific collaborative practices. They then used the coded field notes to write narrative accounts of how the cases would proceed through county agencies. These narratives were revised by the editors to produce the chapters that follow.

READING THE CASE STUDIES

What follows are the case studies of current collaborative practice in six counties, here pseudonymed as Brady, Treir, Pickard, Secord, Fox, and Holderness. In addition to the county names, the names of all locations, people, and organizations have been masked. In reading through the six counties, certain common themes emerge. For example, many of the case studies deal with conflicting viewpoints of the client-contact worker and the administrator, agencies' impressions of each other, agency expectations of the family, chronic work overload and staff shortages, and questions of technology, the law, and confidentiality. By examining all of the cases in comparison with each other, the reader may develop a sense of when, where, how, and why interagency collaboration does (or does not) happen. This section was written to provide rich description of the possibilities for collaboration in a range of situations. Again, we encourage the reader to compare the case studies to their own situation and to use the case studies and the cross-site analyses in discussions about the possibilities and problems with interagency collaboration in their locale.

The case studies of the six counties are presented in four chapters, both to reduce redundancy and to highlight important themes to consider. Chapters 2, 3, and 4 each present the case of a single county, emphasizing the unique lessons of each of the three counties. Chapter 5 presents more focused discussion about the three remaining counties, concentrating on alternative definitions of collaboration in each place and the problems each has experienced. Chapter 6 presents three different cross-site analyses and concludes part I.

2

Making a Virtue of Necessity: Organic Collaboration in a Rural County

Catherine Awsumb
Rhonda Jeffries

Brady County, a rural county with five small towns and a total population of less than 10,000, exemplifies the kind of organic collaboration that emerges within an extremely limited social services network. *Organic collaboration* is defined as the spontaneous emergence of support and information sharing among personnel at different agencies who come to know and trust each other. As opposed to the formal collaborative policies and structures that characterized some of the larger and more bureaucratized counties in the study, most of the interagency collaboration that exists in Brady County is informal and based on personal contacts or relationships. A teacher in the county summarized the situation by saying that "collaboration is the norm here because we are so small we know who everyone is." Workers in different agencies made frequent contact and there appeared to be fewer barriers to information exchange than in larger counties.

Although there did appear to be a good deal of fruitful collaboration in Brady, this poor, rural county's service network was not without its limitations. A school social worker in the county agreed that collaboration was the norm, but she emphasized that it arose out of necessity: "We have a lot of collaboration in the county. We have to because resources are so scarce." Whereas workers in larger counties often had a great deal of functional specialization in their jobs, Brady social service employees defined themselves as generalists. No matter what the client problem was, the same set of names kept coming up as referrals. Workers in Brady are used to coming together to devise creative solutions to client problems because there are basic gaps in what the county can provide: Brady has no full-time mental health or juvenile justice personnel and no hospital. Almost any specialized service from disability testing to child-support investigation requires referring clients out of county.

Researchers found that a core group of five women (the Child Protective Services worker, the Mental Health liaison, and the school social worker and counselors) did most of the collaboration in the county, relying on each other for information, ideas, and support no matter what the client problem. They had a tight network based on friendship and long-standing professional trust, which served well for informal exchange of information outside of formally defined agency-to-agency channels. Although this kind of organic collaboration has obvious strengths, it has serious drawbacks as well. Because the range of resources and expertise within the network is so limited, solutions may not be well tailored to specific client needs. Such a network, defining itself by personalities rather than by job roles, is extremely vulnerable to disruption by personnel changes. Newer employees may lack access to the informal norms and practices that determine how things get done in the county and may be shut out of opportunities to collaborate.

This chapter explores the strengths and weaknesses of organic collaboration as practiced in Brady County, focusing on the fact that this style of collaboration is rooted in the resource limitations of a poor, rural county. The *Caseflow* section traces the six fictional clients through the social services system, showing how the same network of friends across agencies works together no matter what the situation or client point of entry into the system. The *Analysis and Conclusions* section discusses the strengths and weaknesses of organic collaboration in a small county and some possible next steps Brady social service workers believe they need to take to improve collaboration.

CASEFLOWS

Mental Health: Justin

The case of Justin, the 5-year-old living with his younger sister and their recovering alcoholic mother in a homeless shelter, immediately exposed the limits of Brady's social services resources. Most significantly, Brady has no emergency shelter, so that a battered woman and her children would have to be referred out of county. Many interviewees spoke of the difficulty of following through on a case when referrals must necessarily go in all directions outside the county or even the state (the closest major city to Brady is in Virginia rather than North Carolina) and both clients and workers must deal with an entirely different social services bureaucracy.

Even if shelter were not an issue and the case stayed within Brady, options were limited. Although the case was written so that Mental Health was Justin's point of entry into the social services system, we soon discovered that the Department of Mental Health consists of one part-time social worker, Ann, an on-loan agent who covers several counties, visiting Brady roughly three times each week. Ann indicated that although she frequently participates in collaboration, she rarely initiates it. Her part-time status puts her in reactive mode, struggling to keep up with the referrals she gets rather than reaching out. Ann emphasized that her background is in social work, not therapy. Several other interviewees, although praising Ann's ability and dedication, indicated that some clients needed a level of treatment that Ann was not qualified to provide. Justin's case might ultimately be referred out of the county for mental health services which Brady does not offer.

Ann said that her first course of action after Justin was referred to her would be to draw an extensive developmental history and determine what services he was already receiving. She mentioned the paperwork and confidentiality issues which could be involved in developing this history, but emphasized that the task could be accomplished more efficiently through the informal channels of her network of friends in other agencies. She said that she would phone Dawn, the Child Protective Services worker, or one of the school counselors to see what they knew about the case. Ann noted, "Paper between agencies is really unnecessary. Each agency has its own paper system." She said that a written recommendation takes a while to work its way through the system, but a verbal recommendation could be acted on in about a week.

After initial testing, Ann said she would work with the teacher in whose classroom Justin was placed to develop a behavioral plan. This plan would be reinforced by individual counseling, possibly at the school site. In cases like this there are usually team meetings at the school involving Ann, classroom teachers, school counselors, and, if at all possible, Justin's mother. Ann felt strongly that Justin's mother could benefit from individual counseling herself. The emphasis would be on dealing with her alcoholism, stabilizing her life, improving her parenting skills and helping her manage Justin's behavior. Ann said she would work with Dawn, the Child Protective Services (CPS) worker at DSS, on this. Dawn agreed with Ann that offering services to the whole family needed to be a priority. She mentioned group meetings for her alcohol problem and parenting classes. For help in stabilizing the family financially, Dawn would refer Justin's mother to Kitty, an income maintenance worker in DSS, to determine eligibility for programs like Food Stamps, Aid to Families with Dependent Children (AFDC), and Medicaid.

Despite her heavy caseload and the difficulty of scheduling meetings around the days she is in the county, Ann seems to be a core part of the informal network. These same five women discussed each other constantly in interviews and obviously rely on each other a great deal. They go out of their way to share information through informal channels and form a virtually closed circuit, passing referrals back and forth among themselves.

Although interviewees suggested possible sources of support for Justin and his family within their limited informal network, most roads seemed ultimately to lead outside the county. Brady simply does not have the resources, specifically, a homeless shelter and full-time Mental Health personnel, which all interviewees agreed this family needs. Given the unlikelihood that the family would or could travel across state or county lines to access needed services, Justin's might be a case that would fall through the cracks of Brady's limited social services network.

Juvenile Services: Cal

The point of entry for Cal, the 15-year-old being released from training school, was Juvenile Services, and the first contact was Bonnie, the court counselor who serves several counties and usually visits Brady County only every other week. Although she was not in the county very often, Bonnie clearly had close working relationships with the high school social worker, the mental health liaison, and the Child Protective Services worker, three of the key members of the core informal network that conducts most of the interagency collaboration in Brady. She mentioned that these same three women are involved in every case she handles, either as sources of informal advice or for formal referrals.

Bonnie's role in Cal's case would be to monitor his compliance with the terms of his conditional release from training school and put together a comprehensive package of services to support his re-entry into home, community, and school. Bonnie thought that Cal might benefit from some Mental Health assistance, and would contact Ann, Brady County's part-time Mental Health liaison. She would also contact the high school guidance counselor, Shirley, to try to access the resources of the Community Based Alternatives (CBA) task force, which Shirley chairs. The goal of CBA is to provide services in the community to juvenile offenders that prevent them from having to go to training school, but Bonnie felt there might be something there for Cal. Bonnie said she and Shirley would make a home visit together soon after Cal's release to discuss getting him involved in CBA programs such as mentoring or tutoring.

When Shirley discussed Cal's case, she said that if he had been convicted of a felony he would require an advocate to re-enter the school system. Shirley would play that role and would work with Bonnie on monitoring and supporting compliance with the conditional release. Both Shirley and Bonnie stressed the importance of helping the mother improve her family's situation and suggested several educational programs or support groups that might be appropriate. Bonnie admitted, "We have very little mandate to make changes in the family. In cases of obvious abuse we refer to DSS." She speculated that the mother is already probably getting Medicaid and AFDC, so she would have an eligibility specialist but perhaps no case worker. Even if there were no evidence of abuse Bonnie and Shirley said they would call Dawn, the Child Protective

Services worker, to discuss the case on an informal basis and solicit suggestions for services that would support Cal's re-entry into the community.

The challenge in a case like Cal's is to design a comprehensive and integrated plan to support his transition out of training school. In this case, the tightness of Brady's informal network of contacts across agencies would be a big advantage. All of the major players already know and trust each other and could serve as a ready-made transition team, the kind of case management that is much more difficult to organize in counties with more formal cross-agency barriers and lines of communication.

Social Services: Jerome

The first contact for Jerome, the young adolescent with learning and behavioral problems and an unemployed, alcoholic single mother, was Susan, the income maintenance supervisor for Brady County DSS. Susan's approach was a straightforward one of determining eligibility for various programs that DSS administers. Specifically, she mentioned ensuring access to AFDC, Medicaid, and Food Stamps if the family met eligibility requirements. She would discuss these programs with the mother and then refer her to Kitty, an income mainte-nance caseworker, to complete the paperwork. When we interviewed Kitty we were struck by the fact that one entire wall of Kitty's small office was covered with baskets of different colored forms. She told us that Jerome's case would require at least six different eligibility forms, some as long as 16 pages.

In addition to describing the in-house paperwork, Kitty emphasized that she was required to refer any AFDC applicants to child support and employment security agencies. Because these agencies do not have offices within Brady county, these referrals can represent a major stumbling block. Kitty said wearily of these referrals that "it takes a long time to follow through." She also noted that "transportation is often a major problem and going out there is often fruitless. We've started taking those forms ourselves to facilitate the process, but it would be nice if they could come out here to meet clients every so often. Lack of public transportation is a major barrier to coordinated services."

In addition to referring Jerome's family to Kitty for eligibility process-ing, Susan, the supervisor, said she would make another in-agency referral to Dawn, the Child Protective Services worker. She felt that Dawn would be best positioned to deal with the issues of Jerome's frequent absenteeism, his moth-er's alcoholism, and the family's lack of adequate clothing. When we spoke with Dawn she said that she would work with Jerome's teachers and school counselor on his behavior problems and help his mother learn how to manage his behavior constructively. She felt that counseling or an alcoholism support group would be important resources for the mother.

The pattern of referrals in Jerome's case suggests that there are two distinct cultural elements within DSS: service workers and eligibility workers.

The terminology was introduced by Susan, the income maintenance supervisor, who noted that her experience with interagency collaboration was limited because it was "the service workers who would tend to have more back and forth with other agencies and sit on interagency councils." Kitty, the income maintenance caseworker, agreed that "it is the social workers who talk to the schools a lot." Service workers seem to focus on the client; eligibility workers focus on the program. Service workers handle things informally, with a phone call; eligibility workers have strict paper trails to which they must adhere.

The agencies that Kitty says she works most closely with are child support, employment security, and social security—agencies that seem to have a similar culture of program eligibility and administration. It is also interesting to note that all of these agencies are outside the county and thus collaboration with them rarely involves face-to-face contact. Therefore, for eligibility workers the definition of collaboration seems to be following defined paper flows from agency to agency.

Dawn, the primary service worker at DSS, provided a stark contrast to Susan and Kitty. Her name came up in virtually every interview outside DSS, and she was the only person at DSS mentioned by name by any school personnel. Along with the school social worker and counselors and the mental health liaison, she was part of the county's core informal network. She said that most of her referrals in and out are by phone rather than paper and she stressed the importance of keeping in touch with other agencies even when there was not a specific referral to be made:

> The more you interact with other agencies in and out of your county the better resource access you have when you need to call on them. I try to go to their meetings whenever possible. Sometimes it is good to use other agencies just as a listening ear. I like to just call up and say 'What do you think I ought to do?"

The contrast between eligibility workers and service workers was also clear in terms of the ways they defined client relationships. Susan said that her interaction with a client like Jerome's mother was typically limited to a single appointment in which she makes referrals and "then the paperwork comes back across my desk." She commented that "it is not our responsibility to follow up or keep track," but she also said that "if we know it's a really bad situation, we will call and make sure they are getting the services they need." An eligibility worker's relationship with a client lasts as long as it takes to guide them through the paper trail. Whereas eligibility workers deal with issues which can be quantified in terms of financial cut offs, service workers focus on the "softer" issues like abusive behavior, parenting skills, and alcoholism. Their relationships with clients have no clear termination point, so they are much more likely to follow up on other services the client is receiving over time.

Jerome's case made it apparent that possibilities for collaboration vary based on agency culture. Whereas some interviewees took a straightforward eligibility approach—focusing on matching discrete client needs with available programs—others emphasized a more comprehensive approach to treatment—stressing the need to address the family situation as a whole. It is only when agency personnel focus on treating root problems, as opposed to isolated symptoms, that real collaboration is likely to emerge.

Schools: Tina

The initial contact for Tina, a physically handicapped child with severe attacks of anger, was Pamela, the counselor at Fillmore, Brady's K-3 school. Pamela stated that her first step would be to recommend to the principal that Tina be discussed by the School-Based Committee (SBC), which would make referrals for testing and eventual placement. The principal at Fillmore, Tom, later outlined several steps that the school would take with Tina *before* arriving at the SBC. He emphasized that there was a very well-defined process flow for dealing with all at-risk, learning disabled (LD), and Behaviorally and Emotionally Handicapped (BEH) children. The point of this process, according to Tom, was "to do everything we can within the building," before having to call on outside resources: "Collaboration within the building comes first. We want to use all the resources here before we go outside the building."

According to Tom, the process begins with what he described as "assertive discipline" and progresses to individual counseling with Pamela. When guidance counseling alone does not seem to make a difference the next step in Tom's process is the School Assistance Team (SAT), which works with the classroom teacher to develop behavior modification and learning strategies. Only when these strategies have been given a chance to work is the child referred to the SBC—"the last in-building step." The SBC is empowered to obtain permission for testing and the case is then referred to the Director of Exceptional Children, Cindy, who works out of the school system central office. Tom estimated that the entire process for placement into special education, from guidance to the SAT to the SBC to testing to placement in a resource classroom, takes approximately 6 months.

Interviewees felt that the SBC would likely recommend that Tina be placed in the county's special BEH class for all ages, which is held at Central Middle School. Marcia, the BEH teacher, and Ken, the on-site counselor, felt that it would be important for Tina to receive services beyond those of the school. Their first action would be to call in Ann, the county's only mental health worker. This referral would have to be informal: "The family has to go in and make the first move. All we can do is set up the appointment and offer transportation." They felt that getting Ann involved would be an important step in getting the whole family to take an active part in addressing Tina's problems. "Getting the parents in is half the battle," they stressed; ideally there would be regular meetings between the parents, the BEH teacher, and the counselor. They stated that Ann also frequently comes into the school for such meetings. Although they spoke positively about Ann's involvement in BEH cases, they added the caveat that "if the child or the family doesn't click with Ann there is really no one else to go to in the county. It becomes a transportation issue and a financial issue." Ann herself pointed out that because she is only in the county 3 days each week, scheduling can be extremely difficult. She also noted that her training is in social work, not psychology, and that some children and families need more services than she is able to provide. Marcia and Ken mentioned that Sam, a counselor who formerly worked in Brady county but is now in nearby Lackawanna (about 25 miles away) still gets some referrals.

There was some hesitation among school personnel interviewed about the role DSS would play in a case like Tina's. Pamela, the initial contact, felt that the history of abuse would warrant a call to Dawn, the Child Protective Services worker at DSS. Although she obviously trusted Dawn on a personal level and valued her input, Pamela was somewhat ambivalent about involving DSS formally, saying that "social services is very hush-hush. They don't collaborate." Tom, her principal, was even more dubious about the necessity of calling DSS and again emphasized his desire to manage the situation within the school: "Time is the major barrier in going outside. They already have a caseload. I would want to handle it in the building anyway if possible." He clearly preferred to call DSS only as a last resort. He felt that once a referral to DSS was made, they completely took over and the school was out of the loop: "They come pick her up and do all the follow up. I don't know what they do with her."

Marcia and Ken, the BEH teacher and guidance counselor, also saw DSS as a last resort, indicating that DSS only became involved in clear-cut cases of current abuse. Marcia said that because Tina's case specified a *history* of physical abuse, but no signs of current abuse, she presented a dilemma for school personnel in terms of whether to seek interagency collaboration. Because DSS is required to investigate abuse cases within 24 hours, Marcia expressed reluctance about getting them involved in Tina's case unless there was concrete and immediate evidence of abuse. "You have to ask if it is worth getting them in to do an investigation which may only endanger the child more. Often you make a referral to social services and they don't find anything. Once you get burned reporting things, you think twice."

Despite their hesitations, because all four of our school-system interviewees mentioned Dawn, the Child Protective Services worker, as a potential referral for Tina, she was consulted. Although the schools had indicated she would only become involved in an extreme situation, Dawn assumed she would be involved at an earlier point. She talked about working with the school counselor, teacher, and parent on a consistent discipline plan. She agreed with school personnel that "a history of physical abuse is difficult to prove without bruises," but said she would encourage the school to keep a log of "suspicious things" on Tina and monitor the case closely on an ongoing basis.

A final contact on Tina's case mentioned by Pamela was Shirley, the high school social worker. Although Shirley primarily works with adolescents through the Juvenile Services-funded CBA program many people in the county call on her for informal advice on programs and services. Shirley formerly worked at DSS and is a native of the county, so she is very familiar both with the social services bureaucracy and with many county residents. The younger school counselors look on her as a valuable mentor, and she is the linchpin of the informal network we identified. Someone mentioned calling her for advice on every case, even when there was nothing "official" she could do. Shirley was asked what she would recommend if Pamela called her about Tina's case. She felt that one of the specialized developmental testing facilities in nearby counties should already have been involved by this stage, but if not they would be an important resource. She also felt it would be important to get Tina's mother into Mental Health, beginning with Ann. Shirley said she would also recommend a private, nonprofit intervention and treatment program for child victims of sexual and physical abuse located about an hour away.

A severe and sensitive case such as Tina's highlights the fact that even in a close knit county like Brady suspicion and defensiveness exist between agencies. Both schools and DSS wanted to prove their competence to handle the case internally and were concerned that outside referrals might actually be detrimental. Unfortunately, Tina's needs do cross traditional agency boundaries; by trying to protect her from what they perceived as threatening or inadequate intervention by other agencies, personnel may actually be keeping her from the help she needs.

Schools: Tommy

One of our interviewees described Tommy, a boy with inadequate food and clothing, persistent minor medical problems, and poor school attendance as "not endangered but quite needy." His caseflow began with Cassie, the counselor at the Brady school serving grades 4 through 6. Before determining what services would be most appropriate for Tommy, Cassie said she would need to make several calls to supplement the basic information in school records, which she characterized as sketchy and rarely useful. Cassie stated that she would first contact Pamela, the counselor at the K-3 school, saying "the biggest help is having Pamela at the lower level. The kids have already gotten some services, and I can get her at-risk list." Cassie said she would particularly want to discuss with Pamela how receptive the parents had been to help. The next call Cassie would make would be to Shirley, the high school social worker. She viewed Shirley as not necessarily a formal referral for specific services, but as "someone who has a lot of ideas. She has worked at DSS and is from the county. She is aware of a lot of resources and may know the family background." About Tommy, Shirley said that her main advice to Cassie would be to "involve the parents early and encourage the family to request assistance, particularly from public health." She would also want to make sure that Tommy was referred to the SAT as soon as possible to start the testing process for possible learning disabilities.

Cassie's next call would be to Suzanne, the attendance counselor, to see if she had made any home visits and had any more information about the family. Suzanne said that if she had not already made a home visit based on attendance records, she would do so on Cassie's referral. Her philosophy is that "adequate health and clothing are key for getting attendance back," so she would try to find out what help they are getting and work with them to set up appointments at the Health Department and at a local religious charity that provides second-hand clothes. Suzanne stressed that it was important to work with the family over time, encouraging them to request needed services and giving them a chance to do that for themselves before making a direct referral to Dawn, the Child Protective Services worker at DSS.

Once she had gathered as much information as possible about the services Tommy and his family had already received, Cassie said she would begin addressing specific needs. She said she would start by calling Ginger, head nurse at the Health Department. Ginger said that because Brady had recently moved away from having school nurses "(the health department nurses) serve in that capacity but not to the extent that we used to." Ginger explained that if the family could be convinced to accept the help, Tommy would be eligible for up to $100 in assistance from the School Health Fund.

To address Tommy's difficulties with writing Cassie recommended initiating the standard testing referral process, which moves through the SAT to the SBC to the central office. Cassie's first step would be to meet with Florence, the exceptional children's teacher in the building. Florence said that she and Cassie would try to set up a conference with the parents in which they could obtain a comprehensive developmental and social history on Tommy. She stressed that it would be important "to handle it in a personal way rather than bombarding the parents. The parents may have uncomfortable feelings about school." If Florence then felt it was warranted and the parents agreed, she would initiate the formal SAT/SBC/testing process. Although most other school personnel did not feel there was much if any paperwork involved in working with these cases, Florence noted that "as the resource teacher I am primarily responsible for record keeping." She described the testing referral process for testing as "hectic," particularly as she has no planning period (she met with us over breakfast).

The generous and multifaceted response to Tommy's case illustrated the strengths of organic collaboration based on personal contacts. In a small county like Brady a needy but not actively endangered child would be treated like a neighbor in need rather than shunted into formal channels. This personal approach, when allowed to flourish, is doubtless less traumatic for clients and represents collaboration at its most caring.

Health Department: Maureen

Maureen, the possibly pregnant teenager, would enter the Brady social services system via Martha, a family nurse practitioner. Martha indicated that the usual Health Department referral pattern in cases involving young people was in from the schools (or self-referral) and out to DSS. There did not seem to be as much back and forth as in cases that centered on schools or Mental Health. Health cases tend to have more discrete time limits (such as the term of pregnancy), which define the client relationship.

Martha said that if Maureen's pregnancy test came out negative she would be referred to the Family Planning Clinic where she could receive contraceptives. If Maureen is in fact pregnant Martha would give her counseling about her options and immediately involve Dawn, the Child Protective Services worker. If Maureen wants an abortion she would have to travel to a facility approximately 60 miles away. If transportation is a problem it could be provided either by DSS or by the high school social worker. Adoption could be arranged through Dawn at DSS. Martha said she would definitely want to involve Shirley, the high school social worker, if Maureen decides to keep the baby. She said that Shirley knows many of the families in the county and could help Maureen break the news to her parents.

Martha said her first priority would be to try to get Maureen enrolled in a maternity care coordination program that she runs called Baby Love. This program is very crowded, and they receive more applications than they can serve. Eligibility is determined through DSS, and Martha indicated frustration with the long, slow process. Martha explained, "I make a list of the documents and information they need in an attempt to shorten the process. If they go and they're missing even one piece of information, they have to start all over again. This can make the process take forever." It is imperative to have a social security number in order to get help from Social Services and a lot of her clients do not have this. Until Maureen is cleared through the eligibility worker at DSS and receives her Medicaid card, it will be difficult for her to get prenatal care. As Martha put it, "Without the card, most doctors do not want to see the patient. They've been burned too many times." Once in the Baby Love Program Maureen would see Martha at least once a month, and Martha would keep a file documenting prenatal care.

In order to qualify for Baby Love or for Women, Infants, and Children (WIC) payments once the baby is born, Maureen would have to go through a large stack of eligibility paperwork with Kitty, the eligibility worker at DSS. Kitty said that Maureen must have parental permission in order to enroll in the Baby Love program, but usually by the time the case gets to her the parents already know about the pregnancy. If the parents do not know she refers the client to Dawn, the Child Protective Services worker. Whereas Kitty would handle the "hard issues" like paperwork and eligibility, Dawn would deal with "soft issues" like counseling and moral support. DSS encourages high school completions, and they could also offer Maureen assistance in paying a child-care provider.

Because time is of the essence for Maureen whether she chooses to keep her baby or not, this case revealed tensions and frustrations in the way paperwork is handled. Martha indicated that she does everything she can to jump start the process at DSS but feels her hands are often tied. She feels that she has to compile a great deal of repetitious income information. Martha has also found confidentiality regulations to be a barrier to getting clients the services they need, although she feels the situation is improving:

> It hasn't always been this good in terms of collaboration. People used to hide behind confidentiality. I independently drew up a permission form for parents to sign and ran it by an attorney that has helped facilitate more sharing of information between agencies.

Her release form is specific to the Baby Love program and limited to the term of pregnancy. Unlike most interviewees, who prefer to work over the phone, Martha feels that in urgent cases it is often more effective to "go wave a paper in their face." Kitty at DSS agreed that the paperwork was cumbersome, particularly in a delicate and time-sensitive situation like this, but she seemed resigned to the system and saw no way around it.

Because of the state-mandated Baby Love program, Brady is well-equipped to handle a case such as Maureen's. In this case the structure and resources of the state program meshed neatly with the existing informal network for collaboration in the county. In such a situation, collaboration rather than being an artificial mandate or an extra layer of bureaucracy actually leverages resources that are already in place at the local level.

ANALYSIS AND CONCLUSIONS

Not surprisingly, interviewees in Brady County expressed universally positive sentiments about interagency collaboration in the abstract. After all, being against "collaboration" in social service circles is a little like being against "quality" in business or "motherhood and apple pie" in politics. Interviewees were unanimous both in their abstract assertion that collaboration is a wonderful thing and in their specific praise of their county's small, informal network based on personal relationships. Most of the interviewees felt informal collaboration works well and would like to keep it at that level. Ginger, head nurse at the Health Department, said:

> Most of our interagency work is phone contact. I don't really know if meetings are needed monthly. Maybe quarterly. The real work gets done over the phone and then we just meet for coordination. The interagency idea is good, but forcing it too much is bad.

Almost every interviewee identified close personal relationships as the greatest facilitator of collaboration in the county. Marcia, the BEH teacher, told us that "collaboration is the norm here because we are so small we know who everyone is," and Cassie the school counselor said that "interagency involvement develops over time because of personal relationships."

As researchers walked interviewees step by step through the hypothetical case flows it became clear that the county did indeed have a high level of organic collaboration, particularly among five key players, and relatively relaxed bureaucratic barriers to information sharing. The caseflows also revealed, however, significant weaknesses and even gaps in this organic network. Interagency collaboration in Brady County is best described by saying that the county's small size is both its greatest blessing and its greatest curse. Many interviewees expressed this paradox and identified the strengths and weaknesses of a small informal network. Several phrased it in terms of making a virtue of necessity. According to Bonnie, the court counselor who covered several counties:

> In Brady we have few facilities and no alternatives, so we must work together. It's getting done because if we don't do it, it doesn't get done. It is happening out of necessity. Necessity is the mother of invention. Everyone knows everyone else, and it's an active group of people. You keep seeing the same faces at meetings.

Shirley, the high school social worker and linchpin of the informal network, pointed out:

> We have a lot of collaboration in this county. We have to because resources are so scarce. The network is so small that the same people have to be called over and over again. This is a pro and a con. You know who you are working with and what their skills are, but they are all so burdened.

The benefits of organic collaboration are obvious and interviewees discussed them openly and at length: workers in different agencies feel free to consult each other informally, to share information, and to devise solutions that are not necessarily dictated by written rules and procedures. The drawbacks of organic collaboration are less immediately apparent and is the focus of this section.

One major drawback of person to person as opposed to systemic collaboration is its hit-or-miss nature. Cassie was emphatic about the limitations of the small, informal network: "There is only one person to call in each agency and they are out doing their job." Such heavy reliance on informal patterns of collaboration below the defined channels of interagency collaboration also raises serious continuity questions. In most cases, high turnover is endemic to poorly paid and stressful human services positions; although Brady County seemed to have strikingly low turnover, it would only take a few people leaving their jobs to shatter the informal network.

A reliance on informal networking also becomes problematic when it shuts newcomers out of the loop. This perspective was expressed most forcefully by a school counselor who has been working in the county only a few years and still feels that she lacks the personal relationships needed to navigate the informal network. "It takes a couple of years to build trust," she said. "People here are not hot to jump on the ideas or recommendations of a new person." She cited one incident in which she complained to the Sheriff's Department about not being included on a committee on sexual abuse cases. "I was told, 'Well, you'll find out anyway, you'll hear it through the grapevine.' But by then it may be too late for me to work with that student."

The most obvious limitations to collaboration in a small county like Brady are limits of time and money. Brady workers rely on informal collaboration not only because they know and trust each other but also because it is less resource-intensive than formal collaboration. Small agency staffs and heavy caseloads made scheduling interagency meetings "a luxury" according to several workers. This was particularly true for teachers, who doubted they would be granted release time to participate in formal interagency collaboration. Many interviewees felt that the network was already maximally burdened and that people did not have time to collaborate more. Tom, the principal, told us that "time is the major barrier to going outside for help. They already have a caseload." Marcia, the BEH teacher, suggested, "The main thing we need is more people to call."

The scarcity of resources also inhibits collaboration by forcing agencies to focus narrowly on their own defined missions rather than addressing broader issues or operating in a more preventive way. ("It's all we can do to get our own jobs done first.") Although a few interviewees took the opportunity to complain extensively about inadequate funding, most seemed to take it for granted as the nature of social services and did not dwell on it. Sometimes, however, a small resource gap can be a major barrier to collaboration. The most striking example of this in Brady County was the school counselor who had difficulty discussing cases with colleagues at other agencies because the only phone she had access to was in the principal's office, "where there are always a lot of people milling around."

One resource constraint that inhibits collaboration and may be particular to small rural counties like Brady is the lack of public transportation. For families without access to a car this can be a major barrier to receiving integrated services or following through on referrals. Although DSS is able to provide transportation for clients to medical services, situations like a meeting with a school counselor or an employment agency must be dealt with on an ad hoc basis and sometimes fall through the cracks. This is where a surprising number of interagency referrals seem to break down.

The fact that many services simply are not available in Brady County taxes the ingenuity of the informal network. The issue that emerged most strongly was the sheer lack of Mental Health resources and services on which to call. As Cassie put it, "Ann is only here 3 days per week and when she is here she is too busy to talk. Also, she is a social worker, not a psychologist. We need both. Some families need more services than she can provide." Counseling services in nearby cities were mentioned over and over again as possible alternative referrals, but financial and transportation issues often made their availability to Brady County residents somewhat theoretical. Clients often have to be referred to cities an hour or more away, sometimes even out of state. Hospitalization, AIDS treatment, foster care, emergency shelter, and medical psychiatry all require referrals outside the county. Following up on these clients to ensure they get the services they need can be very difficult. Sending clients across county lines also means dealing with a different set of rules and regulations. This problem was especially apparent to Ann, the part-time Mental Health worker. She covers three neighboring counties, all of which are in a different judicial district from Brady. She must remember that there are certain things she can do in other counties that she cannot do in Brady and when she refers clients across county lines the rules may change. Ann felt strongly that "standardizing these rules among districts would improve consistency of service."

Because Brady's social service workers relied so much on informal communication to solve client problems they were often uncertain about formal procedures or policies that might constrain solutions. In their daily practice workers often considered agency boundaries somewhat fluid or permeable and were then shocked to bump into the hard realities of differing eligibility requirements or legally mandated procedures. In many cases workers at one agency lacked information about income cutoffs and paperwork required for services provided by other agencies. This made them uncertain about making referrals that might turn out to be fruitless for the client. One of the school counselors expressed a desire for a "symposium" in which public and private agencies could present their programs to each other, "especially so we can understand how their finances work."

The strict legal constraints on DSS activity were particularly at odds with the free-flowing norms of informal collaboration. Despite their friendship with Dawn, school and Health Department personnel were wary of getting her involved in possible abuse cases because of the legal requirement that DSS make a formal investigation within a certain time period. Cassie explained that "their caseloads are so heavy that I hate to bother them. I'm hesitant to report when I know they are required to act. I wish I could just *talk* to them more." Marcia, the BEH teacher, spoke of "having been burned" by investigations that turned up nothing and the fear that bringing in DSS sometimes endangered the child more than helping him or her. There was also the perception that once DSS became involved, they took over entirely and allowed for little back and forth with the schools. Thus DSS was only likely to be called in extreme cases and was to some extent shut out of informal collaboration with a more preventative emphasis.

All of these perceptions contrasted sharply with the account of Dawn, the Child Protective Services worker and a key member of the informal network, of working with the schools. She said that "although confidentiality is a big issue in our agency, we share a lot with the school system. We're just careful to get a signed release from the parents and let them know who we'll be speaking with." She also spoke of working with counselors and teachers on at-risk kids when no charge of abuse was involved. The way Dawn defined her job role indicated that she was able to participate in collaboration because she was more attuned to the norms of the informal network than to the procedures and regulations of her own agency.

Although Brady is able to rely on informal collaboration because of its small scale, this intimacy can become a drawback in situations where, because of the stigma that attaches to many forms of public assistance, clients might actually prefer a more anonymous, impersonal bureaucracy to having their neighbors know about their personal problems. Stigma can be a significant barrier to collaboration in that it influences referral patterns. Workers seemed to be concerned about stigma in an inverse proportion to the degree it is attached to their own agencies: the least stigmatized agencies saw it as the most significant barrier. School personnel seemed to be especially sensitive to this issue when making referrals to DSS and Mental Health. One teacher noted that "if it is a health issue I would go directly to the Health Department, but in DSS cases we try to work with the family first." In many such cases non-DSS personnel prefer to make referrals to private charities or to try and meet the needs of the families on a personal basis. The head nurse at the Health Department said:

> If any of us here has used clothing our outreach worker might dispense it
> directly rather than passing them through DSS. That way it is like folks just
> kind of sharing, like passing clothes in a family. That is a lot easier than for
> a client to accept than going to DSS.

It was generally concluded that parents are even more hesitant to come into other social service agencies than they are to the schools. In fact, the schools were mentioned by both Health and Mental Health workers as a relatively "neutral" and unthreatening site for conferences involving parents.

The stigma attached to Mental Health services was even more severe and personnel in other agencies felt it was often fruitless to encourage families to get the services they need. Tom, the elementary principal, expressed the opinion that "some parents just don't want the state to do that sensitive work." Florence, the exceptional children's teacher, said that "on occasion I will refer hardcore BEH cases to mental health but there is great stigma attached. A lot who need the help simply won't go." Cassie felt that "we really don't have anyone to refer families to for counseling. They see the Mental Health center as negative and too expensive. There is a stigma attached. In a small community people don't want to be seen going in and have everyone know their business."

An important point to be made about the informal network in Brady County is that it exists almost exclusively below the level of agency heads. Administrators were more oriented toward the formal mission of their agencies and wanted to keep things "in the building," whereas "front-line" workers saw agency boundaries more flexibly and were more likely to reach out to their peers (often close friends) in other agencies to meet client needs. Workers in several agencies used "us/them" language to describe how their informal interagency networking had increased over time while expressing doubts that "the heads are any closer."

It was generally felt by line workers that administrators were more concerned with protecting their turf and more likely to view collaboration as an admission that they could not handle their own jobs. Shirley, the school social worker who came over from DSS, stated explicitly that "people from the top must be willing to collaborate as well as people from the lines. It is beyond my comprehension why agencies say no to help and don't ask for suggestions. It all boils down to territory: 'I know what I'm doing.'" Administrators in the schools and at DSS bore out the assumptions of their staff by using identical language about "keeping collaboration in the building" and exhausting all internal resources before going "outside the building." It should also be noted that the line workers were all women, whereas the administrators were almost all men, a factor that may reinforce the cultural rift.

The schools provide a particularly clear example of how even in a small county administrative role definition can erect walls limiting informal collaboration. A school counselor opined that part of the reluctance to go outside the school system to seek services was due to disagreement about the proper role of the school: "Principals often feel things can be handled at school. They like to know when a report is made and don't always think one *should* be made. Principals never call outside. They may not feel it is our business if it is a *family* issue." She felt that counselors could play a vital buffer role in these situations. Her principal's assessment of the role of guidance counseling reinforced the inside/outside language: "The guidance counselor is brought in when the teacher refers the kid and says that problems from outside the building are being brought in."

The desire of administrators to keep it "in the building" raises the issue of turfism. Although most interviewees, especially those who had worked in larger counties, were quick to stress their belief that turfism was not so bad in Brady County as in most places, the issue was clearly on everyone's mind. Particularly when we asked what fears people might have about increased interagency collaboration, interviewees discussed the unwillingness that others might have to "having people looking over their shoulders" in a more formal system of collaboration. Although people were generally willing to reach out on a personal basis to peers in other agencies whom they liked and trusted, they were wary of collaboration being mandated from on high. One school counselor noted that "a big fear would be the protection of territory. People like to prove they are competent at their own jobs, to say 'We can handle it ourselves.'"

It was generally recognized, however, that this attitude, although it preserves the organizational integrity of agencies, is not in the best interests of clients with multiple needs. At a follow-up meeting in which researchers presented their conclusions to agency heads, the head of the Health Department put it this way: "People try to take it as far as they can within their own agencies. We need to find a mechanism for identifying problems in their infancy stages and not waiting for people to exhaust their internal limits. It just isn't efficient to do it that way." Although this comment received hearty assent from the administrators around the table, there was also much nervous discussion at this meeting of how interagency collaboration would affect individual agency funding streams and autonomy.

Confidentiality is a particularly sticky issue within an informal collaborative network, because information tends to be shared on the basis of personal trust rather than stated policies. When such trust exists information sharing is expedited, but where close relationships do not exist vague notions of confidentiality can become an excuse for doing nothing. Brady agency heads were in agreement that current statutes are unnecessarily ambiguous and overlapping and that better ones need to be written. Statutes are interpreted in widely different ways across agencies and levels within agencies and can be used as much to protect turf as to protect clients. As one admitted: "Confidentiality is really more of a territorial issue than a legal issue."

Although Bonnie, the court counselor, felt free to exchange information with the two or three people she worked with most closely outside her own agency, she had a great deal to say on how confidentiality requirements and the fear of lawsuits inhibit collaboration. In describing confidentiality as "a built-in barrier to collaboration," Bonnie referred us to an article in the state judicial code which states that "juvenile records and social reports," shall be "withheld from public inspection and may be examined only by order of the judge." The statute continues for almost a full page detailing specific provisions for the protection of information before concluding in a vague and seemingly contradictory fashion that "nothing in this section shall preclude the necessary sharing of information among authorized agencies." Bonnie urged, "Look at that last sentence. The legislature put it there for a reason." Despite that intention to promote cross-agency collaboration, she noted that "agencies have been successfully sued and are skittish and wary." She said that people try to protect themselves by drawing up their own release forms, talking about cases without using names, and working below task force level.

Shirley, the school social worker, felt:

It is hard because of confidentiality to get information appropriately. Coming out of DSS I know more informal ways. Confidentiality is important but it inhibits what you can do. It is difficult to know what your responsibility is. If there is immediate danger to the child, I err on the side of action. The bottom line on confidentiality is territory. People are concerned that others will think they are doing their jobs wrong. Workers generally respect the need to share information; administrators are more protective. Over time you learn who you want to work with at each step.

Therefore, differing interpretations of confidentiality are another factor favoring front-line collaboration based on personal relationships over more formal interagency connections. Indeed, people calibrated their definition of collaboration to specific individuals; when there was no close personal relationship they were likely to adhere to a stricter and more formal interpretation than when working with someone with whom they had developed trust. School personnel in particular seemed to feel that a looser view of confidentiality set them apart from the rest of the social services bureaucracy. In general, people whose jobs involved a great deal of paperwork and documentation were very aware of the legal status of the information they handled. People whose jobs consisted mostly of verbal communication found this attitude incomprehensible and suspected that territory was the real reason other people were reluctant to share information.

At the follow-up meeting in which researchers presented their findings about collaboration in the county, Brady agency heads emphasized their strong belief that informal networking served the county well. There was hearty assent around the table when the head of DSS expressed his concern that more formal mechanisms would be "just another layer of bureaucracy." Several agency heads had questions about the wisdom of diverting funding from "the real tangible problems we address like vaccination" to "this vague interagency thing." The administrators were particularly resentful of "mandates from Raleigh without the resources to back them up," and hoped that interagency collaboration would not prove to be another of those.

Despite fears of increased bureaucracy, many interviewees stated explicitly that the lack of formal mechanisms for discussing specific cases was one flaw in the current state of interagency collaboration in Brady county. Ann, the Mental Health worker, reported that any formal interagency meetings she had been to in Brady County tended to be "updates on policies, sharing information about resources, discussing attendance figures, that kind of stuff. We never talk about individual cases. That would be helpful. They do more of that in the other counties I cover and it is needed here."

Several people cited the creation of the state-mandated CBA task force meetings as a turning point in the awareness of the need for collaboration in Brady County, but wished it could go further. CBA, with representation from most public and private agencies, focuses on the needs of young people in the county and new programs that are being developed. They share general information about resources that are available, especially for at-risk children and those who have dropped out. Bonnie, the court counselor, explained that the CBA meetings opened the eyes of the task force members to a wide range of community needs and possibilities of collaborative efforts to address them. "Getting us all together in one room made us realize that we have all the issues of Raleigh/Durham, but just in microcosm. The CBA task force meetings brought many of the issues to the forefront." Interestingly, most of the participants in the CBA meetings felt that it was not the program itself which facilitated collaboration, but simply the opportunity for representatives of different agencies to be in the same place at the same time. School counselor Cassie concluded that, "It's good to have built-in time just to talk to people from other agencies where you don't feel guilty. Now it is a luxury. It's so helpful to get information that someone else has already found out." Bonnie said that the state-mandated CBA task force meetings had been a real catalyst because they enabled agencies to come together in one place and begin a dialogue about what is going on within each agency and the issues with which they are confronted.

Several participants expressed frustration that the CBA meetings were devoted to program administration and that it was not a format which allowed discussion of actual cases. As Cassie put it, "Unfortunately, we don't do any interagency collaboration at that meeting. They are just for program administration. It really could be used for other purposes. We need to do more collaboration—all of us feel that." She said that several of the participants at the CBA meeting including school counselors, the local Mental Health representative, and the child welfare social worker from DSS tried to get together either before or after the CBA meetings and use the opportunity to share information about actual cases. This is the same core informal network that came up over and over again as doing most of the real ground-level collaboration in the county. Although they felt their informal network generally worked well, many line workers believed they could serve the needs of clients more effectively if there were a more systematic mechanism for exchanging information about actual cases. If a way could be found to do this while protecting confidentiality and without imposing cumbersome bureaucracy, this could take formal collaboration in Brady county to a more meaningful and sustainable level.

3

Collaboration and Complexity in an Urban Center

Penny L. Richards
Brian McCadden
Jackie Blount

Pickard County is an urban retail center with a diverse population of about 500,000. The county seat has grown rapidly since the construction of an industrial complex nearby, which has confounded efforts at city planning. Traffic is usually heavy, with long delays, and road construction is the norm. Meanwhile, tiny rural communities also exist, presenting a broad range of conditions to county agencies. Demands on the county's social service agencies have also increased significantly in recent years, as the region's economy suffers growing pains.

Very busy roads and a freeway prevent easy pedestrian access to municipal services. Construction is underway to relocate and centralize the complex of social services, to avoid the congestion of city traffic. Although this relocation may improve the working conditions of social service agents and locate them in a setting conducive to cross-agency contact, clients with limited access to private transportation may not find the change as beneficial.

Unlike most of North Carolina, efforts at collaboration in Pickard County, whether at the agency or individual level, are more likely to be stymied by overabundance than by scarcity. There are so many programs, and so many faces and voices attached to those programs, that a client-contact worker seeking information may quickly become overwhelmed (to say nothing of the potential client's dilemma before even choosing a door to enter). When, in the following caseflows, agency personnel were asked where a hypothetical client might go next, many possibilities were offered. Further questioning, however, revealed that much of the potential of the county's resources is never really tapped: in order to function in such a complicated system, most workers develop a few standard referrals that they use for most clients. This in turn creates case bottlenecks and paperwork logjams as everyone's favorite next steps become flooded while other possible paths remain unexplored; worker burnout, client frustration, and lost opportunities are among the predictable results of this complex urban web.

CASEFLOWS

Mental Health: Justin

The case of Justin, the 5-year-old living with his younger sister and their recovering alcoholic mother in a homeless shelter, was first shown to Rosalind, a case manager who has had experience working in at least one other local social service agency. She began by explaining that Justin's case is very similar to those Mental Health Services regularly sees, except that at 5 he is a little younger than most clients. Around 90% of the cases taken by Mental Health, she estimated, are sexually and/or physically abused children and Justin may have suffered as much. At least half of the children are in custody of DSS, which means that Mental Health must regularly work closely with that agency.

Rosalind explained that Mental Health would first arrange for an outreach consultation to evaluate Justin's needs at no cost to the family. This assessment would include an interview with the mother (at which time she may be referred to the local alcohol rehabilitation program, or Substance Abuse Center [SAC], as well as SafeHaven, a service that aids abused women); discussions with the mother's therapist, if she has one; meetings with representatives of Justin's school; a meeting with Justin's little sister, Julia, who is also likely to need assistance; and an evaluation of the mother's financial situation. If Justin is found to be in need of Mental Health services, then he would be referred to private therapy programs if the family can afford them. Otherwise, he would be assigned a Mental Health intake worker, who would set up a doctor's appointment to assess Justin's need for medicine such as Ritalin. The intake worker would then assign Justin either to a clinic or to a treatment team, which is the more likely outcome.

If Justin were assigned to a team, either a Mental Health case manager or therapist would assume primary responsibility for his progress. Team members would include the therapist and representatives from Justin's school, from the Department of Social Services, and from SAC and SafeHaven, should Justin's mother seek such treatment. Mental Health would act as the lead agency at periodic meetings of the treatment team. Because individual therapy may not work with such a young client, the team might suggest play therapy. The team would also arrange to work with the mother to insure that her mental health needs were being met. They would try to get the family into their own home as a stable environment. If this meant changing schools for Justin, his new teachers and counselors would be invited to work with the team. The mother may be referred to the Pickard County Schools' Project Enterprise, which offers workshops and in-home counseling on effective parenting skills. Should Justin's behavior become dangerous, the team might decide to seek Willie M. program assistance. (Willie M. refers to the NC court order to serve violent and aggressive youth.) Finally, the family's basic needs might be met by the Catholic Parish Outreach, a private charity that provides clothing and other necessities, DSS, which can offer emergency rent money or utility bill relief, and school nurses, who can serve as liaisons to Health Department services.

When asked if such intensive team collaboration was common throughout the county and in various agencies, and, if so, how a team leader is selected, Rosalind responded that every agency practices some case management, but for overwhelming cases, one lead agency evolves. Mental Health Services takes the lead for Willie M. cases, for example. Large, demanding cases usually require the combined effort of several agencies, however, and in Pickard County such cases are coordinated through the "Hard-to-Serve Committee." This local committee is composed of representatives of DSS, Mental Health, Juvenile Court, and others. At meetings, case managers or lead case workers present cases and ask for assistance in planning.

Rosalind explained that there is also a great deal of informal cooperation among agencies. Case workers and managers regularly call on their contacts at other agencies around the county. This system works particularly well in small counties, she said. In large counties such as Pickard, however, the success of a particular case worker/manager depends on his or her ability to establish a strong and broad network of contacts throughout the social service systems. She suggested that perhaps new workers could begin with a 2-week orientation to the county to learn the services, the community, and the individuals at other agencies.

Regarding general obstacles to coordination among agencies, Rosalind, without hesitation, said "statutes." She explained that Mental Health has a system of regulations by which it must operate to deliver services. Substance abuse agencies, however, have different and even more stringent requirements. DSS operates by yet another set of procedures and regulations. Confidentiality is obviously one of its greatest concerns. At times these different applicable laws prevent easy coordination among agencies. To make matters even more confusing, Rosalind believed that many of these statutes serve important functions and cannot be done away with entirely.

Rosalind felt that other systemic problems hindered successful interagency collaboration as well. "There have been lots of attempts at interagency collaboration but these have been around individual cases. There needs to be something more ongoing." Also, she said, "People get wrapped up in an agency identity. It's scary for them to change. Some people are afraid of growth." Some of these people are also afraid of job loss. Increased paperwork can cause backlogs at the administrative level, which can result in underestimates of service delivery. These underestimates translate into workforce reduction by layoff. Rather than provoke such a chain of events, workers in vulnerable positions might well prefer not to enter into formal collaborative ventures.

Rosalind believed that Mental Health Services has invested substantial effort in working well with other agencies, and that teamwork was the most productive form for social services agencies to pursue. These cooperative relationships, however, have their bounds (the work of therapists, for example, must be private). Despite these, Rosalind maintained that Mental Health case workers and managers have made great strides toward cooperation with other agencies.

Justin's case was next followed to Project Enterprise (PE), the Pickard County Schools' project designed to offer proactive help for anyone concerned with effective childrearing. Rosalind suggested that this service might be asked to assist Justin's mother. Wesley, a busy but enthusiastic staffer, said that PE would establish contact with the teacher who had referred Justin to Mental Health Services. Justin's mother then would be contacted and told about the programs offered by PE, including individual counseling for Justin and his mother. PE would also try to help the mother coordinate transportation. Should she decide to take advantage of services offered by PE, someone could observe Justin in the field. If Justin manages well at school, someone would just check up on him. Wesley indicated that most referrals for PE come from the school system, and from parent's self-referrals A smaller number of clients are referred by a wide variety of social service agencies, individuals, and organizations. Once a child is referred, some services are delivered in the home, but most are offered at the PE facility.

In assessing the state of collaboration in Pickard County, Wesley explained candidly, "It's my sense that in small counties, things are easier to coordinate. In large counties, it's harder to coordinate." He said that, essentially, the human factor is important. Whenever there is large turnover, it is difficult for other social service providers. These workers need personal trust: "The key is an individual's trustworthiness." Turnover is a problem in a large system. Wesley also thought it difficult when work is divided among so many agencies. Everyone gets spread thin: "Committees work best, but then there are time problems." With so many agencies involved for each child and family, Wesley wondered, "How must it be for the families?" He recalled a family that had recently received home visits from representatives of five different agencies. The mother, exasperated, asked Wesley, "OK, where are YOU from?" Wesley suggested that to prevent such scenarios, some centralization might be good.

Wesley thought the movement toward offering services in informal neighborhood centers was a good idea. We should "integrate and decentralize" (in a bureaucratic sense). We should "make schools serve more functions for kids because that's where kids are. People prefer going to schools rather than to various agencies. Maybe there could be mobile units, not administered by schools, but available there. This could provide one-stop shopping." He explained that the problem with this model is that in so many cases, schools do not serve neighborhoods because of busing. Wesley also mentioned "nondeficit services." Too often, he said, services are available only to people in extreme and well-documented need. Nondeficit services are instead available to all families and children, alleviating the stigma of need, the issue of labeling, and the wait-until-crisis timing of traditional services. For example, Wesley suggested that universal daycare would be more efficient and humane than the bureaucracy involved in determining which high-risk children qualify for subsidized day care.

With Mental Health and Project Enterprise serving as coordinating bodies, Justin's case would be seen by a broad spectrum of public and private social services agencies. This may work for and against the child: many agencies working together may assemble a package of services to meet multiple needs of the family, but they also may catch the family in a tangle of regulations and forms from which little service may actually result. Rosalind and Wesley indicated that, although the former is the goal, the latter is always a danger, especially in a city where agencies are struggling to handle enormous caseloads.

Juvenile Services: Cal

Cal, the 15-year-old with a past involving gangs, weapons, and drugs, encounters the county system anew on release from training school. As a Juvenile Court (JC) counselor, Will said that he would officially serve as the agent of change for Cal on the youth's release. Will would seek appropriate referrals to other agencies. Cal's family, he noted, had transportation problems and financial needs, as well as the issue of Cal's self-esteem. Will would refer Cal's mother to DSS for a variety of subsistence programs like AFDC, Medicaid, and transportation services. If the stepfather were disabled, Will would see if he qualified for disability income. The county alcohol and drug treatment programs would also be recommended for Cal's stepfather. If Cal's family refused to seek public assistance after such counseling, Will would then look for child neglect. If neglect were a problem, Child Protective Services (CPS) would investigate. Will would touch base with CPS anyway, perhaps asking their advice in the form of a hypothetical situation. If neglect were not found, the case would be documented in the event that Cal's situation changed for the worse.

Will then described his own role in Cal's case more specifically. As a conditional release counselor, it is his job to provide prerelease (from training school) counseling for students, to meet with schools and other services, and to arrange a package of services to help Cal make a smooth transition out of training school. The conditional release counselor meets with Cal's transition team comprised of school-based and central office staff who work to determine school placements like grade levels and special programs. The transition committee usually consists of Will, a school psychologist, a guidance counselor, and the Special Programs coordinator at the school district's central office.

After consulting with this team, Will would meet with Cal to discuss the programs that might best meet his needs. Will might recommend that Cal participate in a buddies program such as Partners, or the YES program. In either case, Will only needs to make a phone call for the referral. Homesteaders brings counselors into the home to work with the family over the short term (6-8 weeks), and might be another appropriate referral. Will would also suggest that the school counselor test Cal to see if he qualifies for an Academically Gifted school placement. Communities in Schools (CIS), a private initiative, might be contacted. CIS targets at-risk students, seeking to modify the curriculum and provide reality-based instruction. Mentors provide individual tutoring for these students. Will also might contact MHS to see if Cal qualified for counseling, if he were not already receiving such service. Finally, Will might also suggest a Drug Action referral depending on Cal's present involvement with drugs.

In listing the possible referrals, Will noted that collaboration outside Juvenile Services is mainly informal. He maintains a solid and reliable network of contacts in agencies throughout the county, contacts on whom he can rely for help and good information. To build and maintain these contacts he performs services beyond his job, as Juvenile Counselor, such as sitting on the boards of various service agencies in the county. From these positions he learns a great deal. For formal collaboration, he described the "Hard-to-Serve" Committee (see Justin's case for a description).

Impediments to collaboration, according to Will, are funding constraints, case overload, and clients who are unwilling or unable to follow through on the multiple services arranged for them. As examples, he cited clients whose insurance would not cover the private referrals agencies had given them, or who became discouraged in the face of daunting waiting periods. He puts his best efforts into line-up services, however, for the kids who willingly participate. In this sense, a strong incentive for caseworkers to collaborate, even in the face of obstacles, is a positive client attitude.

Cal's case was next presented to the school district's Special Programs Specialist, Lavonne, whom Will had indicated would be part of Cal's transitional team to prepare Cal's school placements and services. First she would see if Cal needed a Special Programs (SP) placement (such as for BEH children). If he did need SP, then she would see if Cal's projected school had the special programs to meet his needs. If the school's resources were inadequate, she would see if Cal might be transferred to another school, or to an alternative high school or one with alternative hours. Then Lavonne would check for involvement with the Mental Health agency in Cal's case, and if his family were an active DSS case. If either of these agencies were involved, the transition committee would initiate contact with them. If Cal's family were not involved with either agency, Lavonne might call them anyway and arrange appointments with intake workers. She might also see if Cal qualified for Medicaid on his own. Finally, Lavonne might line up a referral to Wilderness Camp, a program that works with BEH children in a setting somewhat like Outward Bound. (At Youth Services the administrator of Wilderness Camp said that students like Cal with weapon and gang histories would not be taken into this program.) Lavonne would probably also suggest that Cal be referred to Drug Action, a local addiction-assistance program.

Several nonprofit private agencies were mentioned as possible resources for Cal. The Neutral Zone is an umbrella organization of agencies to serve the needs of troubled boys and girls according to their pamphlet. One program's coordinator, Patricia, considered how Cal might benefit from Youth Action Resources (YAR), a mentoring program. She began by explaining that Cal is somewhat typical of the cases she sees, except that YAR also does not accept clients with drugs or weapon involvement. Usually Juvenile Courts are selective about the cases they refer to Patricia. More importantly, as the coordinator of a small program like YAR, Patricia must be aware of other options for clients she must reject. Some youth, she felt, are better served by other area mentor programs, with which she maintains good relationships. Such organizations offer each other high levels of support and information sharing, and Patricia feels comfortable making referrals to such familiar, cooperative agencies. The only special difficulty she noted in such collaborative arrangements was the problem of communicating confidential or sensitive information to remote locations.

Cal's case, according to Will, Lavonne, and Patricia, would need interagency attention, because individual agencies might avoid concentrating their efforts on such a difficult youth. With the right combination of programs, and solid commitment from Cal and his parents, it is possible he would receive the services he needs to make the transition back to society. It is also possible, however, that such programs may be overloaded, or place Cal on a waiting list just when timely service is so crucial. Interagency collaboration at best may improve Cal's chances of receiving appropriate, timely help. Scarce resources and the nature of his case prevent any certainty of such aid being available or successful.

Department of Social Services: Jerome

Jerome's case would pass from the DSS-Protective Services secretary to an intake worker. The troubled adolescent, with learning, family, and behavioral problems, would then be assigned to an investigative case worker, Beverly, who would assess the severity of the problem and work with the family to improve

Jerome's health and home environment. Beverly would first interview Jerome, his siblings, his mother, and other family members and relatives, in an effort to assess the child and the family's stability. Physical and psychological evaluations would be performed, the former by the county hospital, the latter by internal DSS therapists. Beverly would have Medicaid, Aid to Families with Dependent Children (AFDC), Food Stamps, and other applications completed if the family was not already enrolled in such programs. Beverly, along with Jerome's mother, would develop a plan for caring for the children while getting the mother back on her feet The plan would tap outside resources, such as the Substance Abuse Center (SAC), daycare for the youngest child, Big Brothers/Big Sisters, SafeHaven, and perhaps temporary group homes for the children while their mother worked things out.

Beverly collaborates with other agencies on an as-needed basis. The contacts are mostly one-way: Beverly contacts them, they do not contact her. Collaboration, to Beverly, means telephone conferences to deal with situational dilemmas. She shares information only when others need to know it; for confidentiality reasons she discourages other agencies from actively seeking information from her regarding specific cases. She said that she might mention the threat of court subpoenas to keep school personnel from involving themselves in Jerome's case, although she would not further disclose that very few such cases actually reach court.

If the abuse/neglect charge is substantiated, Beverly would transfer the case to a treatment case worker (either high- or low-risk, depending on the assessment) from 1 to 3 months after being assigned. Although Beverly did not find anything in Jerome's case to warrant her initiating the lengthy process of permanently removing the children from their mother's care, she did consider the possibility of temporary removal to a group home. Such an action is considered a "last resort" by DSS, whose mission is not to break up families but to mend them, a point emphasized repeatedly by both Beverly and Marina, the treatment caseworker.

In the most likely outcome, Beverly classifies Jerome's situation as low-risk and transfers his case to a low-risk treatment case worker. Physical abuse, sexual abuse, or severe neglect qualify a case as high-risk, none of which appear as conditions in Jerome's life. No low-risk case worker was available to consult, but Marina, a high-risk case worker, agreed to discuss Jerome's further progress through DSS. Marina would collect background information from Beverly, review it and meet with the family to verify Beverly's assessment. In accordance with treatment policy, Marina would develop a relationship with the family, which in Jerome's case means his mother's cooperation and commitment would be sought. This is often done through home visits, to revise the treatment plan based on prior progress. Much of the decision making here is shared. Marina noted that some treatment case workers shy away from a relational policy because they are unwilling to invest the necessary time and energy.

Marina agreed with Beverly's assessment that the children would not be removed right away, as from the vignette it appears that there is no physical threat. Activities may be found for the children either in school or outside school to help their socialization process. The school would not be included in locating such activities: DSS handles all such details themselves. Beverly's care plan would be continued, and modified if necessary to include the systems to which the family is connected: relatives, their church community, the children's school, the neighborhood, and other social services. The church would not be accessed for "faith-healing value," but for its social services. Psychological testing and family or individual therapy might also enter into the plan, but through either private or DSS therapists, not Mental Health. Marina said that she could be on Jerome's case as long as is necessary to get the family "righted."

If Jerome's mother took a belligerent turn when DSS entered the situation, becoming abusive or uncooperative, Marina would act to remove the children from the home. In this case, Marina would contact Child and Family Services, another DSS unit, and together they would review the case biography, determining the best resources to fit Jerome's and his siblings' needs. At all times the case worker leads the procedure, and CFS acts as their resource. Contacting CFS does not automatically mean that Jerome will be removed from the family. They may advise that it is premature to remove him, or they may act to find a temporary place for Jerome while the case worker continues working with the mother. A wide variety of services might be considered as alternatives to removal, including church organizations, because North Carolina has a long tradition of churches taking care of unwanted or troubled children.

If removal is finally decided on, the court petition is filed, the removal is made, and the battle begins. Both Beverly and Marina agreed, however, that DSS policy and Jerome's situation would not indicate such an action be taken without first exploring every other option. If Jerome's mother resisted such options, however, removal would always loom as a possibility. Little interagency collaboration seems to exist to ease Jerome's troubles, or to help his mother, or to relieve DSS of some of these responsibilities.

Schools: Tina

Tina—a child with physical handicaps exhibiting severe outbursts of anger— enters the service network through the school. Tasha, an elementary school counselor, read Tina's case, commenting that more details would help her to outline possible responses to Tina's needs. To address Tina's academic needs, a special placement team composed of the counselor, teacher, and parent would be organized. If Tina were obviously suffering from physical abuse, DSS (specifically, Child Protective Services) would be called immediately. If Tina already had an active case with DSS, Tasha would ask about the current status of the case and the case worker's name. If Tina's behavior presented safety problems, Mental Health services would be contacted, but the parents must first be contacted for consent. (Tasha's sense is that the parents would be unlikely to consent to this service.)

Within the school, Tasha has a variety of resources to offer Tina: special classes, counseling, and a nurse's evaluation. Although Tina is borderline emotionally mentally handicapped (EMH), Tasha thought that Tina should receive a full-time EMH placement, perhaps with some outside counseling. For Tina to receive this placement, she must first be screened by the School-Based Assistance Team, which would coordinate the necessary testing and documentation. Tasha also said that family counseling might be in order, but that the family would likely resist. Cooperation becomes unpredictable, she finds, when alcohol is involved. Tasha would offer Tina some counseling herself, both to determine the level of abuse and to find outlets for Tina's anger. If Tina had medical problems beyond spina bifida that contributed to her anger, Tasha would arrange for the school nurse to examine Tina and then recommend any further medical referrals.

Some of Tina's problems, however, would prompt Tasha to seek services beyond the school's resources. If abuse were clearly involved, Tasha would contact DSS; however, she noted that DSS is sometimes resistant to serving the child's best interests because DSS primarily tries to keep families together. In order for DSS to intervene, Tasha explained, there first needs to be a crisis. Tasha tries to document cases like Tina's carefully so that the groundwork is laid for future DSS intervention. Usually, she noted, Special Programs children are much more likely to garner DSS attention than other children. Tasha would also make a home visit. She would work to build rapport with Tina's father, a relationship she views as key to helping Tina. The father may need help to deal with his own problems. Also, Tina's mother is being abused and probably needs services such as a shelter where she can be safe.

Throughout the process of finding and coordinating services for Tina, Tasha said she would stay in contact with Tina's teachers and the parents as much as possible. Generally, Tasha would build a network of support to deal with Tina's problems, an ongoing and evolving network rather than one built from sporadic, incomplete contact. She noted, however, that keeping this sort of network process strong is difficult considering that she serves over 800 children. Other service providers are similarly overloaded. The school nurse, she pointed out, can visit each school site for only around 3 hours each week because each nurse is responsible for several schools. Tasha is persistent and maintains a wide variety of contacts. Heavy caseloads, reluctant parents, and other agencies' rules do not deter her efforts; they are the real conditions she has come to expect while seeking services for the students in her school.

Mabel, an intake worker at DSS, picked up the scenario at that agency. Assuming that the abuse Tina and her mother were enduring was ongoing, Mabel would make a referral to CPS. Because the family seemed to have problems making ends meet, Mabel noted that there were many services she could offer, such as AFDC, Food Stamps, Medicaid, housing, utility bill relief, and the like. Mabel believed that Tina's emotional needs probably justified a referral for in-depth counseling. She would recommend Family Services of Pickard County, an agency that provides counseling on a sliding fee scale. Because the mother was being abused, Mabel would refer her to Interact, an agency that assists abused spouses.

Mabel discussed some of the technology that helps her deliver services. She said the telephone is the mainstay of her work: she estimates that she uses the telephone for at least 95% of her referrals. She has built a large and cooperative network of people at other agencies on whom she can consistently call. In addition to the telephone, she described the computer resting on her desk as part of a pilot program designed to provide case workers with exhaustive information about available services, programs, and funds. Also, this computer expedites case processing because many forms of client information (e.g., drivers license records) are available online. She explained that eventually the agency would process all documentation on the computer rather than through paperwork exchange. Although only a few case workers were yet using this system, Mabel felt that it had already dramatically improved her work flow.

Mabel offered other ideas for improving interagency collaboration in Pickard County. She said that it is important to "meet face-to-face with other agencies in order to get clear on what each does. We need a two-way feedback system. Generally, though, we don't have enough time for this. We need more people to handle cases. When new people come, we need to let them have brief presentations about how services work." She explained that confidentiality tends to keep information inaccessible, which further hinders interagency communication. Another barrier to effective collaboration Mabel saw was a concern among administrators about maximizing client contact workers' time. As it is, "income maintenance workers must work within certain time limits even if there is a significant overload." Because collaboration takes time, administrators end up serving in formal collaborative roles so that case workers can spend more of their limited hours working directly with clients. Mabel said one person in DSS goes to a half-day meeting once a month to discuss interagency referrals and cooperation. This person's work has proven invaluable to the agency's service delivery, and Mabel wished there could be more such collaboration. Ultimately, more time devoted to collaboration and to becoming familiar with the procedures and services of other agencies could make client contact hours more efficient.

Mabel's referral to CPS led Tina's case to Bracey, a former intake worker who currently screens referrals. She explained that a case like Tina's is not typical for CPS because children with severe handicaps are not usually referred into the CPS system. Most children referred either have less severe mental or physical problems or have been neglected. Bracey, like Tasha, wanted more information about Tina before proceeding. Unlike Tasha, Bracey indicated that she would address this need by beginning a formal investigation.

The focus of the investigation into Tina's case would be the suspected physical abuse, and the father's alcoholism as it affects the child. Bracey would probably work with the CPS treatment unit that deals with cases of child physical abuse. (If sexual abuse were suspected, however, she would instead contact the Sex Abuse unit for investigation and treatment.) If the investigation revealed that the abuse was severe, Tina would be removed from the home and placed with relatives or in a foster home. To remove Tina, there must be a petition that bears a judge's signature to do so. If the investigation instead revealed that Tina's abuse is less severe, Bracey would work with the family to find support groups, parenting classes, and home health services. "Sometimes families of kids like this are severely stressed." Bracey would also want to get the father into the Substance Abuse Center (SAC), a local agency that deals with alcohol abuse. Bracey noted that Tina's mother needed relief. Although she does not usually encourage parents to quit work, doing so might help this mother enough to allow her to care better for Tina. "The mother sounds like she cares. She can be helped."

Bracey said that she collaborates extensively with other agencies, but also revealed that other agencies tend to call her more than she calls them. Bracey basically accepts referrals and then screens them. One problem she regularly faces in making calls to other agencies is the need for strict confidentiality in CPS cases. "Parent contact is the dividing line for allowing collaboration. Have them call me, but I can't call them." Bracey further emphasized the considerable legal requirements and liabilities she faced in her work. Generally she "cannot make collaborative calls by state law until a case is under investigation." Bracey's vision of an ideal collaborative setup reflects the bind she works within: she would like to see a unit or group of people who could make initial contacts with the family in order to look at the situation without necessarily taking the case. She added, however, that she thought her agency worked well in spite of these limitations. She said she did not find that lack of collaboration presented significant problems in handling cases well.

School counselor Tasha's mention of a possible EMH placement took Tina's case to Jean and Rhonda, chairwomen of the School-Based Assistance Team (SBAT) that screens and processes Special Programs placements. They explained that the SBAT, composed of the principal, a school psychologist, three grade-level teachers, the school counselor, and the contact teachers, would begin the placement process by discussing Tina's needs. The team may sit in a circle and brainstorm, discuss similar problems faced in the past, or try to identify resources that might help deal with Tina's needs. The county school office would be contacted to obtain resources for particular problems. Often the team finds that the paperwork and decision making necessary are overwhelming. Jean and Rhonda indicated that Tasha's help has been very important in recent years. Because she usually makes the phone calls to other agencies, however, most everyone contributes ideas and some expertise.

While the SBAT discussed Tina's problems, every effort would be made to include parents in the process. Formal assessments—a battery of tests as well as observation sessions—would be conducted to better determine Tina's needs. Then Tina's main teacher would design and implement three classroom interventions intended to mediate Tina's anger. If unsuccessful, the attempts would be documented and attached to the rest of the assessments. Finally, when all assessments were conducted, the team would reconvene to decide whether or not to place Tina in a school-based special program. If the parents agreed to the placement, Tina's program would be adjusted and the case would be closed for the team. Should Tina's parents disagree with the placement, their action and rationales would be documented; if a pattern of chronic child neglect is later found, this documentation will contribute to the case.

In all cases, throughout the screening and placement process, team members take care to follow guidelines for paperwork, for deadlines, and for procedures. The Central Office insists that the school protect itself by complying with processing requirements, and there is a constantly implied threat of lawsuits if things are done improperly. If federal investigators were to find the paperwork out of compliance, the school would lose $2,000 per child per year. A shortage of school psychologists slows the assessment process, making deadlines hard to meet. Jean and Rhonda said that this extra pressure has them working overtime with little compensation. For this reason, both agreed that teachers should not double as resource people; instead, they would favor specialized staff positions. "Teachers are already too busy. The paperwork for the SBAT is a full time job. There should be a separate position. We want to teach!"

Finally, because Tasha and Mabel had indicated that Tina's medical condition needed to be more fully investigated, perhaps referred to a school nurse, her case was presented to Nanci, a school nurse at the Public Health Department. She began by explaining that she thought Tina and her mother would benefit from Al-A-Teen and Al-Anon programs to help them cope with the father's alcoholism. Problems with transportation or child care could be addressed. The father, she said, clearly needs help to get to the point of going to Alcoholics Anonymous himself.

Nanci would contact DSS because there was physical abuse and a possibility of sexual abuse. She also thought Tina should see a school psychologist, and that perhaps Communities in Schools could offer assistance by providing some mental health services. Regarding Tina's physical health, Nanci suggested that Tina needed a complete evaluation. She wondered who was taking care of Tina's daily living needs. If the mother handled all day-to-day care, then she is undoubtedly overburdened; an aide could help take care of Tina's immense ongoing physical needs. Tina's Individual Education Plan (IEP) could specify that she needs to have special assistance for such physical needs as catheterization. If DSS were involved, then an aide could be provided automatically, if deemed necessary. Despite these suggestions, Nanci clearly worried about saying anything about difficulties in collaboration that might get her in trouble. She did indicate that the critical shortage of nurses leaves a school nurse so overloaded that she cannot effectively provide screening, treatment, and referrals to all the children who need her.

Tina's case would be seen by several agencies, all of whom would recommend other programs for possible investigation. This is not surprising. Her problems are multiple and some are at a crisis point. Her school's willingness to classify Tina as having special needs gives her access to programs other children would not as easily enter. That Tina's parents are both experiencing difficulty brings further attention. It appears that a child with so many discreet problems—educational, medical, emotional, environmental—has hooks that qualify her for many discreet treatments; the challenge to the service system comes in finding more coordinated approaches, rather than symptom-by-symptom solutions.

Schools: Tommy

Tommy, a child with inadequate food and clothing, persistent minor medical complaints, and a spotty attendance record, would be referred to his school counselor, Tasha, by a teacher, the school nurse, or school social worker. Because Tommy's most immediate need is medical, Tasha would first check with the nurse to make sure the child is being attended. In Tommy's school records, Tasha would examine test results; they may indicate whether his home environment or a learning disability are involved in his poor performance. A home visit or other meeting with Tommy's parents would give Tasha an idea of the boy's home life, and let her gauge whether her interventions will meet with parental cooperation or resistance. Tasha would work with Tommy's teacher to help find him a "buddy," which he appears to need. She would also use informal means to address some of Tommy's other problems; for example, she keeps an emergency supply of children's clothing (solicited from school staff) from which she could offer Tommy something clean and suitable.

School social workers would probably not be involved in Tasha's plans. Their primary concern is Tommy's poor attendance. The county places a high priority on keeping kids in school, and there are only 3.5 social workers to work with 80,000 students. Surprisingly, given such daunting workloads, there is a services overlap here. Especially with his chronic absences, the social workers probably want to talk to Tommy's parents or make a home visit, repeating Tasha's actions with a similar motive of assessing his home environment. The separate tracks taken by the school social worker and counselors have the dual disadvantage of reinventing the wheel (collecting the same information twice) and of subjecting Tommy's family to unnecessary intrusion. According to all school personnel, Tommy's case, it seems, would hinge on his parents' level of cooperation. If they are cooperative, the case probably would never leave the school. If they are uncooperative, the case would spread to other agencies.

Parents Cooperative. If Tommy's parents are willing to work with school officials, his case would be easy for the school to handle without much outside help. The school's internal intervention team, which may consist of teachers, the school counselor, the principal, the school psychologist, special education teachers, and the school nurse, would work with the parents to develop a plan for helping Tommy and his family. The plan might consist of medical treatment (by the nurse and perhaps Public Health officials), home or after-school tutoring, programs such as Boy's Clubs or the church choir (mentioned in the vignette), outside sources of food and clothing (this may include private agencies and churches), and a referral to the Department of Social Services (DSS) for financial assistance. This team, however, can only get involved with parental consent.

Tasha noted that one problem in services delivery is that parents are often unaware of available programs until their situation reaches a crisis point requiring intervention. She believed that many problems could be prevented by making resources known to parents before critical need arises. However, Tommy's parents' pride and their church involvement indicate to Tasha that the DSS route might be less successful than the less official private services route. The team's recommendations may include psychological screening by the school psychologist, which could eventually involve Mental Health; that, however, would depend on the family's ability to pay or eligibility for aid, and Tasha was doubtful they would really need or want to receive such services. (The family's eligibility process, channeled through DSS, is much as described elsewhere in this chapter.)

Parents Uncooperative. If Tommy's parents do not cooperate, his case becomes more difficult for school staff to manage, according to Tasha. Tommy would continue to have ailments that the nurse could treat when on campus, but he would receive no long-term health maintenance. Tasha would continue to give him clothing as necessary and food while he is in school, both from her own and outside private resources. She did not discuss how his parents might react when Tommy came home from school with clothing he did not leave the house wearing.

Tasha also has a network of public and private agents she calls on for strategy assistance. Careful not to breach confidentiality codes nor force official entrance into the case by other agencies, she may pose hypothetical scenarios and ask, "What would you do?" Her confidants include private therapists, public mental health workers, the DSS information line, drug action agencies, churches, fellow school counselors, and public health nurses. Tasha said that the school could better serve Tommy if full-time medical, psychological, and social services staff were available. The need to conduct so much "business" on the phone takes away from the timely treatment of Tommy's case.

Tasha speculated that if Tommy's parents initially resist, the whole situation would grow tense. On one hand, Tasha would maintain contact with the boy's parents, trying to make them see Tommy's need and their own responsibilities. She might involve the family's church because the parents might listen to their pastor more than a counselor. This sort of collaboration has no formal procedures or structures. Tasha takes particular pride in being, as she called it, "out in the neighborhoods and in people's faces." She likes to build relationships with community members so that seeking help becomes a more comfortable experience.

But even while working to bring the parents to see their son's problems, Tasha would be building a case against them. She would continue to document the case and Tommy's condition, meeting with him periodically. With such documentation, she could possibly compile enough evidence of chronic neglect to convince DSS to intervene without parental permission. Tasha stated that a case such as Tommy's—involving no clearcut abuse—would take a year to get accepted by DSS because DSS primarily deals with more extreme cases than Tommy's. Tasha also uses the possibility of DSS involvement as a tool to get the parents to cooperate. The intervention of DSS here is seen as a threat, with implications of Tommy's removal from the family, court appearances, and the like. Both gently and with more muscle, Tasha would work with outside contacts to bring about the parental cooperation initially withheld.

Tasha's documentation efforts are paper-intensive. Besides DSS referral forms, Tasha has standard forms for the multidisciplinary intervention team analysis, the tracking of exceptional children, the tracking of "regular" children, parental notification and consent forms, attendance problem forms, and Individualized Education Program (IEP) forms. These forms are unique to the county in design—there is no state- or even region-wide uniformity. The only documentation that is computerized is attendance information and form letters. Tasha indicated that computerizing information and more uniform paperwork would, at the very least, save time in dealing with cases like Tommy's.

The process at DSS when parents are uncooperative is different than if the family willingly seeks assistance: investigation and notification procedures are strictly codified and can be swift, intense, and unpleasant. On accepting Tommy's case, Bracey would assign it to a Protective Services investigative case worker, who has 30 days to complete the following steps: talk with Tommy's parents, talk with Tommy, talk with school staff if necessary, begin developing a treatment plan with the family, and decide whether to close the case or reassign it to a Protective Services treatment case worker. All of Tasha's documentation can only get the case accepted by DSS; once it is accepted, the Protective Services investigative case worker begins new documentation and interviews, drawing on Tasha's information only as necessary or convenient. Bracey indicated that Tommy would be a borderline neglect case, and his case would be closed down quickly—if accepted at all for investigation. At no time in the process would Tasha be updated on the progress of Tommy's case (although she may be subpoenaed if the case goes to court). Once the case leaves the school and enters the more formalized DSS process, collaboration is closed out.

Although she uses the threat of DSS intervention, and prepares to seek it, Tasha's knowledge that she will be excluded from any case once accepted causes her to avoid actually involving DSS with students like Tommy. For such a child, the realities of interagency contact mean that he may be monitored and his family pressured, but little action will be ventured. Tommy's case exposes the complex relationship between agencies and parents in seeking the child's well-being.

Department of Health: Maureen

Maureen, a teenager, may be pregnant, may have been raped, and may have been exposed to the virus that causes AIDS. She may wish to follow up on her teacher's referral to the Health Department, but this may prove to be difficult in practice. The most obvious obstacle is that public transportation will not take her to the right neighborhood. She would have to miss a day of school, but the suspected pregnancy may also cause missed days, and such spotty attendance may draw unwanted attention. After three absences, the school social worker sends a letter home to inform parents. A teenager trying to hide a pregnancy or to find a way to tell her parents might well avoid visiting the Health Department under these conditions.

If and when Maureen did visit Public Health, her first contact would be with a family-planning representative like Renee. This initial counseling would focus on discussing Maureen's test results: a pregnancy test and a sexually transmitted disease (STD) test would be administered (Maureen would pay for materials only), and she would be offered an HIV test. If it turns out that Maureen is healthy and not pregnant, she need not return to the Health Department, after Renee counsels her about birth control and disease prevention. If tests show Maureen to be HIV-positive or infected by another STD, but not pregnant, and if she is not covered by health insurance, she would be given an application for Medicaid, and would begin appropriate treatment. In the case of both an HIV-positive result and a confirmed pregnancy, Maureen would be enrolled in early intervention AIDS treatment either through the Health Department or through a nearby university-sponsored program for HIV-positive mothers.

The most likely situation, however, is that Maureen is pregnant but not HIV-positive. Renee's role, therefore, is to help Maureen decide what to do by providing resource information and discussing the options presented. Although Health Department policy favors including the teen's parents in this decision, the agency is not required to inform parents of a minor's pregnancy. If Maureen chooses an abortion and she has no money, Renee would refer her to DSS, which has two Service Intake workers stationed at the Health Department facility. DSS would then help her apply for state funding and refer her to an abortion clinic. If Maureen has money (or her parents are willing to help), Renee would refer her to a private abortion clinic.

If Maureen decides to continue the pregnancy, she would again be referred to DSS, where she could apply for Medicaid, child care, and AFDC, among other things. Having DSS people physically in the Health Department is seen as a spur to collaboration, especially by DSS; according to DSS coordinator Jody, when Medicaid became available to pregnant women and indigent children, DSS approached the Health Department about placing intake workers at the latter agency's site to smooth the processing of the increased application pool. Applications are filled out at the Health Department and sent to the main DSS office, which can save the client time and effort. On the downside, there are concerns that the convenience may actually make enrolling in other DSS programs less likely or more difficult (because they are not promoted at the Health Department site). The cooperation benefits the agencies, too. Jody noted that being onsite allows DSS workers to access birth certificates, which are located in files only open to the Health Department. Health workers were less enthusiastic about the arrangement, wishing for more meaningful face-to-face contact and exchange.

Maureen would also apply for WIC, an internal Health Department program providing nutritional help to pregnant women. Many programs, including a number of private and church-affiliated offerings, are available to pregnant women through the Health Department which keeps an impressive library of material on these resources.

After deciding to continue the pregnancy and enrolling in the basic programs, Maureen would receive more physical tests (in the case of pregnant women, the HIV test is automatic). Maureen would also be assigned to one of five Maternity Care Coordination (MCC) caseworkers because she is young, alone, and somewhat at risk. Dianna, an MCC caseworker, said MCC is the social work unit of the Health Department. Assignments are made according to address. The county is divided into five sections, with one MCC case worker to each section. Caseloads average 70 to 80 at any given time. Dianna would contact Maureen within 30 days of the assignment. Dianna's role is to make services and resources available, work with Maureen's school nurse, advocate on Maureen's behalf with people who "don't accept or understand" the situation, and help Maureen with her physical and material needs.

Dianna might decide later in the pregnancy, with Maureen, to include an Outreach worker in the case. Janet, who supervises Outreach workers, described them as special help in crisis cases. This worker can attend more closely to Maureen's needs, because she is a paraprofessional—often someone who was once in Maureen's position and wants to help others, but does not have professional credentials—with a smaller caseload, about 10 women at a time. One service only an Outreach worker can provide, besides more contact, is transportation. Because MCC caseworkers have other responsibilities and are professionally liable, they cannot offer clients transportation to appointments or meetings. At 2 months postpartum, Maureen's case would leave Dianna and be transferred to a Child Services Coordination (CSC) team, but the Outreach worker could stay with Maureen, providing continuity for up to a year postpartum.

The main role of CSC is to attend to the child's developmental needs from birth to age 2, tracking potential developmental problems and offering preventative maintenance. Unlike MCC, CSC is a primarily a medical program, working mostly with the county hospital staff. Carol, a CSC supervisor, said each team consists of a nurse coupled with supervisory, medical, and administrative support. MCC and Outreach are not effectively included in the CSC team, an internal miscoordination that Renee and Dianna found more troubling than Carol did. A certain amount of tension exists between the two units, seemingly stemming from status and pay issues (CSC nurses have higher status in the Health Department and are paid better than the MCC social workers). With so much internal complexity, it is not surprising that DSS social workers are seldom called to assist in Health Department cases like Maureen's. The Health Department, it seems, attempts to do it all for each client.

However, if Maureen wants to return to school after becoming a mother, and her parents have withdrawn all support, her needs exceed even the Health Department's broad range of services. Daycare is the major problem, for which she would be referred to Kira, a DSS Children and Family Services (CFS) representative. Maureen, she said, would have to be eligible for AFDC and actually living on her own to qualify for enrollment in the JOBS Program, which would help her find and fund daycare. Both JOBS and most reimbursable daycare programs, however, have waiting lists, according to Sue, a representative of the Department of Facility Services-Child Care Section, the state level daycare funds distribution unit. Kira pointed out that because Maureen is a pregnant teen she would be prioritized on the waiting list at JOBS and for daycare. Choosing a childcare facility would be Maureen's decision; she would have to investigate to find facilities that accept Medicaid reimbursement. Maureen would more than likely pick several facilities and get on the waiting list at each. Although daycare is obviously crucial to meeting Maureen's needs, the process of obtaining it appears to be hazily understood by many agency personnel; it is a service existing on the margins of several agencies that is not clearly monitored or served by any one agency. Maureen, therefore, in seeking daycare so she can return to school, would face not only multiple waiting lists, but caseworkers who cannot themselves be as helpful on this point as they have otherwise been. Every day that passes in waiting, Maureen may feel more and more that continuing her education is a distant, lost ideal.

ANALYSIS AND CONCLUSIONS

The caseflows traced earlier were shaped by their urban context. In such a complex system, the challenge is to assemble a sufficient, efficient package of services for the client, without incompatible or redundant services that trap the family in a thicket of regulations and paperwork with little helpful result. Some urban crises demand collaborative attention because no one agency is constituted to address them; however, the demand is not always met, and such cases (Cal's, for example) are most vulnerable to repeated rejection or abandonment—the hot potato problem. The impersonality of urban life may make difficult decisions about children seem callous to parents and teachers. The scale of services in Pickard leads to some fragmentation of roles. A smaller county may have one office supplying multiple treatments, but in Pickard each individual facet of a child's life may attract a different caseworker, resulting in enormous teams that resist coordination.

Agency workers, in general, appeared to be committed to client interests, a commitment that persists in spite of enormous job stress and obstacles. This commitment to children's interests, however, often manifested itself in a protective or even controlling approach to cases. Workers use phrases like "I know what's best for this person," and believe themselves to the point that they may be unwilling to share responsibility for a case. Whenever several agencies worked together on cases, each seemed to prefer assuming the lead on case management rather than playing merely cooperative or secondary roles. This preference for leadership may stem from idiosyncrasies of paperwork requirements or funding regulations. For some agencies, leading the case is the only way to receive full funding reimbursement in a cooperative arrangement. This tendency to own cases, at both the caseworker and agency levels, works against collaborative relationships among service providers.

Client contact workers in all agencies routinely carry enormous caseloads in Pickard County. Although this would seem to recommend the building of interagency support networks, the opposite is actually the result here. Caseworkers explain that they would like to pursue more leads for each of their clients, but that heavy caseloads keep them too busy to do so. Numerous interviewees experienced ongoing frustration over this discrepancy between desired and actual service delivery.

Interagency collaboration, the focus of this study, was itself a term with various meanings. It was striking to discover that in Pickard County the meaning of the term varied more by position within agency hierarchy than by individuals or particular agencies. Generally, client-contact workers tended to view collaboration as a process, as calling on particular other persons at various agencies for advice, for joint action, or to make referrals. These webs of contacts are unique for every client-contact worker and are usually built over a period of years. Almost every such person interviewed indicated the importance of these systems of connections and stressed that the work of new persons is complicated by the necessity of first establishing these networks. "Collaboration" to these people usually meant informal exchange of information or services rather than a formally structured organization or system.

In contrast, individuals in administrative positions tended to view "collaboration" in structural terms. To them, a collaborative process is one in which agency roles are formally designated, case responsibility carefully delineated, and information flow defined and routinized. Many agency administrators described collaborative efforts where representatives of other agencies would meet together and discuss better means of client service delivery. These groups usually consisted of administrators rather than client-contact workers. Client-contact workers did not seem to have the schedule flexibility or time to participate in many formally organized interagency efforts.

Information management—its collection, protection, and accessibility—presents constant challenges to would-be collaborative arrangements in Pickard. Agencies collect data uniquely: unique forms, unique storage, unique pieces of information. Collaboration, therefore, may be impeded by the redundancy, or by the incompatibility, of these processes between agencies. Confidentiality laws, as mentioned earlier, may further prohibit information sharing; interviewees also emphasized a more intangible condition, the personal relationships between agency personnel. The degree of trust and rapport existing between workers can be the most important factor in the ease of access to information. Perhaps one of the most overarching limitations on easy information exchange between workers in social service agencies, however, is lack of time. Client-contact workers expressed frustration that they did not have the schedule flexibility to attend meetings and access the information about other agencies that administrators routinely share. All of these conditions combine to create information jams that limit effective collaboration. Over time, this reduced level of communication has created a system where agencies often do not fully understand the roles and capacities of other agencies. In such an atmosphere, information may be withheld entirely, partially shared, intermittently inaccurate, or imprudently confided, all to the detriment of the client and interagency relations. In a large system like Pickard County, the mere quantity of information flowing through such a poorly coordinated stream leads to case bottlenecks that further strain limited resources.

In such a system, there is a sense of isolation within agencies. Profound differences existed between the jobs performed by client-contact workers and administrators. Often the people who worked most closely with clients were the ones receiving the least pay, facing the greatest overload, enjoying the fewest job-related perks, and having the least flexible schedules. Chronic understaffing and rapid turnover exacerbate the stress. Overall, very little systematic effort goes into caring for and nurturing the client-contact workers. Although there are some programs designed to help reduce stress or to provide counseling, generally these resources were not accessed because of their poor quality, expense, or time demands. A general sense seems to permeate the agencies visited, a sense that the welfare of the client-contact worker is not important in the overall functioning of each organization. It follows that clients will be affected adversely by the agency's neglect of their only possible advocates.

What did the service providers of Pickard County think would improve their ability to collaborate? Not surprisingly in this massive network, interviewees repeatedly said that they would like to have time to get to know the other social service workers throughout the county. Some said that they simply wanted to know more about the services offered in the area. Others specifically indicated that they wanted to build their web of contacts. Still others felt that increased contact would certainly lead to better relations between agencies and that collaboration would then naturally follow. Although several people believed that turf battles and fears of job loss keep agencies from collaborating as fully as possible, increased contact among and between agencies was usually viewed as a promising avenue for service improvement.

4

Collaboration in Crisis: Fragmentation as Status Quo

Amee Adkins
Kathy Hytten

Treir County is a relatively rural county in eastern North Carolina with a population of 50,000 to 60,000 people. The median family income is a little over $30,000 annually. In the winter the unemployment rate averages 10%, whereas in the summer it is approximately half that. The education system includes 13 public schools, serving a population of a little over 8,000 students. There are eight elementary schools, three middle schools, and two high schools. The county also sponsors a community college, which offers vocational, technical, and general education programs.

All of the social service agencies in Treir County are located in the two largest municipalities: Haight (population 6,000) and Vista (population 3,800). The Mental Health Department operates in Haight, and it is the largest branch of a mental health network that serves four counties in the area. The Departments of Health, Juvenile Services, and Social Services are located in Vista, all within a few blocks of each other. The Board of Education is about one mile from this area. Organizationally, these five agencies are independent of each other, and each has its own bureaucratic structure.

Contact and cooperation between and among the various agencies in Treir County is frequently informal. Case workers in the agencies, for the most part, report good working relationships and fairly frequent telephone contact with each other, usually arising in the context of advice and referrals. In addition, Treir County maintains four formal collaborative instruments: three are the result of state mandates and the fourth is an ad hoc task force that responds to perceived local "crises" in service delivery. The research in Treir County suggests that the informal "collaboration," as denoted in the interviews is often simply the logical extension of service delivery to clients with typical needs; that is, needs to which agencies are equipped to respond. Therefore, service providers might pick up the phone and call someone in another agency to tell her to expect a referral—one that is easy to discern, such as a need for AFDC support. The formal collaborative teams, however, each respond to atypical client issues; that is, confounding problems that no existing service pathway can accommodate. The application of this implicit criterion to case management enhances interagency collaboration for the exceptional cases, but, at the same time, it allows normal agency processes to remain unchanged. That is, it both perpetuates a lack of collaboration and reinforces the claim that the separate agencies should proceed without collaborating. In other words, it reifies existing agency cultures and structures, making them seem natural, rational, and immutable (Berger & Luckmann, 1966). The reification of such processes poses a substantial barrier to interagency collaboration because service providers take them for granted as the way to meet client needs. Further, as these cultures and structures play a role in the client pathways, they themselves present a number of barriers to interagency collaboration.

This chapter looks at the adaptive sorting mechanism in Trier County that, on the one hand, assures interagency collaboration for exceptional issues among clients and, on the other hand, denies it on behalf of typical clients. In doing so, we present the formal collaborative structures cited during the interviews, the client pathways for each vignette, and an analysis of the conditions of case management in Treir County that promote and impede interagency collaboration.

EXISTING COLLABORATIVES

As mentioned earlier, there are four formal collaborative structures in Treir County. Of these four, only three were implicated sufficiently in the field work to justify their analysis. All four are described here, but the reader should note that the Early Childhood Development Council will not be represented in the conclusions presented.

The first two collaborative structures, the Children First Council (CFC) and the Children First Case Review Team (CFCRT), are related formally. They originally were constituted to review cases of children's sexual abuse/assault and to attend to issues concerning perpetrators and victims. The Children First Council considers broader issues at stake in serving these populations, whereas the Children First Case Review Team collaborates on serving specific cases. As these two teams have developed, they have expanded the focus of their attention from only cases of sexual abuse to other complex issues facing service providers. Members of the Children First Council include representatives from the Department of Social Services (DSS), Mental Health, Juvenile Services, and Education (school psychologist), as well as members of other relevant public and private agencies (e.g., physicians, attorneys, law enforcement, and the Domestic Violence Council). Members from public agencies on the CFC are also representatives on the Children First Case Review Team, whereas members from the private sector include two pediatricians, the District Attorney, two guardians ad litem, and an attorney. Both groups include a broad range of service professionals from the public and private spheres; the only notable exception is the Health Department, which has no seat on either team. Another important feature of these teams is that, although they boast broad representation, the majority of members hold higher level, administrative posts in their home agencies. This carries two effects: first, this creates a gap between formal structures for collaboration and the day-to-day practice of service delivery because very few on these teams are front-line service providers; second, administrators are able to deliberate collaborative service provision from a "bird's-eye view" of their agencies and thus work from a more informed understanding of a wider array of services that might be appropriate and available.

The CFCRT meets regularly every other week to discuss strategies for problematic cases. It is administratively independent of all agencies, and a new facilitator is chosen annually by the members. Everyone must sign a statement of confidentiality before each meeting, and, likewise, the team must have a signed waiver from the client's parents releasing information to each member of the team. Parents may decline all or some of these waivers, in which case the CFCRT will break down into approved subgroups. The purpose of the CFCRT is to deal with child victimization from a multidisciplinary approach. The Children First Case Review Team seeks the following objectives:

1. Identify resources in the community on a case-by-case basis;
2. Facilitate information sharing for better coordination of services;
3. Strengthen agency relationships;
4. Identify deficiencies in the community and make recommendations;
5. Work directly with the District Attorney when court involvement is indicated;
6. Facilitate interagency education.

The CFCRT discusses an estimated three new cases at each meeting (six new cases per month), as well as updating past cases. Occasionally the CFCRT sets aside a meeting to discuss a particular issue and how best to address it. At the time of this study, for example, the CFCRT elected to discuss the increase in the number of incidents of students caught with weapons in school and the school board's response of "long-term suspension" (suspension for the duration of the academic year).

In contrast to the administrative-level personnel on the CFC and CFCRT, direct service providers comprise the Early Childhood Development Council, which collaborates to serve infants with congenital developmental problems. Participating agencies include the Mental Health Center, DSS, and the Board of Education, each represented by its early childhood professional. There are also positions for the Director of the local Child Development Center, a speech pathologist (also from the Development Center), and one slot each for the Exceptional Family Member Program, parents, the area School for the Deaf, and the local Head Start agency. This group is not involved with developing broad policy; they only consider particular cases, working to compose comprehensive medical, psychological, and developmental service packages to prevent long-term disability. In accordance with their state mandate, their formal consideration of cases closes when such children reach 2 years of age.

The last existing collaborative mechanisms to be discussed are the ad hoc task forces that convene in response to emerging crises, such as dramatic increases in teen pregnancy. Participation in these task forces is more fluid than the teams described previously, depending on the nature of the problems and the agencies and level of personnel responding to them. When asked about the staff composition of these meetings, the Director of the Health Department included himself, the supervisor of field workers from DSS, an Adult Protective Services worker, an assistant county manager, and, in the case of the AIDS Task Force, the STD counselor from the Health Department, among others. Generally, their discussions are limited to the breadth of an issue, rather than specific cases, and the goal primarily is to encourage agencies to anticipate new demands and, perhaps, to brainstorm responses.

CLIENT PATHWAYS

Mental Health: Justin

Justin, the 5-year-old living with his younger sister and their recovering alcoholic mother in a homeless shelter, entered the network of human services through the local Mental Health agency's child therapy division. The Child Therapist, Serina, said that most of her cases, or "consumers,"[1] are identified or

---

[1]The Director of the Treir Mental Health Agency pointed out that their staff refers to their clients as "consumers" in an effort to distance themselves from the medical community, an association which might be made if they used the term "patient," and from the rest of the human services system, which is connoted by the term "client." Also, by using the term "consumer" the Director hopes to promote a sense of accountability among her staff through this subtle reminder that individuals *choose* to submit to their services.

referred by the schools and DSS' Child Protective Services (CPS). She has almost 60 active cases and said she tries to meet with each consumer at least once weekly, sometimes once every other week.

In the children's interests, Serina prefers to conduct initial intake interviews herself, to begin forming a relationship immediately and to reduce embarrassment for the child. The purpose of the interview is to collect information for a preliminary screening sheet (e.g., name, address, problem, brief social history, medical history, and mental assessment). In addition, at this initial meeting she would schedule an appointment with Justin's mother to discuss his case and the family's situation further. For instance, Serina would advise Justin's mother about other social services support she may not already receive, such as AFDC from DSS, the Early Childhood Intervention Clinic for Julia (Justin's younger sister) and peer counseling for herself through the Mental Health agency.

Serina routinely develops initial service plans for her consumers, although each plan is subject to adjustment once treatment is in progress. Justin's service plan would include additional assessments, if any were necessary, to complete a psychological evaluation. To collect this information, she would call the school for any of their records of Justin; she would refer Justin to the local Developmental Evaluation Center (in the neighboring county) for any other necessary assessments. Describing the likely course of Justin's treatment, Serina said she would exchange evaluation profiles with the school, meet with Justin on a weekly or biweekly basis, and perhaps observe Justin in school (although this is unlikely).

As Serina and the Director of the Mental Health agency described services for Justin and his family, it appears that no measure of collaboration enters into this case. Serina would advise Justin's mother of other available services, based on her own working knowledge of county agencies; beyond that Serina offered no indication of formal referrals, much less collaboration. It would be up to Justin's mother to make the connections herself. Interviews indicated that the needs and issues that Justin's vignette presents are typical of the client population for Treir County's Mental Health center. Consequently, the Child Therapist is equipped to handle Justin's case within the boundaries of her own agency.

Juvenile Services: Cal

Cal, the 15-year-old with a past involving gangs, weapons, and drugs, encounters the county system anew on release from training school. Two Juvenile Services counselors were interviewed regarding Cal's client pathway. These counselors opted to recreate Cal's probable course leading up to the vignette as written, because that is where the majority of services would be invoked. Gary and Sheila framed Cal's situation with the acknowledgement that state law requires "all community resources be exhausted" before the courts may invoke the option of training school.

On Cal's arrest for possessing drugs and a weapon, the police would contact Sheila, an intake counselor from Juvenile Services. As he was charged with a "nondivertible offense," a court appointment would be approved automatically. Sheila would conduct a prehearing investigation, first requesting from his school a copy of Cal's disciplinary record and a report on his academic status. Sheila said she would also communicate with the Department of Social Services (DSS) to find out if he or his family were being served by them in some capacity. Given adequate time (more than 5 weeks) prior to Cal's court date, Sheila mentioned Cal might be referred to a private psychologist for therapy. Juvenile Services has resources to contract for a private therapist for individual and family counseling and for a private psychologist who does psychological evaluations.[2]

Sheila assumed the judge would grant Cal "conditional release," at which point his case would be transferred to Gary, who would explore the alternatives available for Cal from the community. Gary's task would be to design a treatment plan for Cal with specific goals and objectives to address his problems and needs. He described several options that would be appropriate for Cal, including Tough Love, in-home therapy from a therapist at the Mental Health agency, a group home setting, and Wilderness Journey Programs.

The Juvenile Services counselor indicated that Cal's case, in all likelihood, would be referred to the Children First Case Review Team (CFCRT) because they could expect that his family is receiving services from several agencies. The caseworker introducing his case to the CFCRT (in this case, Gary) first would ask Cal's parents to sign consent forms for the release of information to members of the CFCRT. Gary then would be able to introduce Cal's situation at the next meeting, when the extent to which he receives services from other agencies would become apparent. The members of the CFCRT would discuss the range of service alternatives for Cal and evaluate their effectiveness in his case, although decisions regarding his treatment belong ultimately to the caseworker who introduced him.

After exhausting all community resources to no avail, Cal would have been sent to training school, where he would have been assigned a new case worker. Resuming when Cal returns from training school, Cal's training school counselor would meet with Gary, his counselor through Juvenile Services, to design a posttreatment plan. Among the issues determined in his posttreatment plan would be where Cal would go on release—be it home, a relative's home, or a group home. The vignette indicated to the Juvenile Court counselor that he would return home, at which point he would be reassigned to his original Juvenile Court counselor and regular contact would resume. Cal's counselor would contact the school regularly to keep track of his performance and would continue to seek effective treatment for him until Cal's probation is fulfilled. Were Cal to commit any additional offenses after he turned 16, he would enter the adult system.

---

[2]For a brief explanation of some of the complications that are created with referrals to the Mental Health Agency, see Jerome's client pathway.

The Juvenile Court counselor commented that Cal was a "worst case scenario" and that Cal "needs a miracle." Interagency contact would have begun before Cal left for training school; in compliance with the state mandate, all potential contributions from any agency would have been employed. According to the interviews, this interagency contact would have been facilitated by the collaborative mechanism, CFCRT.

Social Services: Jerome

Jerome is a troubled adolescent, with learning, family, and behavioral problems. Tracking Jerome's pathway began with a group interview at DSS including the director of Child Protective Services (CPS), the supervisor for Adult Services— Emergency Assistance Authority (who formerly was a case worker), and an income maintenance worker with AFDC. The details of Jerome's case warranted a variety of agencies' services; thus the course of research led to interviews with an investigator, a treatment worker and a foster care worker in DSS, a school counselor and school psychologist, a nurse from the Department of Health, and a therapist in the Mental Health agency.

At DSS an intake worker would receive the report, take down the available information, and give the report to a CPS investigator, who would interview Jerome at his school and probably the school counselor. Assuming that Jerome's case is substantiated, a treatment worker would be assigned to him and his family, unless "the child is at risk for immediate harm." If so, the investigator would petition the courts for immediate custody, and Jerome would be placed in foster care; otherwise, the case would be transferred to a regular caseworker. According to Jane, a treatment worker from DSS-CPS, after the initial visit, Jane would talk with family members, other agencies with which the family might be involved, and the school counselor. Because this is a case under CPS, she may access any records concerning Jerome without violating the principle of confidentiality.

Jane, using "the least authoritative approach" in working with the family, tries to act primarily as "a facilitator to get the family where they want to be." To do this she would draw up a service contract that "spells out problems and goals for the parent, and the consequences if goals are not achieved." For example, part of this service contract would require Mrs. Johnson to seek treatment for substance abuse at the Mental Health agency. Although the treatment worker could not "force" her to comply, she ultimately has the power to remove the children from the home. Also, Jane would advise Mrs. Johnson of other resources available (e.g., food stamps, AFDC) and help her with any applications she may need to make.

Regarding Jerome, Jane would refer him for a medical evaluation, most likely to a private physician, whose fee would be paid either by Medicaid or perhaps from a special fund maintained by DSS for that purpose, if available. She also would write into the service contract mental health counseling for Jerome. According to the treatment worker, this would begin with a telephone referral from the treatment worker to Serina, the child therapist in the Mental Health agency, followed shortly by a brief written description of Jerome's situation.

The child therapist described this referral process differently. Serina said "DSS and Juvenile Services have money to obtain therapy for children from private [therapists and counselors]." When this money is available, DSS refers clients to private therapists and counselors, using funds that provide treatment for approximately four sessions. If the client needs further treatment following these sessions (and many do), he or she would be referred to the Mental Health agency. According to the child therapist, regardless of any treatment before this, they (the therapist and the consumer) "have to start over," building a therapeutic relationship and settling on a treatment pattern. In other words, therapists are not simply interchangeable. Whether Jerome would go initially to a private therapist or directly to the Mental Health agency, he apparently would be referred there eventually.

The specific procedures followed within the Mental Health center are similar to Justin's client pathway. The treatment alternatives for Jerome's family would include individual counseling for Jerome, counseling for Jerome and his younger sister, Angela, together, and family therapy including Mrs. Johnson (to be conducted by the child therapist). Serina also mentioned possibly involving the children in some form of group therapy. In addition, Mrs. Johnson would be assigned a substance abuse counselor at the Mental Health center who would meet with her and design her treatment plan. Treir County's Mental Health agency has a substance abuse counselor who specializes in group therapy for women substance abusers and women recovering from a substance abuse problem.

While Jerome is in therapy, the DSS-CPS treatment worker and the child therapist would share information about Jerome's progress. Both DSS and Mental Health would maintain case files kept separately for the sake of legal accountability. Because the case involves Child Protective Services, DSS has freer access to Jerome's records at the Mental Health agency, but the reverse is not true. Nevertheless, the child therapist and the treatment worker freely exchange information about the case informally, but they "don't always write it down." The treatment worker described how, with the child therapist, they "would compare how Jerome is doing, because they may pick up on different problems." Jerome would remain in counseling for as long as the child therapist thought it necessary.

According to Christy, the foster care worker interviewed, "if Jerome has not responded to treatment" (e.g., Mrs. Johnson violated the service contract, was sufficiently uncooperative, or resisted responding to Jerome's problems) the treatment worker would refer the family to a foster care worker. This process would require Jane to prepare a court case and to petition Family Court for foster care for Jerome.

Christy then "would set up a relationship with the school and a health agency," and would refer Jerome to a private physician, if possible, or the Health Department for routine health care, such as immunization. The second priority would be to address his situation at school—"Does school adequately meet his needs or does he need to go to a Development Center?" The school psychologist would need to refer Jerome to the Development Center (for evaluation or therapy). The foster care worker indicated that if DSS had funds available, they would contract with an independent therapist to work with Jerome. In either case, Christy would pursue private services before tapping existing public sources. Collaborating with other public agencies, in other words, is a fall-back rather than primary option.

Several people interviewed indicated that Jerome probably would be introduced to the Children First Case Review Team (CFCRT), due to the complexity of his and his family's needs and problems. As with Cal, Jerome's mother would have to sign consent forms for release of information for every member of the CFCRT, and at the meeting, they would discuss alternatives for him. Reflecting on other information gathered during the field study, however, it is rather doubtful that Jerome's case would be placed before the CFCRT, because although his needs are complex, they also are all typical of the needs readily served by the various agencies. In short, Jerome and his family would receive services for their various problems through a network of logical and legally required referrals, rather than through formal interagency collaboration. We are emphasizing the distinction here between adequate service delivery to respond to a variety of client needs and the coordination of that delivery through a collaborative team, each member of which "keeps up with" the status of the client and family.

Schools: Tina

Tina—the child with physical handicaps exhibiting severe outbursts of anger—enters the service network through the school. Although the complex mixture of severe medical and emotional problems in Tina's vignette seem like natural stimuli for interagency collaboration, interviews indicated that in Treir County her case would remain in the school system. Tina's client pathway begins with the school counselor receiving a referral from Tina's teacher and their discussing Tina's situation. The counselor, Pat, would arrange a meeting with Tina to assess her needs. Tina's parents would be invited for a meeting with the school counselor, who suggested that "the mother is going to need someone to take charge." The vignette did not indicate the likelihood that Tina's father would cooperate (or attend this conference), although the school counselor would encourage him to attend.

Pat and Tina's mother would discuss Tina's problems, as well as some of the problems at home, which are a source for the secondary problems at school.

They would also discuss alternatives for dealing with these difficulties. The counselor would encourage Tina's mother to contact the Mental Health agency to address her own problems, although Pat noted people's reluctance to follow that advice because of the stigma associated with that agency. If physical abuse appeared to be an issue, she would have to report the suspicion to Child Protective Services and would advise Tina's mother that this report would be made.

In response to Tina's educational needs, Pat would reassign her to the fifth grade and reassess both the amount of time she should be assigned to the resource center and Tina's diagnosis as educably mentally handicapped (EMH). Further, the counselor would investigate the possibility of an alternative educational setting, which might be more appropriate for Tina. If her current elementary school did not have an adequate alternative setting, Tina might be recommended for a local development center, where her needs could be more sufficiently addressed.

In Treir County, Tina's pathway remains in the educational system, and largely in one elementary school. Aside from the recommendation that her mother seek help with the Mental Health center, the school counselor would manage both the educative and therapeutic aspects of Tina's case "in house." The EMH tag and the allotment of instructional resources are typical assignments required of elementary school personnel.

Schools: Tommy

Tommy is a child with inadequate food and clothing, persistent minor medical complaints, and a spotty attendance record. Pat, the school counselor, reasoned that Tommy's case would also probably begin with a teacher referral. Based on this referral, the counselor would make an appointment to talk to Tommy and to assess his needs, then request a meeting with Tommy's parents. Pat would explain to them that Tommy has been having difficulties, and it "is my job to make Tommy feel successful." They would discuss Tommy's medical history and when he last saw a pediatrician. She would urge the parents to take Tommy to the doctor to deal with his skin condition. The counselor would try to establish a relationship with Tommy's parents, perhaps by turning the situation around by asking them "How do you think you can help Tommy?" rather than accusing them of bad parenting.

After allowing Tommy's parents some time, Pat would follow up with the parents to ask whether they had taken him to a pediatrician. Based on the parents' apparent financial need (and assuming that they were not eligible for Medicaid), she would inform them about a state-wide philanthropic organization sponsored by an interfaith church council and underwritten by Blue Cross/Blue Shield. She would also describe other community resources for which they might qualify but of which they might be unaware. During this first appointment the counselor also might ask them to sign a consent form to release

Tommy's medical records. Assuming that Tommy's parents would respond to Pat's recommendations and would address his medical needs, the counselor would continue to work with Tommy regularly, becoming his "personal counselor." She would probably involve him in "discovery groups," which ideally would help Tommy make some friends at school while also working through some of his problems.

If his parents seemed uncooperative and did not address his medical problems, the counselor would strongly urge them to reconsider, advising them of the ramifications of their failure to respond. If they continued to resist, she would file a neglect report with Child Protective Services. This report would include all of the relevant information and would be filed with an intake worker at DSS, and an investigator would pursue the report and decide whether or not to substantiate it. Additionally, the counselor might contact the Health Department regarding Tommy's rash.

Pat would call a school social worker to address Tommy's truancy if that also did not improve. The school social worker, Matt, would contact Tommy's parents and likely would make a home visit to discuss with them his attendance. Matt would inform them of available community-based programs that could provide new clothes for Tommy and any other children in the family because this seems to be affecting his attendance. If his attendance still did not improve and the parents seemed uncooperative, the school social worker would petition the courts to intercede.

Despite the collaborative prompts in Tommy's vignette, both the school social worker and the school counselor suggested that, as with Tina's pathway, Tommy would remain within the perimeter of education, and both of them first would concentrate on convincing the parents to improve Tommy's situation. To address the lack of interagency collaboration—indeed, outside referrals generally, for both Tommy's and Tina's cases—at least two factors help explain. First, as outlined in the introduction to this chapter, neither of these clients present particularly atypical conditions—the schools deal with the kinds of issues they present fairly regularly, albeit not necessarily concentrated in one child or family. Second, at the building level, schools generally are not represented on any of the collaborative teams. Representatives for the school system are from the district offices; usually they are school psychologists, who in Treir County rarely perform counseling services, conducting test batteries for special programs instead.

Health Department: Maureen

As a teenager who may be pregnant, may have been raped, and may have been exposed to the virus that causes AIDS, Maureen's client pathway wanders through several offices in Treir County's Health Department, including a registered nurse (RN) from the General Clinic, two Child Services Coordinators, two

Maternal Care Coordinators, and a WIC case worker. As indicated by the list of interviews, her case would also be handled in-house, explained largely by the typical qualities of Maureen's circumstances.

Maureen's first encounter would be an appointment at the pregnancy clinic. If Maureen is in fact pregnant, she would meet with one of the Maternal Care Coordinators (MCC). We interviewed Jenna from that program. Jenna would guide Maureen through several processes simultaneously: counseling her about her feelings about her pregnancy and issues she needs to consider, enrollment in the WIC program, and enrollment in DSS's Baby Love Program (maternal Medicaid). The MCC would discuss with Maureen issues such as how to tell her parents the news, what proper prenatal care entails, and how to prepare for the baby.

Jenna would schedule Maureen for an appointment at the WIC office (located in the Health Department), where a case worker would help her complete an application and determine if she qualified financially. Maureen would schedule a second appointment to assess her nutritional needs and obtain the appropriate food vouchers. Maureen would return every 2 months to receive a new supply of vouchers until she delivered the baby.

The MCC also would refer Maureen to the Baby Love Program to initiate Medicaid benefits. Once maternal Medicaid is available, she would help Maureen find a private obstetrician, but until then she would schedule regular appointments (i.e., monthly during first trimester, biweekly during second trimester, and weekly during last trimester) with the Prenatal Clinic at the Health Department. When Maureen established herself with an obstetrician, Jenna would ask her to sign a release that would allow her and the doctor to exchange information on Maureen's behalf. Also, once Maureen left the Prenatal Clinic for a private physician, she and her MCC would arrange monthly consultations—sometimes at the Health Department, sometimes in Maureen's home, and sometimes via telephone.

Jenna would help her schedule an appointment with the Sexually Transmitted Diseases clinic for an HIV test, which requires pre- and posttest counseling regardless of the results. If Maureen is HIV-positive, the clinic maintains a counselor on staff to provide ongoing therapy. The MCC would record Maureen's medical history, perform a physical assessment, and would learn the nature of the sexual encounter—date rape. She would encourage Maureen to contact the Rape Crisis Center: "You just about have to take them by the hand . . . you try not to be too pushy."

Asked about contact with school personnel, Jenna reported that in most cases there would be none. Contact between the MCC and Maureen's case worker at DSS would also be minimal. The only specific instance offered was in the case of emergency environmental material needs such as electricity, heat, or water, when they would consult DSS for emergency funds.

Maureen would remain in the Maternal Care Coordination program until 2 months after delivery, at which time she would be eligible for Child Service

Coordination (for mothers with children from infancy up to age 3, and sometimes up to age 5). Her MCC probably would arrange a transfer visit with a Child Service Coordinator (CSC) before Maureen was due to deliver. The CSC program is a voluntary program for "babies at some risk for developmental disability." In her first postpartum meeting with a CSC, Maureen and the coordinator would complete a needs assessment, including financial status, areas of public assistance, and material needs (e.g., baby furniture, clothing). They schedule meetings at least once every 3 months to track the infant's health and development.

The Treir County Health Department has developed a maternal care program that attends to more than the expectant mother's physical needs so that they can provide a network of support tailored to her emotional needs as well. At issue here is the means by which they generate the sources of support within their program, rather than appropriating external, existent services from other agencies. The MCC and CSC staff who were interviewed both emphasized the personal and durable relationship they cultivated with their clients. As a result of these relationships, they also discussed their inclinations to do a great deal for these women beyond the bureaucratic descriptions of these programs, such as providing medical care for their children past the prescribed age limit and counseling them for economic self-sufficiency.

ANALYSIS AND CONCLUSIONS

Based on the client pathways described earlier, it appears that collaboration among agencies in Treir County is minimal, if not nonexistent. In the course of many interviews, however, the researchers collected information about the status of collaboration among the county's six human services agencies; it is only because the vignettes which structured the field work are not appropriate to Treir County's collaborative structures that the Children First Council, Children First Case Review Team, and ad hoc interagency task forces received so little attention to this point. This analysis, therefore, begins with some efforts to explain that discrepancy, in particular how it implicates certain structural and cultural barriers to interagency collaboration in Treir County.

We must begin by considering what kinds of cases and issues are targeted by interagency collaboration in Treir County. The key factors that lead to a referral to the CFC and CFCRT, according to several interviews, are the complexity of the child's needs and problems and the number of agencies likely to be involved. However, comparing all accounts of the CFCRT, it appears that most cases referred to the CFCRT involve children who are victims of sexual abuse or who have extreme behavioral problems (often identified as BEH). The correlation between referrals to the CFCRT and circumstances of sexual abuse or BEH seems due in part to the complexity of these issues and the treatment that they require. Also, both of these issues apparently are relatively new to Treir County and an effective treatment protocol has yet to be determined. The CFCRT appears to be a mechanism through which professionals from various agencies may explore together appropriate responses to new challenges as they arise.

Similarly, the ad hoc interagency advisory groups respond to problems perceived to be growing in the county. These groups convene as task forces whenever service providers or agency administrators perceive an urgent pattern among the county's population, a pattern that will require concerted attention to accommodate it. Whereas the CFC and CFCRT respond to types of cases/clients, these ad hoc advisory groups are organized to respond to categories of issues. Nevertheless, in both collaborative structures the issue is the exceptionality of the circumstances, and the working definition of "exceptionality" seems to hinge on the inadequacy of existing services for new clients' needs.

Another way of expressing the circumstances that lead to interagency collaboration in Treir County is to characterize the cases which are directed to the CFC and CFCRT as exportable, in the sense that they are easily transferred from the receiving agency to the interagency team on the basis of the intractability of the client's needs. By contrast, those matters that lead to the creation of ad hoc task forces are those determined to pose more generalized "crisis conditions" for the county. As if escaping through a pressure valve, exportable cases and crisis conditions are shunted out of established service conduits, reifying existing agency structures and organizational cultures. That is, traditional service delivery patterns are left intact and reaffirmed in their adequacy to meet more typical client needs. This mechanism makes these bureaucratic features seem real, immutable, and natural, by "permitting" agencies and service providers to declare themselves incapable of sufficient response. For example, neither Juvenile Services, the schools, nor the Mental Health center in Treir County has the resources or expertise necessary to respond fully to the needs of children identified as BEH. Rather than developing their own resources to serve these clients, they export them to the interagency team for collaborative service provision. By exporting "extraordinary" client problems to interagency teams or creating ad hoc task forces, agencies avoid the challenges of adapting their structures to meet these emerging needs. Rather than making their own structures more flexible, they create superstructures to respond.

This critique of Treir County's CFC, CFCRT, and ad hoc task forces is not aimed at the process of interagency collaboration they sponsor. Instead, it is directed to the by-product of this collaboration; that is, to the reification of some of the shortcomings in the human services network. Service providers on Treir County's interagency teams self-report successful collaboration on behalf of those clients referred to them. They and their fellow service providers working in the agencies themselves, however, do not provide parallel evidence from their dispensation of the more "typical" cases that there is any transfer of learning from the collaborative approach on the teams to within the various agencies. In other words, at home in their organizations, it is business as usual, no matter how successfully innovative they are abroad.

The assertion that Treir County's collaborative mechanisms reify existing shortcomings comes out of the authors' analyses of field notes. It is one of our interpretations of what occurs in the processes of service delivery, and it is not an observation that any of the interviewees ventured themselves. They, however, did offer a variety of experiences that constituted some of the barriers and enablers for increased interagency collaboration. The following paragraphs summarize these factors, sorting them into two categories—structural and cultural—both of which refer to organizational dimensions of human services agencies.

The reference to "structural barriers" implies simply that there are obstacles inherent to the current organizational structure of the agencies themselves. They stem from the bureaucratic organization of human services agencies, restrictions placed on certain practices in compliance with federal and state funding requirements, and from the generally underprivileged status of public services in U.S. society. Many of the structural barriers to interagency collaboration are represented in several of the other case studies. For this reason, this summary here is brief.

The most commonly perceived barrier in Treir County is the overall condition of the agencies—understaffed—and of their employees—overworked and underpaid. Contributing to the fact that agency personnel are overworked is the lack of money for more advanced technology, and especially apparent is the lack of computers. As a result, most case files are handwritten. The amount of paperwork required to document cases in the various agencies is also a barrier. Beyond the duplication of information both within and among different agencies, the sheer volume of forms can intimidate clients.

Aside from lack of resources, service providers noted that issues of legal liability also interfere with potential collaboration. Within the question of liability, the issue of confidentiality is of particular concern according to the interviews, suggesting that the need to maintain confidentiality thwarts potential collaboration among agencies. In the United States, service providers from many fields recognize that we are in an age of increased litigation, and state employees in the human services arena are not immune. Service providers in Treir County must make their decisions about consulting with their associates in light of this risk.

Treir County service providers also cited what can be grouped together as "cultural barriers" to interagency collaboration, in the sense that the professional culture of service provision elicits certain behaviors, perceptions, and practices that inhibit collaboration among service personnel. Perhaps the most immediate cultural barrier to collaboration is the notion of stigma associated with public assistance. Interviews with agency personnel, especially on the level of direct service provision, referred frequently to the negative images of other agencies, perceptions such as "only crazy people" go to Mental Health.

Lack of understanding about available services, agency procedures, and referral processes among the agencies impedes collaboration because service providers cannot adequately forecast occasions in which other agencies could be helpful. In Treir County, service providers specifically discussed their ignorance of other agencies' capabilities; many of them simply did not know what was available through other offices. In the case of DSS and Juvenile Services in Treir, counselors appeared to not realize that their agency's capacity for limited funding for private therapy, for example, complicated later services from, in this case, the Mental Health center.

Coupled with the lack of understanding of other agencies, there is also a general assumption among various agencies of the heavy congestion of the other agencies. This makes providers reluctant to involve other agencies unless absolutely necessary, and thereby leads them to refer only the most severe cases. For example, the school system maintains its own social workers, psychologists, nurses, and counselors to respond to the needs of their students, thereby foregoing some outside referrals. During the interviews regarding this issue, the school social worker and elementary school counselor acknowledged that they perform a clearinghouse function for DSS by handling what they can and forwarding only the more serious cases. Both Juvenile Services and DSS also have resources that preempt outside referrals in the form of special funds to refer people to private physicians, therapists, and psychologists. They thus avoid the need to collaborate with other public agencies for these services, until these funds are exhausted.

In part, this is a function of professional courtesy, but from the interviews there is also an underlying theme that caseworkers are "protective" of their clients' interests. They question how effectively another agency will respond to their clients' needs or how capable the system in another agency may be to serve their clients. This "protectiveness," quite a different matter from the turfism discussed in other chapters, is complemented by different philosophies among agencies regarding what is "in the best interest of clients," particularly when the clients are children. An example of this conflict is that whereas one agency, especially DSS, might think foster care is the best option for a child, another agency, in particular Mental Health, might believe keeping the child in the home is crucial. This disparity came up several times in Treir county between the Child Therapist at Mental Health and the Treatment Worker at DSS, who have tried over the years to build a more interactive professional relationship and have yet to overcome this barrier. The issue of the availability of private funds in DSS and Juvenile Services for therapists, doctors, and counselors similarly reflects these concerns to protect clients and defend particular definitions of client welfare. These agencies are able to "shop" for what they deem the most appropriate treatment for their clients, are able to avoid adding to the caseload of other agencies, and are able to pursue their own agenda for their clients.

The relatively small size of Trier County acts as both a barrier and an enabler to interagency communication and collaboration. Because the county is so small, people know each other, can work with each other on an informal level, and call each other for support. Also because of the familiarity of a small county, however, personality conflicts or negative relationships can more readily jeopardize communication and interaction among agencies. Because of these social dynamics in a small county, the turnover rate among social services personnel (approximately 3 years in Treir, according to an administrator at DSS) is especially problematic. Cooperation that takes place frequently involves a personal relationship between two people; whenever a new person comes to work in an agency, new relationships must be cultivated, which is a time consuming process.

In the case of Treir County, it is difficult to identify enablers to interagency collaboration, not because of a particular lack of it, but because according to the interviews it takes place in such particular isolation—the CFC, CFCRT, and the ad hoc teams. Those organs work because the individuals who participate do so willingly, rather than out of some requirement by their superior, and because their home agency affords them some release time for it. Based on the interviews, these teams constitute an exclusive group, which, culturally speaking, presents an incentive to sustain participation if you are a member. Many of the council and case review team members have worked together in Treir County for years. At the same time, these groups offer a cultural disincentive to avoid participation if you are not a member. The elementary school counselor, for example, had tried to participate in their meetings, but she felt isolated and subordinate. As a result, she not only no longer attends, but she also disparages the work the teams do.

Treir County hosts a situation in which one can see effective collaboration among various human service agencies to serve narrowly defined, complex client needs. In this situation, collaboration is defined as service providers, certain community members, and agency administrators meeting regularly to plan, advise, and monitor case management for clients in critical need. The conditions that prompt such collaboration for some clients are directly indicative of the conditions which preclude it for others. This occurs as the incapacities for agencies to serve complex, "atypical" clients and issues compel service providers to seek innovative service provision and implicitly reaffirm the belief that their capacities to meet the simplified, typical needs that match their agencies' service categories. In addition, the research in Treir County supports the conclusion that despite successes for the CFC, CFCRT, and ad hoc interagency task forces in terms of collaborative service provision, participating representatives do not use the knowledge they accumulate in the process to inform their regular practice in their home public service agencies.

5

Interagency Collaboration: Alternative Forms and Their Problems

Laura Desimone
Deloris Jerman-Garrison
Jean Patterson
Maike Philipsen
Susan M. Manley
Wanda Hedrick

In tracing the fate of our six fictional client vignettes, certain regularities emerged. The differences between a major urban center such as Pickard and a sparsely populated rural area like Brady obviously have a strong effect on the possibilities for and parameters of interagency collaboration. Despite these differences in structure and culture, we did find that social services professionals across the state do share some common vocabulary and practices. In all six counties, for example, a physically and emotionally handicapped child such as Tina would have her needs addressed through an Individualized Education Plan. Similarly, all of the counties mentioned that a pregnant teenager like Maureen would likely be served by the Maternity Care Coordination program. In most cases, these common approaches to client problems were dictated by state-level policies rather than being spontaneous responses of the individual counties. To avoid repetitiveness in presenting our findings, we have described full sets of caseflows for only three of our six counties (in chapters 2-4 of this part). These three chapters should give readers a comprehensive sense of current collaborative practice (or the lack thereof) in North Carolina.

In this chapter we present condensed findings from the three remaining counties, focusing on what is distinctive about collaborative practice in these counties and glossing over results that mirror those presented in detail for other counties. Each of these short cases presents a unique twist on collaboration, an approach that emerges from the structural and cultural particularities of the county in question. The experience of Fox County sheds light on the strengths and weaknesses of bureaucratic specialization. Secord County demonstrates how a "loosely coupled" school may have trouble fitting into a more tightly structured social services network. Finally, Holderness County presents an example of how the quest for agency autonomy can result in isolation and replication in service delivery.

FOX COUNTY: BUREAUCRATIC SPECIALIZATION AND TRAINED INCAPACITY

Fox County, a semiurban county with a population of almost 200,000 located near a major city in western North Carolina, demonstrated many of the barriers to interagency collaboration that arise from the increased bureaucratization and specialization of social services in larger counties. In comparison to smaller counties studied, the lack of an informal network among social service professionals in Fox county was striking. The system had simply become too large and formalized for many people to simply pick up the phone and engage in the kind of casual, almost social, information exchange that tended to grease the wheels of collaboration in small counties like Brady.

As agencies expand to meet the needs of a growing population, they tend to adhere more tightly to formal rules and procedures to manage their increased workload with some degree of regularity. Theories of bureaucracy and organizational development describe the process whereby at some point in an organization's growth reliance on common sense, "folk wisdom," about organizational norms, and personal relationships is no longer sufficient, and decision-making structures become standardized. Instead of operating on a case-by-case basis, issues with which the organization must deal frequently are categorized and treated according to standard operating procedures. The role of the agency and the roles of individuals within the agency become increasingly specialized along the lines of formal procedures.

Although bureaucracy has become a dirty word, it has undeniable advantages in terms of organizational efficiency. No one expects or desires large public agencies to operate on a completely nonformalized basis, making up the rules as they go along and reinventing the wheel afresh with each case that comes across the desk. Organization theorists also recognize, however, that the efficiency of specialization and standardized operating procedures leads to corresponding *inefficiencies*. In Fox County the research identified many examples of a phenomenon known as *trained incapacity*, whereby professionals are unable to recognize and deal with issues that fall outside the boundaries defined by their specialized training and socialization within a given organization (Knott & Miller, 1987).

It should be noted that the concept of trained incapacity is a somewhat benign interpretation of the failure of agencies to work together in the best interests of clients. This interpretation assumes that agencies have the *will* to collaborate but are prevented from doing so by limited understanding of the total picture of social services in the county. A less generous interpretation of failure to collaborate would be turfism, in which agencies compete for limited resources and attempt to justify their existence by laying exclusive claim to particular clients or problems and deliberately foiling the attempts of other agencies to operate within that turf. Certainly there was some evidence of turfism in Fox County, best exemplified by the administrator who said that there was no "competition" between agencies over a particular client population because "that's our market." In general, however, the data from Fox County better support a hypothesis of limited vision than one of deliberate defensiveness.

Symptoms of trained incapacity identified in Fox County included the use of specialized jargon incomprehensible to anyone outside a given agency, the definition of worker roles according to agency structure rather than client needs, and a general unwillingness to take responsibility for client problems that did not map neatly onto the defined mission of any agency. Perhaps the most obvious example of trained incapacity in Fox County and in every other county in the research was the lack of attention to clients' transportation needs. Nearly every interviewee told some anecdote about a client who did not follow through on a referral to another agency because of lack of transportation. Everyone recognized the problem, but because transportation falls into no one agency mission, no one has an institutional incentive to take responsibility for this basic client need that can prevent access to so many other services. Trained incapacity is a critical problem for interagency collaboration, which requires that social service professionals begin with the needs of the client rather than the programs and procedures of the agency. In Fox County, as in the other larger counties included in the study, the professional socialization of agency personnel often sharply limited the range of possible solutions they could imagine to a client problem, stifling interagency collaboration and causing clients to fall through the cracks.

The phenomenon of trained incapacity among social service professionals in Fox County emerged most clearly in the contrast between the hypothetical fate in this county of Tina, the mentally handicapped 12-year-old suffering from spina bifida and severe emotional problems, and that of Cal, the violent adolescent just returning to the community after a stint in training school. When researchers presented Tina's case to interviewees, the well-oiled machinery of the Department of Exceptional Children (DEC) roared into gear. This specialized network of teachers, nurses, and counselors is a separate fiefdom within the schools, including a wide array of resources and services purposefully designed to meet the multiple needs of a child such as Tina. In effect the DEC institutionalizes interagency collaboration for a specific client population, providing well-defined channels through which clients who fit the network's definitional criteria can pass to receive appropriate services.

The response to Cal's case reveals that no similar network exists for the violent juvenile offender. Rather, such a client is likely to be passed from agency to agency like a hot potato. Each interviewee expressed profound pessimism about the prospects for success with a client like Cal and endeavored to prove how the logic of the system required that this case be shifted to a different agency. Because no one agency had a program or a policy that they believed would successfully address Cal's needs, the main incentive of interviewees was to keep what they perceived as a probable failure out of their agency's case load. Looking through their individual agency lenses, all any interviewee could see was frustration and failure. The limits of these lenses resulted not in a collaborative approach in which agencies would link up to address multiple aspects of Cal's problems, but in no one at all stepping up to claim responsibility for a case like Cal's.

The Department of Exceptional Children: A Well-Oiled Machine

The fit between the needs of the child like Tina and the services available in Fox County was evident immediately. Interviewees at all stages responded to her case unhesitatingly with specific names, referral patterns, and available services. Clearly, the bureaucracy had specialized to the point where a standard operating procedure would come into play in a case like Tina's. The case began at Rourkeville Elementary, the heart of the DEC network in Fox County. Rourkeville, the school in the county to which special needs children are most often assigned, has three special education classrooms for children with different types of problems. The two special education teachers interviewed began by reeling off tests and procedures they would use to work with Tina within the school, then quickly progressed to explaining how Tina and her family could access Mental Health and Social Services through special DEC channels. Consulting with the regular school social worker on Tina's case was briefly mentioned, but one teacher shrugged off the suggestion with a doubtful expression and the dismissive comment, "She's only here 2 days a week." Neither special education teacher seemed to consider the nurse, social worker, or counselor who were provided for the entire school population as important resources, preferring to rely on DEC resources. For example, the DEC in Fox County has a special liaison with the Department of Mental Health who has appointments reserved for his referrals. The DEC also has a specialized school nurse who would be called in on a case like Tina's and would facilitate access to other social services.

As Tina's hypothetical case moved through the system it became clear that her needs would likely be well met in Fox County because of the existence of the special DEC network designed precisely to handle these kinds of cases. Members of this highly insular network defined themselves by the distinct population they served and were almost disdainful of the ability of other county social service providers to contribute to the fulfillment of their unique mission, mentioning referrals almost exclusively within their tightly knit group. Several interviewees noted the benefits of their specialization, noting that they were "more tied in," "better informed" about available resources, and "better able to focus" because of the their concentration on a specific population. The DEC in Fox County is an example of an efficient, highly evolved, but self-contained pocket of collaboration. In a case such as Tina's, where the diagnosis precisely matches the self-definition of the specialized network, such a system provides extremely efficient services. However, in cases in which the fit between client and network is not so neat the very specialization of the network may cause paralysis and inability to act.

The Troubled Teenager as Hot Potato

The case of Cal, the juvenile offender, exposed the downside of specialization in Fox County. Confronted with a deeply troubled adolescent with multiple problems, most interviewees seemed relieved to say "That's not my job," and pass the case on to another agency. By emphasizing the boundaries of their professional role they could protect themselves from getting involved with what seemed likely to be a frustrating, even fruitless, case. This retreat into specialized roles was best exemplified by the Juvenile Court counselor interviewed who emphasized that "my job is to enforce the orders of the court. We don't become personally involved." At several points she stated that "I am not a social worker" or "I am not a parent." She summarized her approach to her job by pointing to a thick manual titled *Handbook for Juvenile Justice Procedures* and explaining that "as much as possible I go by the book."

In a case like Cal's, however, if every social service professional goes by the book and no further, large gaps and contradictions may remain from the client's point of view. For example, a frequent condition of probation established by court counselors is a family consultation at Mental Health or the Department of Social Services. Although such appointments can be ordered and failing to keep them is a violation of probation, the court counselor stressed that it is not her responsibility to actually set up the appointments, so she simply gives the client the phone number. This procedure ignores the fact that many clients have transportation difficulties or fears of stigmatization which prevent them from making the first move in accessing social services. It also ignores the potential benefits of direct collaboration between the Juvenile Justice system and other agencies in facilitating Cal's reintegration into the community.

School system personnel interviewed about Cal's case also took a "by the book" and partial approach to his problems. Two assistant superintendents spent most of their interview time defending themselves against the perception of other agencies that the school system tried to "dump" kids like Cal by channeling them into the special Promenade School for troubled adolescents. Before such a placement decision would be made, they stressed, proper bureaucratic procedures would be followed, including having Cal's case reviewed by the School Based Committee and designing a "modified Individualized Education Plan" that would "give him an opportunity to utilize his particular strengths and weaknesses" in a regular school. Even if Cal did end up at the Promenade, they were anxious to defend and justify this option, saying that it was the best route for "teenagers who can't make it in the mainstream and need a higher level of counseling and services." They emphasized that this year the Promenade had adopted "a new therapeutic model" and was "no longer a dumping ground or a punishment," tacitly admitting that in the recent past the special school *did* serve as a dumping ground to which the school system could send students whose needs were not easily addressed by standard operating procedures.

Interviewees at Juvenile Justice and the schools carefully outlined the proper procedures their agencies would follow in Cal's case but everyone agreed that ultimate responsibility for Cal would land at DSS. Given Cal's family situation it seemed likely that Cal would not only receive DSS services but actually be placed in DSS custody. The DSS placement worker interviewed described the referral process for severely troubled cases as "playing dominoes with kids." She saw herself as embattled, constantly fighting other parts of the social services bureaucracy in a struggle over resources and responsibility, and often ending up as the "fall guy" when other agencies feel a case is hopeless. She cited one local official who believed that funds should be spent on preventative programs, not on providing placement for already deeply troubled cases.

In the past 4 years the number of children in DSS custody in Fox County has risen from around 100 to 367, straining resources to the limit. The placement worker interviewed was particularly bitter about the fact that children are often remanded to her custody with no warning: "We are expected to go to court for placement hearings with no prior notice. We may not even know the name or the offense and the kid is sitting in the lobby. It is very unfair to a child to get placed in the custody of DSS with no plan." She was not optimistic about Cal's chances for successful reintegration into the community, indicating that because there are few placement options for older and violent adolescents the most likely scenario was for him to end up back in training school until his 18th birthday, when he would be released from DSS custody. Her final assessment of how the system deals with a case like Cal's was "These kids are throwaways—by the parents, by the schools. DSS will take them. It's not that we don't want them. Just don't criticize what I then have to do."

The case of Cal in Fox County illustrates how specialized social service agencies can add up not to collaboration but to a whole which is less than the sum of its parts. Juvenile Services would define its role neutrally and legalistically, going by the book to design a probation plan but making no effort to support the client in fulfilling the conditions. The schools follow the mandated procedure of referring Cal to the School Based Committee to recommend placement and design a "modified Individualized Education Plan." Ultimate responsibility would fall to the DSS placement worker, with her wall map covered with 367 pins, each representing a child she is constantly shifting around to find placements. Unlike Tina, who seemed to elicit concern and compassion from interviewees, Cal's case was greeted with pessimism, resignation, and a desire to keep involvement and responsibility to the bureaucratically defined minimum. The court counselor interviewed in this case defined collaboration as "each agency taking care of their responsibility," and going on to say that "It's easy to get upset when they are not doing their job." Apparently, however, Cal is no one's responsibility and no one's job. Although each agency would utilize their discrete procedures for discrete problems, no interview expressed any hope that the whole child would be any better off.

The Double-Edged Sword of Bureaucratic Specialization

The research in Fox County demonstrates the truth of the maxim that bureaucratic specialization is a double-edged sword: on the one hand it can efficiently provide highly focused services to a well-defined clientele; on the other it can limit flexibility and the use of common-sense responses to clients whose problems do not appear easily solvable or do not fit into preexisting categories of agency programs and services. Tina's case represents the most positive end of this continua, Cal's the most negative. A similar dichotomy existed within the case of Maureen, the pregnant teenager. Because of North Carolina's persistently dismal showing on national comparisons of infant mortality, the state has mandated intensive services for at-risk pregnant mothers. In Fox County, this effort would mean Maureen would be immediately referred to a Maternity Care Coordinator (MCC), a nurse or social worker who would coordinate Maureen's access to prenatal care and other social services during her pregnancy. Most importantly, the MCC would provide the kind of personal follow through and advocacy that is often lacking as clients attempt to navigate the social services labyrinth, setting up appointments, providing transportation, and interpreting complex eligibility requirements and forms for various programs. There are currently eleven MCCs in Fox County, handling a total case load of 1200 patients. Thus, as with Tina, in Maureen's case a network exists in Fox County that has been specifically designed to provide a particular clientele with access to a comprehensive range of services. An interviewee at the Health Department emphasized that Fox was particularly well-equipped to handle Maureen's case and that she was "proud of what we could offer a girl like this."

Ironically, however, the same specialization that successfully delivers targeted services to a client like Maureen could leave her infant child in the lurch were ongoing services required. Interviewees on this case expressed concern about the gap in services for preschool children, indicating that current agency structures and mandates let this group fall through the cracks. Until they reach school age there is no institutional point of contact. As one nurse put it, "we have 1200 mothers in the prenatal program each year. Nowhere near that many are seen in child health. Where do they go? We know where they are. Nowhere. They don't go anywhere. . . . By the time they are picked up again by the school it may be too late." The sporadic attention of the social services system to Maureen and her child, shifting on and off according to agency mandates and structures rather than client needs, is a classic example of how a bureaucratic system with many rational, specialized components can be irrational as a whole.

Another important aspect of the phenomenon of trained incapacity is the tendency of members of one organization to reify their institutionalized way of seeing a problem as the only correct way and to either dismiss competing interpretations or fail to recognize them altogether. In Fox County this symptom of trained incapacity was evident in the tendency of members of one organization to consider themselves "professionals" and everyone else in the social service system amateurs. This trait was most marked among members of the highly specialized DEC network, all of whom discounted the value of working with "regular" nurses, counselors, and social workers. One DEC specialist spoke at length about his belief that most school personnel were not qualified or "good enough" to provide effective counseling and suggested that they needed more supervision from "lead people" with specialized training, presumably people such as himself. A Health Department employee spoke in similar dismissive terms about school personnel, indicating that she preferred to collaborate with other social welfare "professionals" and did not consider school personnel to be attuned to "the whole child." By thus privileging their own professional knowledge and training, specialized professionals may miss valuable opportunities to collaborate with those who operate under a different paradigm.

In Fox County collaboration was stymied by bureaucratic specialization not only among agencies but within them. Many front-line workers interviewed could conceive of collaboration only as working with other functionally specialized units of their own organization. It often seemed a stretch of the imagination for teachers and counselors within the school or eligibility workers and case managers within DSS to work together, much less for them to collaborate with people across agency boundaries. For example, in the case of Jerome, who suffered from possible neglect, interviewees at DSS described a standard operating procedure that would begin with an "investigator" visiting his home to make a report, followed if necessary by a "treatment worker" who would recommend solutions and manage the case on an ongoing basis. Although there may be some efficiencies for DSS in differentiating the investigation/diagnosis function from the treatment function, from the point of view of the client this division of labor, which asks them to admit not one but two total strangers into their home and personal problems, must seem even more threatening and invasive than it needs to be. Interviewees at DSS recognized this and said that "co-visits," in which the investigator could personally introduce the treatment worker to the family, were in the planning stage. This as yet unresolved dichotomy is an example of how bureaucratic procedures are more often driven by the logic and imperatives of the organization than by the needs of its clients.

Another way in which specialization within agencies can hamper collaboration is the communication gap it creates between administrators and employees. Bureaucratic organizations are structured into hierarchies—chains of command in which management and administration functions are separated from direct client service. Often this can lead to a lack of understanding on the part of administrators about the constraints faced by front-line workers as they go about the day-to-day business of the organization. Administrators who meet frequently with their colleagues from other agencies at professional councils and speak to them on the phone about broad policy issues may fail to realize that, at the nitty-gritty level of client service, workers in their agencies are isolated from each other both by time constraints and by technical barriers such as differences in confidentiality policies or program eligibility requirements. Thus most of the discussion of between-agency collaboration in Fox County came during interviews with administrators and was presented at a fairly abstract level. Personnel who deal directly with clients were far less likely to give examples of working with other agencies.

On the surface, it would appear that Fox County has a highly evolved system of interagency collaboration, with at least five formal interagency bodies in existence. Each of these groups has an impressive mission statement and conducts regular meetings, but, oddly, they rarely came up in the case flows outlined by client service workers. When questioned directly about how collaboration was practiced in the county, some client-service interviewees did mention these bodies but were unable to say much about them besides the fact that their bosses went to the meetings. It appears that the functional distinction between administrators and client-contact staff leads to a situation in which collaboration can be valued as a theory or concept without confronting implementation constraints faced on the front lines.

Building Bridges Between Bureaucratic Fiefdoms

Despite evidence that bureaucratic specialization has limited the possibilities for collaboration in Fox County, numerous examples were found of individuals and agencies rising above their trained incapacity to comprehend a larger view of the needs of social service clients. This section concludes by outlining some of these best demonstrated practices for building bridges between bureaucratic fiefdoms with their distinctive professional knowledge, language, procedures, and culture.

The most frequently mentioned facilitator of interagency collaboration was job hopping between agencies. Numerous examples were given of employees who had moved from one agency to another, bringing with them "inside knowledge" of procedures and channels that could be used to facilitate communication and collaboration. In this way a larger county like Fox can replicate some of the strengths of the informal network that exists in smaller counties. An interesting variant of job hopping was "pillow talk," in which a married couple who worked at different agencies exchanged their folk wisdom about the practices of their agencies. It seems unlikely, however, that the state could mandate such a practice.

Another very successful strategy for breaching bureaucratic walls was the establishment of "outposts" of one agency within the walls of another. This is extremely significant for clients, who are unlikely to understand functional distinctions among agencies and simply want their problem solved. A Mental Health counselor spoke of the fact that many clients who came into Mental Health with substance abuse problems never made it to the separate Substance Abuse facility when referred there. Having worked up the courage to come into one agency they felt rejected by being referred somewhere else and did not respond to the message that there was a site better suited to their needs. To respond to this issue, a Substance Abuse counselor now maintains office hours at the Mental Health facility to facilitate the transition. Similarly, one of the major achievements of the Maternity Care Coordination program has been the establishment of a Medicaid eligibility officer on site at the Health Department. Previously, clients had to go to DSS to have Medicaid paperwork processed, creating major gaps in transportation, coordination, and follow through. Such beachheads of collaboration facilitate the flow of information between agencies serving the same clients and, most importantly, are significantly more attuned to how the system looks from the clients' point of view.

Although formal, permanent agency outposts are not always possible, another option is providing workers the incentive and flexibility to accompany clients to another agency rather than just making a referral. This practice addresses issues of stigma and issues of transportation that clients may face when they are referred from agency to agency. It also establishes a face-to-face contact between employees of agencies who may not otherwise interact personally and it smoothes transitions for clients.

Finally, the possibility exists of tackling trained incapacity directly, by establishing a system in which social service professionals are formally educated about the programs and procedures of other agencies. The Health Department in Fox County has used this practice, inviting school nurses, social workers, and counselors for a tour and seminar to make them aware of the range of Health Department services and how to access them. Employees may simply be unaware of services offered elsewhere which would benefit their clients. Even more often, they lack technical knowledge about agency procedures and eligibility requirements. Direct education may be one of the most effective weapons against the inefficiencies of bureaucratic specialization.

The social services system in Fox County illustrates both the strengths and the weaknesses of bureaucratic specialization. Specialization shapes the language professionals use, the way they frame problems, and the solutions they can envision. When, as in the case of at-risk pregnant women or children with multiple handicaps, bureaucratic structures are designed around the needs of a particular population, a high degree of collaboration and efficiency in service delivery can result. When, however, a client's problems do not match the logic of any standard bureaucratic response, the system may be paralyzed. In Fox County the research uncovered striking examples of trained incapacity, the inability of social service workers to recognize and deal with problems outside their specialized professional purview, but also strategies of how this phenomenon can be countered at both individual and institutional levels.

SECORD COUNTY: THE LOOSELY COUPLED SCHOOL WITHIN THE TIGHTLY STRUCTURED SERVICES NETWORK

Secord County is a rural, sparsely populated county with about 100,000 residents. Secord's social service agencies—Health, Mental Health, Juvenile Services, and Social Services—are typical for a midsize county in their record of problems and successes in trying to collaborate on children's cases. Personnel at all these agencies are united, however, in portraying the county's schools as a significant obstacle to their efforts. Schools and school staff are described as incomprehensible, incompetent, and inaccessible by other agency workers. Schools in Secord, partly in response to such common accusations, have little confidence in other agencies, and they seek to meet students multiple needs in-house, both formally and informally. To further complicate the picture, certain types of schoolchildren actually seem to benefit from the less-than-cooperative relationship. The arrangement in Secord thus poses some basic questions about the role of the school and its compatibility with other government agencies serving children.

Schools have been described as loosely coupled organizations (Weick, 1976). This means that although principals and teachers work together toward broad goals, the actual nature of their relationship is often indirect, and open for negotiation. The levels and segments of a schools faculty are linked, but not closely, or predictably. The loosely coupled organization of schools can make them difficult to control or change because the lines of real authority are not necessarily clear; however, loose coupling also gives an organization the flexibility to handle the multiple and novel tasks educators often face. Schools vary in the extent of their loose coupling, but in general schools can be said to be more loosely coupled than most other government social agencies. This can produce mutual frustration, as schools find other agencies unnecessarily rigid in their procedures, and those other agencies find schools capricious and inconsistent. The theory of loose coupling fits well in such situations, and Secord County is a textbook case.

Secord's Schools: The View From Outside

Secord County's social service agencies share a common set of conceptions about the schools their clients attend. They see school faculties as incomprehensible at best, and incompetent at worst: as backwards, lightweight, and counterproductive. Schools, agency personnel indicate, should ideally serve agencies needs by providing neutral and noninterfering settings for investigations and treatments on the students who are legally bound to spend their days there. Instead, agency staff complain that school personnel, particularly principals, are intentionally uncooperative with the rest of the social service network. The school as incompetent and resistant at worst, the convenient host of professional outsiders more urgent enterprises at best, is the cumulative picture offered by interviewees in Secord's Department of Social Services (DSS), Health Department, Mental Health, and Juvenile Services agencies.

The idea that schools, teachers, and administrators are incompetent is not unique to social service agencies; there is a familiar strain of belief in American culture generally that devalues the efforts of educators and questions their professionalism. In the case of social service agencies, however, this opinion is held by those who work with schoolchildren and must (at least occasionally) deal with school employees. The characterization of incompetence is therefore based on and reinforced by professional experience, lending it greater weight among agency personnel. At its most generous, the belief is expressed as mere incomprehension: "We don't understand each other," a Secord Mental Health director admitted. Another Mental Health worker was more critical. The school system has it backwards, she said, schools reward bad behavior. Those with good behavior are ignored. Ironically, Cal's Juvenile Services counselor implied that school guidance counselors were ineffective for the opposite reason: "Maybe they're too busy with gifted and talented students. Most of ours they see as discipline problems." In repeated comments, agency personnel made it clear that they do not expect schools to deal with at-risk children or their parents in a useful, well-informed fashion.

Perhaps as a consequence of this belief that educators are incompetent, other agencies tend to treat schools as mere space, a convenient place and time for investigating, treating, and observing children. A DSS caseworkers' routine in cases of suspected neglect includes visiting schools to speak to children and their teachers. It is also routine for Juvenile Services counselors to carry their work into the clients' first few days at school. Although he says that he tries not to infringe on school time, one such counselor will show up at the school unannounced, to let his client know that he is being watched. Health programs schedule free pregnancy and disease screening—programs likely to serve school-age patients—during school hours. Fast, full access to school records and programs is expected and demanded by agencies for their clients; there seems to be little concern for school procedures and limitations. The loose coupling of schools that makes them appear incompetent to other agencies may also make such interruptions seem acceptable, whereas similar intrusions of school personnel into, say, the Health Departments programs would surely be resented.

More specific to Secord County than the beliefs that school personnel are incompetent and that schools are conveniently open settings for interventions by other agencies, however, is the belief that school personnel intentionally shun and otherwise obstruct efforts by other agencies to collaborate on children's cases. Schools, county workers say, never participate in collaborative teams, even when invited. (In fact, one team has developed alternative mechanisms for notifying the schools of decisions regarding their students, having given up on ever enticing school personnel to meetings.) A liaison position created several years ago to coordinate Mental Health services with school programs soon languished from disinterest on the school's part, according to Mental Health personnel. Likewise, bitterness persists in the wake of a policy change several years ago, in which the school system hired its own nurses and contracted with a private mental health service provider, permanently bypassing the county Health and Mental Health agencies. Social service workers in Secord County, like those everywhere, sense a general resistance to collaboration in the schools—principals don't like to share decision making, and teachers are inaccessible are common sentiments—but in Secord, agency staff also point to specific instances in which such suspicions seem confirmed by school action (or inaction). At least on this point, they agree with several Secord educators: The schools do avoid collaboration.

Secord's Schools: A View From Inside

"I would like the state to take money from DSS and give it to the schools to feed children." So said one principal in Secord County, expressing a common sentiment among the county's school personnel: that schoolchildren do not need outside agencies nearly as much as they need schools, especially if the schools have the resources to address a broad range of needs. Impelled by this belief, in typical loosely coupled fashion, schools in Secord are not waiting for a directive from above before acting. Instead, in various formal and informal ways, principals, teachers, and others are taking steps to make the school as internally self-sufficient in addressing students needs as possible. It is easy to see how such steps have provoked other agencies, and added to the schools reputation for nonparticipation in collaborative efforts.

What is perceived as intentional obstruction by other agencies is, within the school, considered best for the children and for the personnel involved. Yes, a private mental health service provider was hired, they explain, but that agency offered faster, more effective help with fewer logistical hassles. Outside referrals usually require parental consent, which may be elusive enough to stall urgently needed help. DSS and other agencies have, in the past, been uncommunicative when students are referred for help, and school specialists (counselors, psychologists, social workers) feel ignored and insulted by such silences. Ultimately, they seek to avoid such encounters entirely. Educators also say they want to protect the educational functions of the school by discouraging general access to the school plant and hours. In the face of greater public demands on the school, they resent having to share often dwindling resources with other agencies, and they know that frequent interruptions do not promote educational, social, or behavioral progress in most children.

As an alternative to collaborating with agencies they see as ineffective, incommunicative, and disdainful, Secord's schools instead appear to seek greater internal diversity of functions. In this way, more student needs can be met under the school roof, without outside referrals. One principal, referring to the case of Tommy and his poverty-related minor medical problems, wished that the once-a-week school nurse and school social worker visits could be expanded into full-time positions because they barely have time enough to handle referrals regarding rashes, allergies, eyes, ears, head lice, and scabies. "There is not enough time [for them] to deal with this case. Ideally," he continued, "we should have a full-time (nursing) staff. Students are neglected. Someone needs to be assigned full-time." The same principal would also like to see a full-time guidance counselor at the elementary schools. "In general," he said, "the state keeps putting more (responsibility) on schools but gives us no more personnel. We'll have no success until we get more personnel." Additional personnel, additional programs, and expanded roles for existing programs and staff positions are all part of the principal's wish list, and all are intended to increase the school's range of responses to students' needs without necessitating cooperation with other agencies.

New or expanded positions and programs, however, are only one level of this internalization effort. School counselors, social workers, nurses, and psychologists in Secord are well-removed from their counterparts in other agencies, but even these specialists are held to certain restrictions and procedures of their discipline, often out of concern for confidentiality or legal liability. Other school employees—the secretaries, custodians, cafeteria staff, aides, and coaches—may serve to address nonacademic student needs without such constraints. One elementary school principal reported that the most called-on people at his school are the janitor and the secretary, for hugs and kind words. Teachers go the extra mile, too, in ways for which they are not officially designated. One teacher, for example, is trained as an emergency medical technician and examines student injuries when needed. Teachers regularly collect money for a sunshine fund, which may be used to purchase clothing or snacks for needy students. Other teachers simply bring their own children's outgrown clothes when the situation warrants, or visit a nearby church-run clothing bank. Principals in

Secord have been reprimanded for giving students money or extra food in the cafeteria, but the widespread practice continues. Food, clothing, money, attention, encouragement, and advice are readily found within the confines of the school; even medical attention, health monitoring, career information, and job training may sometimes be offered in strictly unofficial, no-paperwork, no-parental-consent fashion by school personnel.

So schools want little to do with other agencies, and other agencies trust schools to do little on their own. How does this impasse affect the at-risk children in the middle?

Secord's Schools: Student Viewpoints

By projecting from some of the vignettes presented to Secord County agency and school personnel, we may see how the noncollaborative arrangement described earlier would impact students in various situations. Tommy's case—a young child exhibiting several low-risk problems and possible parental neglect—appears to be ideal for the school's internal, informal approach. Tina, on the other hand, with her serious medical, emotional, and behavioral difficulties, is ill-served by such a school, as she may not receive timely, appropriate treatments without outside referrals. Cal and Maureen are teenagers, and somewhat less likely to seek adult assistance at school. From the child's perspective, a noncollaborative school is not always beneficial, nor always detrimental.

A young, hungry, poorly dressed child like Tommy evokes such sympathy in most people that he is almost a melodramatic stock character. His facial rash and head lice may not be cuddly, but they are also in all likelihood easily remedied with proper, common-sense treatment. That Tommy's attendance is also erratic assures that his case will come to some main-office attention, and from there the internal resources of the Secord school can be mobilized. Teachers' sunshine funds and the kindness of cafeteria monitors will address his clothing and food needs; his head lice will require immediate attention, but a proper shampooing can easily take place in many schools without notice, perhaps with the help of the school nurse if available. Other needs may be met as well. "Tommy needs warm fuzzies, love, and to be wanted," said the principal. Toward these ends, the principal expressed confidence that a teacher, secretary, or janitor could be persuaded to take Tommy under her wing as a special buddy, to lend encouragement and support. "Teachers go the extra mile," he emphasized. No effort would be made to contact Tommy's parents, despite his poor attendance record: "I could refer this case to the social worker to find out why Tommy's been out of school, but I would not. There's no way of contacting most parents or they are not supportive," explained the principal. In Tommy's case and others like his, the boundaries of the school are never crossed, but his needs are met without paperwork, and without placing his family's pride and privacy in jeopardy in a small, rural community.

Tina's prospects in the same Secord school are less bright. She too is young, but her violent disruptive behavior and serious medical condition do not draw the same sympathetic generosity as the waifish Tommy. Further, her family situation—which appears to involve alcoholism and physical abuse—is frightening, the kind many would prefer not to examine too closely. That Tina is grades behind her age group, and in probable need of special placement, nevertheless, forces the school to get involved. In the noncollaborative arrangement, however, this involvement will not necessarily lead her to qualified treatment. One teacher's comment reveals the isolated position in which school personnel see themselves: "Her mother and father can't help her, so she has to rely on the teacher for help." In spite of internal shortages, timelags, and paperwork, the teacher would not consider seeking outside assistance, but would refer Tina to Special Programs, which sometimes takes an entire year to process an application because the part-time school psychologist is so overloaded. The guidance counselor would refer Tina's parents to external programs like Alcoholics Anonymous and Mental Health, but Tina would be offered only weekly counseling during school hours. "I would assume," the counselor explained, "that DSS was already involved, but would never expect to hear about it directly." Therefore, Tina's mental problems would be addressed by a screening committee composed of classroom teachers, and although her parents would be asked to get Tina a physical, the school would rather have a full-time, on-site nurse to address even such serious health concerns as spina bifida. Tina's needs are many, intertwined, and apparently quite serious; the informal internal responses that serve Tommy so well are clearly, on their own, simply inadequate for a child like Tina.

A noncollaborative school is also unlikely to single-handedly solve the problems of older children like Cal and Maureen. As teenagers, they are usually less huggable, and they may also be less interested in working for adult encouragement and support. Their problems are well beyond the school's ability to respond. Cal has a gang history, and a criminal record; drugs may also be part of the picture. Maureen is possibly pregnant and also at risk of HIV infection. Because each exhibits the capacity for grade-level work or better, there may be little reason for the school to attempt any involvement at all, beyond what is officially required (by court procedure, in Cal's case). In fact, the teacher drops out of the picture completely when Secord's Health Department begins to work with Maureen. High schools in Secord seem prepared to relinquish older students to outside agencies, and to work when required with those same agencies, although both Health and Juvenile Services personnel consider the schools to be less-than-cooperative. One can only speculate whether students' experiences with agency services would be improved if those minimal contacts were more cooperative and integrated in approach.

Working Together? The School and Interagency Collaboration

Secord County's situation is not necessarily unusual. Because schools in general are comparatively more loosely coupled organizations than other social service agencies, the resulting misunderstandings and incompatibilities seen in Secord may also exist to varying degrees in many other locations. Schools are poorly understood beyond their walls: their more flexible, less hierarchical structures appear to other agencies as disorganized and incompetent. Their responses seem unpredictable, their decisions capricious, their actions perhaps downright stubborn. In turn, schools are poorly informed and dubious about county resources available to their students. More hierarchical agencies appear to them as slow-moving, inflexible, and unnecessarily burdened with paperwork and regulations. Teachers regularly defer to the principal and front-office specialists, who (at the elementary level, at least) appear to prefer internal and informal solutions regardless of the problems severity. Even long waits and overloads of school programs do not redirect students cases outside the schools walls. Instead, schools actively develop layers of professional and unofficial expertise to tap as needs arise, further confounding more tightly coupled agencies. Some children benefit from the arrangement, whereas others languish, and the mutual frustration between school and agency continues.

The policy questions raised by Secord are, therefore, of general concern. Should such schools be encouraged to refer all noneducational student problems to outside agencies, unnecessarily placing children like Tommy in the glare of official attention? Should their wishes be granted, and internal resources be improved, so that outside referrals are unnecessary for even the most severe cases to receive proper treatment? Either option would require a school to more closely resemble the agencies that barely recognize it now, and to adopt specific procedures and well-defined chains of responsibility to manage either increased external referrals or increased internal functions. Either option would also attempt to bypass the informal activities of such school employees as secretaries and custodians, who offer individualized attention, advice, comfort, and, at times, material relief to some children in need. Such a loss would be unfortunate for both the children and the employees, and ironic in light of current educational thinking about the value creating a caring atmosphere in the schools. The fate of low-risk cases like Tommy's, and of Tina's more complex combination of serious issues, should both be considered in any effort to reform the way schools fit into the services network of a community.

HOLDERNESS COUNTY: ISOLATION AND REPLICATION IN A CULTURE OF AUTONOMOUS SERVICE DELIVERY

Holderness County is a rural, mountainous county located in western North Carolina. It is remote both demographically and geographically. Half of its approximately 50,000 residents live below the official poverty line, and service providers there note high rates of teen pregnancy among the population, as well as a culturally defined norm of parenting that frequently hovers around statutory guidelines for abuse and neglect. In short, the network of human services in Holderness County interacts with a large portion of the population. At the same time, as is the case with other small, poor counties in North Carolina, Holderness faces the challenging issues of inadequate funding and limited staffing to meet the needs described earlier. This section presents some conditions of interagency relationships in Holderness County that bear significantly on the quality and efficiency of service delivery.

The theme that emerged most strongly from the research in Holderness County was the autonomous nature of service delivery there. Many of the agencies and the case workers approached the client vignettes as if they were the only one on the job, even when they suggested referrals or received the client as a result of a referral. It appears that this autonomy results from several factors; in particular, interviewees talked at length of "mountain culture," as several service providers called it, which makes clients in Holderness County resistant to government involvement, and agency relationships, which steer service providers away from a more integrated approach. The combination of these factors yield an orientation to serving clients that circumvents possible collaborative linkages among agencies. The manifestations of agency autonomy in Holderness County include the ways in which agencies receive and act on referrals from other agencies and the tendency of some agencies to augment their own menu of service options to meet complex client needs internally.

An Existing Model for Collaboration

Before discussing the manifestations of agency autonomy further, a look at existing collaboration in Holderness is in order. The level of formal collaboration in Holderness County is very limited. The only collaborative mechanism that received any attention in the interviews is the Nancy Shea Foundation (NSF), a program funded through Mental Health Services. NSF began in 1990 with the goal of developing a comprehensive system of services for children with serious emotional problems who are at risk of being removed from their homes. Mental Health Services Children and Youth counselors are usually appointed as case managers for NSF clients, and in that capacity they invite representatives from DSS, the courts, Juvenile Services, the schools, and the Health Department to sit on an advisory team to plan services for the client. As a fledgling collaborative program, NSF has had to adopt a narrow definition for client eligibility, thus restricting not only the kinds of clients but also the pool of service personnel who might interact with it in a collaborative capacity. Almost all of the service providers in Holderness County who have worked in conjunction with NSF evaluate it positively. In particular, they praise the program's clearly articulated focus and its established protocol for case management.

The only client vignette that might qualify for NSF services is Cal's. An NSF case manager, Faye, described the process for Cal. It would begin with a commitment from him and his family for in-home therapy, lasting about 6 weeks. Once the family agreed to cooperate, Faye would assemble an intervention team and call a meeting with case workers in other agencies involved in his case. Interviews leading to his referral to NSF suggested this team would include his counselor at Juvenile Services, Mental Health Services' substance abuse counselors, Faye, Cal's high school guidance counselor, and, perhaps, the school psychologist. The first task for this team would be to establish common goals for Cal and clarify each agency's responsibilities. Faye indicated that beyond that, NSF would work with other agencies to see what services they could provide, and she and the representatives from Juvenile Services and his school would exchange updates regularly regarding Cal's status. In sum, as Cal's NSF case manager, Faye would assume the role of "point person" for other county services and orchestrate Cal's service plan.

Serving Clients in a Vacuum

None of the other collaborative structures officially in place in Holderness County (most of which are the result of state mandates) appear in the client pathways. This leads to the conclusion that they simply are not integral to serving the needs of clients in the network of human services there—at least not at the level of direct service provision. Turning to informal collaboration among front-line workers, the picture is similarly bleak. In the case of referrals from the point of entry to a secondary service, only one person interviewed—an elementary school counselor—indicated that he regularly "checked back" with the original agency to chart client progress and follow their lead in his work with children; the others reported frankly that they generally did not follow through when they referred a client for services, nor did they update other agencies involved as to client progress or regress.

In mapping client pathways, this lack of follow through resulted in referrals to the same offices, for example AFDC and substance abuse counseling, being duplicated by two or more agencies, such as Juvenile Services and DSS for Cal's pathway. Such replication is extremely inefficient in terms of expending agency resources, not to mention the degree to which it must tax the client's patience and tolerance. The duplication of referrals by Holderness County case workers seemed closely tied to the infrequency of their contact with each other, even though they serve overlapping populations of clients.

Internal Replication of Existing Services

The strongest manifestations of agency autonomy take place in Holderness County's Health Department and schools. In both of these agencies, the issue was not so much that individual service providers (i.e., nurses, physicians, teachers, and counselors) acted as though they were serving clients "in a vacuum" by disregarding previous referrals; rather, the agencies, as organizations, adapted themselves to provide a wide range of the constellation of human services options available elsewhere in the county.

Maureen's client pathway begins and ends in the Holderness County Health Department. There she would receive services that attended to her social, emotional, and financial needs, as well as the medical attention she requires for her pregnancy and possible exposure to AIDS. Indeed, Janet, the Prenatal Program's head nurse, told the researchers that she rarely refers anyone anywhere outside the Health Department. The Health Department maintains their own social worker who coordinates referrals to private programs, such as shelters and church benevolence offices. Janet indicated that she would direct Maureen to the in-house social worker, especially given the possibility that her parents might kick her out of the house.

As in other North Carolina counties, the Health Department in Holderness County maintains a Maternal Care Coordination (MCC) program and an Outreach Program for which Maureen would be eligible. Case workers from both of these programs would work with her concerning her social needs; at the same time, her MCC would track her medical needs and help her maintain appropriate prenatal care. The Outreach Worker interviewed, Rosemary, would concentrate on Maureen's material support needs, in conjunction with the social worker in the Health Department. Together, the MCC and Outreach Worker would support Maureen through her pregnancy. By providing their own social worker and support personnel, the Health Department in Holderness County bypasses the need to collaborate with other agencies altogether. Although the service providers interviewed said they felt comfortable calling case workers in other agencies, they added that they rarely do because they rarely find it necessary. Furthermore, they suggested that the other agencies, particularly Mental Health Services, seemed overloaded, and, unless the client was in crisis (i.e., suicidal), they generally try to provide emotional counseling themselves.

The case of Justin, who is living in a homeless shelter with his recovering alcoholic mother, also demonstrated the pattern of agency autonomy, but the agency in question here was the Holderness County schools. Although the interview with Dena, the Coordinator of Special Education, took place based on a Mental Health case worker's referral, she focused her discussion entirely on how the school would respond to Justin's needs on their own, to the virtual exclusion of any other agency. In fact, Dena made a point of explaining that the schools no longer contracted with Mental Health Services in Holderness (although they had in the past), opting instead to maintain an increased counseling and psychology staff of their own. The only instance in which Holderness schools would refer students to Mental Health, she said, would be if a child were eligible for the special services of NSF.

The elementary school would respond to Justin's case through its School Based Committee (SBC), including a guidance counselor, the special education teacher, the principal or his assistant, Justin's classroom teacher, and a speech and language pathologist. Dena noted that if they were aware that Mental Health Services was involved with Justin, then a Children and Youth Services counselor would be invited to sit on his SBC conferences. After ordering a series of psychological and developmental evaluations and outlining the results for Justin's mother, the SBC would work with his mother to develop a service delivery plan, including special education placement and its attendant Individualized Education Plan. With that mechanism in place, the SBC would authorize the guidance counselor and a school psychologist to provide counseling and therapy and to continue to monitor his emotional and psychological condition. Justin's case brings out the point that the schools in Holderness County, like the Health Department, have effectively sidestepped opportunities for interagency collaboration by augmenting their staff to provide counseling services otherwise available in the Mental Health agency.

The case of Tommy, with his poverty, absenteeism, and persistent minor medical needs, also demonstrates the phenomenon of the schools augmenting toward autonomy. Audrey, the elementary school teacher interviewed for his case, cited the range of school-based specialists who would be called in for his needs. She would bring Tommy to the attention of the principal, who would access the school nurse, guidance counselor, school psychologist, and school social worker. These specialists would attend to the bulk of Tommy's needs, and all of them seemed to think the school could respond adequately with its district resources. Several of them added, however, that should they find themselves overwhelmed, they would refer Tommy's parents to the Health Department for extra medical services and to several private organizations for material support. Once again, schools in Holderness County generate an internal momentum to serve their students' needs by maintaining their own staff of diverse human services professionals. In doing so, they isolate themselves from other public services agencies, creating a significant breech in interagency relations. In other words, the schools insulate themselves from having to collaborate by providing for these needs themselves.

Service Quality and the Division of Labor

These examples of autonomous service delivery prompt consideration of the quality of these internally provided services. At some point, agencies ought to consider the advantages of division of labor. It seems substantially inefficient for the schools to staff themselves with a professional capacity that already exists in the community. The Health Department is full of health professionals, likewise for Mental Health services and mental health counselors. In a county with such limited resources and such high demand for services, this wasteful duplication is particularly startling. What institutional rationale encourages this quest for autonomy?

This question may be answered in part with the notion of competing agency logics and orientations to their clients. In the examples from Tommy's and Justin's case vignettes, it should be emphasized that schools may feel the need to intervene autonomously with their students in terms of their best interests as *learners*. Implicitly, Holderness schools may be responding to the possibility that when Mental Health counselors attend to these children, they fail to respond to the particular needs of them as students in a classroom with other students. Similarly, in the Health Department in Holderness, the social worker, MCC, and Outreach worker, while caring for Maureen's medical, social, and emotional needs, would be doing so in the unique terms of her impending motherhood without considering her academic development.

The research in Holderness County presents another manifestation of autonomous service delivery, also relevant to organizational definitions of client needs. Holderness service providers offered several examples of how parents and their children could be treated independently of each other. Specifically, this means that their service plans would be pursued separately and apparently without consideration for the other. A striking example occurred in Jerome's client pathway, in which a substance abuse counselor at Mental Health Services would refer his mother to a 30-day, inpatient clinic for recovery treatment. When asked who would care for the children during that time, she responded only with, "That's a good question." Similar, less dramatic examples occurred in Justin's client pathway, again regarding his mother's substance abuse problems. The counselor in that situation stressed that Justin's mother would be her "first client." Service providers in both cases offered no indication of a routinized feedback loop that would coordinate services or progress reports for members of the same family introduced to services by the same complex of problems.

Inefficiency and Inertia of Autonomous Service Delivery

The theme of autonomous service delivery repeated itself throughout Holderness County's human services network. In some situations case workers acted autonomously, recreating referral paths that would already have been in place. In others, agencies positioned themselves autonomously by recreating avenues for services within their organization that already operate elsewhere in Holderness County's human services. Finally, some treatment paths function autonomously, in that they lack mechanisms to link service plans for several members of a single family. To some degree the autonomy is illusory. It was obvious from the research that these clients would have received services from several agencies at once. However, from the perspective that anything perceived to be real is real in its effects (W. I. Thomas in Brown, 1977, p. 97), as the various service providers described their courses of action, they would proceed as if they were the only providers attending the clients.

To be sure, it appears from the pathways that multiple needs in clients would receive attention. As suggested throughout this section, however, a question remains regarding the quality of these services when provided internally by, for example, the Health Department or the schools. Also, one must consider the inefficiencies of autonomous service delivery, particularly when, as a client is referred to a secondary agency, that agency duplicates a range of service referrals already initiated at the original point of entry.

Early in this section, we discussed the Nancy Shea Foundation as the only collaborative structure implicated in the case flows. The discrepancy between the estimated success of this program in bridging some of the gaps and eliminating some of the duplication for their target clients and the inefficiency of the rest of Holderness Counties human services network is dramatic. It seems that until NSF's approach to case management percolates throughout a wider array of the county's service providers, agencies and personnel will continue to work under the self-imposed inertia of autonomy, struggling through unnecessary isolation and duplication to provide for a poor, remote community.

SUMMARY: INTERAGENCY COLLABORATION: ALTERNATIVE FORMS AND THEIR PROBLEMS

The themes of bureaucratic specialization, loosely coupled schools, and autonomy-seeking agencies emerged particularly strongly from the three counties described here, but these phenomena are far from unique. Indeed, examples of all three issues were found in every county studied. Each of these issues presents a trade-off, a balance that must be struck, in order to achieve successful interagency collaboration. Are agency personnel more effective as specialists who can bring state-of-the-art knowledge to bear on specific client problems, or as generalists who attempt to fathom the whole picture of a client's situation? In order to meet the diverse physical, emotional, material, and intellectual needs of their students, should schools adopt more formalized procedures for external referrals or should they develop a broader array of internal capacities? Should agencies strive for autonomous competence, or for greater functional integration? There is no one right answer to any of these questions. As the experiences of the three counties in this chapter make clear, finding a workable balance between each set of poles will depend on the cultural and structural specifics of each county. Although managing these trade-offs is a difficult task, it is a crucial one for improving the delivery of human services for children and their families.

PART I CONCLUSION: Learning from Current Practice

George W. Noblit
Penny L. Richards
Amee Adkins

The preceding cases illustrate a range of policies, conditions, structures, and perceptions that impact service delivery and collaboration thereupon. In this chapter we extrapolate across the case studies to learn more about how these various features affect opportunities for interagency collaboration to serve multiple needs clients. These analyses result from several different syntheses of the data (Noblit & Hare, 1988). First, we consider the range of conditions, cited by service providers, within a matrix that arrays them in terms of barriers and enablers. Second, we apply the matrix to each of the six counties to demonstrate some of the permutations of these barriers and enablers within specific contexts. Third, we present some of the consequences of agency cultures (decision-making logics) for integrated service delivery. Finally, we analyze client characteristics, as portrayed in the vignettes, for the ways they affect the barriers/enablers matrix. This chapter concludes with the implications of these four analyses for state and local level service agencies that intend to pursue interagency collaboration.

One lesson we learned early in the study is that there seems to be no set of terms for enablers/facilitators or barriers/obstacles that do not have other meanings to the professionals who work to serve children and families. For example, throughout this study enablers indicates conditions that make possible or enhance collaboration. Among substance abuse counselors, however, an enabler refers to conditions that prompt relapse among patients. Further, there are two levels to each of these concepts in questions of interagency collaboration. The first level refers to issues surrounding whether or not to collaborate at all. The second refers to issues that arise once one has decided to collaborate and is trying to do so effectively. To resolve these issues, a set of ideas from the study of immigration is applied. *Spurs and reins* refer to the issues involved in deciding to collaborate. *Grease and gravel* refer to things that make collaboration easier or harder, once the decision to collaborate has been made. One final clarification should be kept in mind. Some spurs and/or grease, although fostering interagency collaboration, are undesirable on other grounds. Insufficient funding for the services needed, for example, can be a spur to collaboration while working against the best interests of children and families. Further, some spurs to collaborate may be gravel in the actual process of collaboration. Again, the example of scarce resources is fitting. Service providers may seek to collaborate in an effort to better use their resources, but they find in the process that the effort itself is an intensive drain on already strained budgets, time, and work loads.

This is simply to alert the reader to the point that interagency collaboration is best viewed as a potential technique to improve services. Like all techniques, however, it must not be allowed to undercut the ultimate goal meant to be served, which is meeting the needs of children and families. Collaboration, therefore, is a means to this end. Collaboration must result in effective and timely solutions for those in need, if it is to be considered a successful strategy.

The following example may help clarify how we use the terms. A high school guidance counselor receives a report of a student who may be in need of special attention, whether medical, psychological, financial, legal, or emotional. Will the counselor contact an outside agency—Health, Mental Health, Social Services, Juvenile Services, or any other—about this case? That will depend. Are there conditions intrinsic to the student's problem that would tend to prompt such a move? Is there an atmosphere or tradition among the school staff that encourages outside referrals? Does the counselor have little time but potential contacts' names and numbers handy? Are the parents likely to consent to the student's treatment by a government agency? Is there no person who could possibly deal with this case in the school? If these questions can be answered "yes," the situation includes some "spurs" to attempt collaboration. However, if the counselor anticipates a lot of paperwork in connection with any outside referral, or trouble from the principal, or difficulty in tracking down the appropriate office at a given agency, or if the school has had past problems dealing with other government bodies, or has earmarked funds and hired personnel to handle the student's particular problem, there are "reins" that will restrain the counselor from attempting any interagency collaboration.

Now, assume that the counselor is "spurred" to try interagency collaboration. How successful will the attempt be? If the counselor finds that agency phones are always busy, or caseworkers will not talk about the progress of the student's case, or that confidentiality rules prohibit sharing school records with the person most willing to help, or that the forms required to enroll the student in appropriate programs are voluminous, redundant, and jargon-filled, then the collaboration effort will be difficult, encountering "gravel" that slows the process. If, instead, the counselor discovers that there is a simple process for reporting the student's problem, that a therapist welcomes school interest in a case and sends regular updates on the student, that there are means of transporting the student to appointments, and that referring the case to outside agencies allows access to a whole range of programs unavailable within the school, then the collaboration effort will be eased by conditions that "grease" its track through the system. This second set of conditions—grease and gravel—feed back into the decision making, so that past positive or negative experiences with attempted collaboration are part of the counselor's expectations when choosing whether or not to seek collaboration—they become, therefore, spurs and reins in the next iteration.

SPURS, REINS, GREASE, AND GRAVEL

Figure 1 summarizes the major conditions acting as spurs, reins, grease, and gravel to collaboration in the six counties. Several points should be made about this composite list. First, a full enumeration of all observed factors would be unwieldy and would obscure the major points. Instead, this composite includes conditions frequently noted across the six sites. Other conditions do exist that can fit into one or more of the categories shown. Second, several conditions were found to affect collaboration in more than one way. The geographic proximity of agencies in relation to one another, for example, is always a factor in collaboration. If agencies are close together, they are more likely to try to collaborate and more likely to succeed in coordinating services, whereas the reverse outcomes were seen in agencies far apart. Finally, actual service delivery and the role of private providers, although important, were beyond the scope of this study. This list, therefore, includes major factors that affect formal and informal collaboration primarily among the public agencies studied. There may be, however, different conditions that affect collaboration when private organizations are taken into account.

THE COUNTIES

It is important to realize that although we studied six different counties, in many ways they illustrate some common lessons. The findings for each county are reviewed briefly, focusing on the spurs, reins, grease, and gravel. As noted previously, spurs and reins refer to the issues involved in deciding to collaborate.

I. Spurs (Conditions which appeared to prompt attempts at interagency collaboration)

geographic proximity of agencies	mandates to collaborate	cross-agency friendships
good past experiences with others	invitations to collaborte	multi-needs clients
positive image of other agencies	voluntary/pilot programs	scarce in-house/private resources
access to appropriate technologies	adequate time	recognized need for other perspectives
"pay now or pay later" logic	parent open to collaboration	worker familiar with area services
threat of lost funding if not	closed files	models of successful collaboration studied
will, ability to exceed requirements	sense of isolation from Raleigh	professional specialization
flexible procedures, job descriptions	client crises	help-seeking, proactive personnel
increased application pool	community crises	records on evert child at school

II. Reins (Conditions which appeared to restrain attempts at interagency collaboration)

geographic distance between agencies	legal prohibitions	bad past experiences with other agencies
personality conflicts	confidentiality restrictions	unattractive cases
negative images of other agencies	paperwork avoided	private/in-house referrals preferred
outmoded, incompatible technologies	professional elitism	inadequate time/personnel
no perceived need for other perspectives	"Superman" syndrome	inertia, fear of change
stigma of association with agencies	parents reluctant to consent	new workers not part of network
funding competition among agencies	image of others as overburdened	illusory collaboration
incompatible schedules	internal miscoordination	reluctance to volunteer aid, information
following case across lines costly	client unable to pay for services	potential controvery/court involvement

III. Grease (Conditions which appeared to make attempted collaboration easier)

geographic proximity of agencies	specific mechanisms in place	cross-agency friendships
legal permission to share information	informal ways to cut red tape	access to correct information

Figure 1. Spurs, Reins, Grease and Gravel: Observed conditions in field research

appropriate/compatible technologies
common understanding of client needs
workers familiar with area services
concerted effort to streamline client experience

strong, enthusiastic leadership
worker-level teams
established division of labor
parent motivated to consent by
threat of DSS removal

group-building exercises
"service brokers"
parental consent

IV. Gravel (Conditions which appeared to make attempted collaboration more difficult)

geographic distances between agencies
confidentiality restrictions
asymmetrical relationships
duplicative/contradictory services
high personnel turnover

unrealistic mandates
intertia, fear of change
inadequate time (caseloads)
confusion of jargons, forms
funding complications

personality conflicts
lack of information
rigid agency ideologies
inconsistent rules, procedures
uncooperative parents

Figure 1. Spurs, Reins, Grease and Gravel: Observed conditions in field research (con't)

Grease and gravel refer to things that make collaboration easier or harder, once the decision to collaborate has been made. These separate analyses will build to a series of "lessons learned."

Brady County

Brady County presents the extreme case of the small, rural county; both its very low population and compact size impact interagency collaboration practices, for better and for worse. Resources are scarce, and there are few people working in social agencies: Mental Health services, for example, are the responsibility of one person, who visits the county several times a week. Many clients are referred across county or even state lines to the nearest available provider. On the other hand, the same conditions in Brady County allow for a certain informality that encourages client-contact workers and others to cooperate and form bonds.

The spurs giving incentive to collaborate essentially involve scarce resources, mandates for collaboration, and a small number of agencies and professionals who know each other and who have worked together for some period of time. The reins involve organizational and administrative barriers, the availability of private services, negative evaluations of other agencies, the difficulty in working with school personnel, and fear and uncertainty. Once collaboration is decided on, the grease comes primarily from the existing informal mechanisms and agreements; at the same time, the gravel, in part, are some of what were spurs and reins to collaboration. Key sources of gravel are scarce resources, parent reluctance, personnel overload and turnover, the lack of collaboration by the schools, paperwork, unrealistic mandates, and, once again, fear.

The outstanding feature of the Brady County study, in fact, is the central core of social agency workers: five or six women, in different agencies and roles, whose interactions may constitute the best example we found of informal collaboration. These women are in contact with each other, sometimes daily, by phone, meet often to talk face-to-face, and have developed ways to bypass many of the usual obstacles to collaboration. They have been in place long enough to secure these trusting relationships, as well as to develop a keen knowledge of local conditions and each other's strengths and styles. One worked in another agency before her current placement, and another is a county native, giving each perspectives that the rest appreciate and tap when needed. The downside of this arrangement is that it so heavily depends on a shared history that new personnel may have trouble "plugging into" the circle's expertise, and the departure of any core member may disturb the operation of this delicate network. Although informal networks were observed in all six counties, Brady County's was most visible, as there were few other interagency structures in the picture.

PICKARD COUNTY

Unlike Treir County, Pickard County's large, concentrated, and diverse population has prompted the creation of several interagency collaborative initiatives from which lessons may be drawn. One effort, which reviews sexual abuse cases, put particular energy into the planning stages of the project: models were sought and studied, goals specified, rules established, and obstacles anticipated. A group-building step preceded regular meetings, now directed by a strong team leader. Success has been quantified in a drastic reduction in the average life cycle of cases. A second effort was undertaken "to put a human face on DSS," consistently found to be the most beleaguered of agencies. This initiative, also based on existing models, has been in planning for nearly a decade, and is yet to be fully implemented. Preventive programs, it was explained, are difficult to fund because the effects are long in coming and hard to prove. Neither schools nor Mental Health are regularly involved in these two initiatives.

Pickard's spurs include a positive approach, leadership, increased funds and mandates for collaboration, and considerable experience with collaboration both informally and formally. Some of the reins are ironically parallel to the spurs. Mandates have short lives, informal mechanisms are preferred over formal, and beliefs about the difficulties of collaboration come from extensive experience with it. Others are more mundane, such as agency stigma, overload, and desires to do all for the clients within single agencies; parent consent; administrative barriers; and organizational problems internal to agencies. Once collaboration is decided on it is greased by a set of formal procedures (group-building, objectives, evaluation criteria, leadership, uniform eligibility requirements, record sharing agreements, and models of successful collaboration) and the technology to communicate. The gravel includes services that are less than fully involved (mental health, schools, transportation), bureaucratic and legal constraints, insufficient time and excessive paperwork and workload, outmoded and underutilized technology, ideological differences between agencies, and logjams in service streams.

The large, concentrated, diverse population challenges Pickard County's existing social agency structures. Whereas rural counties experience "gaps" and shortages in service, the experience in Pickard is described in terms of "logjams" and "bottlenecks" occurring in a complex web of services. Clients have the potential to trace any number of pathways through a system of public and private agencies, as, for example, in the case of Justin, for whom an interagency team of five could suggest services from another half-dozen agencies, as necessary. The problem in Pickard arises when service providers rely on familiar standbys for client referrals, producing those bottlenecks and thereby decreasing service efficiency and, at the same time, leaving other potential service underutilized.

Treir County

Treir County, another rather small, rural setting, exemplifies a further phenomenon of interagency collaboration: private providers are not only an alternative to public agencies, but they are often the preferred alternative, perceived as superior by both clients and agency personnel. Justin's experience here gives a clue as to the many bases of this perception. A visit to Accounting in the Mental Health facility to fill out forms is followed by another session of filling out forms (some redundant) with the therapist, so that not until the second visit to the agency is the child's case assessed and a treatment plan established. Tina's case is unlikely to reach Mental Health because her counselor believes that the parents would sense a stigma attached to that agency. Urgent, sensitive cases, therefore, appear ill-suited to the public agency system, and they might indeed be better handled through private referrals, which the other four clients received in Treir County.

The spurs in Treir County are based in both mandates to collaborate and a general attitude that puts the needs of clients first, then working services to fit those needs. The reins include paperwork, overload, limits on access to records, a preference for private providers of services, and problems in interagency relations (especially involving schools). The grease that facilitates collaboration includes the existence of formal procedures, access to phones, the creation of "service brokers," and a case review team made up of service providers, instead of administrators, across agencies. The gravel includes varying levels of participation in formal collaboration, agency ownership of cases, uneven access to client records, interpersonal conflicts, shortages of service providers, and the specificity of the issues dealt with by the interagency teams.

Referral to private providers is not problem-free for agency personnel, however. Although Treir's Child First Case Review Team included a mix of public and private professionals, other formal collaborative efforts are limited to the public agencies. More troublesome is the consequence encountered by Jerome: When the agency's funds for a private therapist are exhausted, the case returns to the public system, and Jerome starts therapy from scratch. Private providers and agencies were significant to service delivery at all six study sites; this prominent role must therefore be understood as part of the present conditions for collaboration in North Carolina. Necessary bridges must be built between private and public agencies so that service to the client is coordinated, continuous, and effective.

Fox County

One of the insights gained in Fox County, a rural county, was that "children's cases" vary widely in the degree of collaboration they command. A teenaged gang member, a pregnant honors student, a neglected kindergartner with a chronic rash, and a low-scoring abused girl with spina bifida all fall into the category of "children's cases." In Fox County and elsewhere, it appeared relatively routine to muster the necessary resources for Tina because her special education placement brought her into contact with a network designed to meet such needs. Outside special education, students were unlikely to receive the same access or quick response, according to interviews.

On the other end of the collaboration-prompting spectrum was Cal, the teenager with weapons, drugs, and gang involvement, returning from training school to a family in crisis. Agency contacts responded helplessly to his vignette, believing that other agencies would be unwilling to take on such a client, and further that the client would be reluctant to cooperate with service providers. One interviewee noted that this case fell into a limbo period, ages 15 to 18, when he is still eligible for services as a child, but may bear adult needs brought about if he legally leaves school, becomes a parent, or is tried as an adult. Maureen's case revealed that ages 1 to 3 are another such gap, when the child leaves newborn programs and before he or she enters preschool. Fox County's range of responses to the client vignettes make it clear that some children's situations are harder than others to deal with collaboratively, although no less in need of coordinated agency services.

Fox County shares many of the issues of the other counties when it comes to interagency collaboration. The spurs to collaboration include a penchant for advocating for the client and brokering the necessary services, an informal collaboration process, considerable experience with collaborating, and the existence of mandates to collaborate. The reins include difficulty in accessing teachers and schools and including them in the process, scarce resources, overload, and problems in interagency relations. The ease of collaboration is greased by existing formal procedures and mechanisms, access to current information, flexible job descriptions, parent support, and common understandings of the needs of clients. Gravel in the collaboration process includes differential power of agencies, illusions of the ease of collaboration, confusion over the rules and terms of other agencies, and scarce resources embedded in an interagency competition for services. This constellation of issues accounts in part for the uneven collaboration that seemed to characterize Fox County.

Secord County

In Secord County, researchers found schools that, like others across the state, were out of touch with the public agencies serving their students. Those agencies perceived the distance. One DSS contact described it as the result of principals trying to handle students' problems themselves and concluded that "we need to be able to talk to the teachers." Juvenile Services has access to school records and performs psychological testing for the schools; nevertheless, there is a sense that "it is difficult to negotiate with the schools," that school representatives "rarely come" when invited to training school exit conferences, and that juvenile offenders get labeled and receive little counseling on their return to public schools.

Schools, for their part, agree that they have little interest in collaborating with other agencies. Past unsatisfactory encounters, the difficulty of obtaining parental consent, and conflicting schedules have led schools like Secord's to develop internal mechanisms to meet student needs: screening committees, school psychologists, guidance counselors, social workers, and school nurses are formally charged with addressing broader life concerns of children at the school. Beyond these, an informal internal safety net of "sunshine funds," extra clothing and snacks, teachers with some medical training, coaches, janitors, and secretaries can provide an array of effective, no-paperwork services in low-risk situations. The danger comes, of course, when serious problems are not referred to more appropriate external agencies. All six counties included instances of this distancing of schools from the rest of the agencies studied, but in Secord we also saw the schools' preferred style of "in-house" services exemplified.

Secord County was spurred to collaborate by the geographic proximity of agencies, existing mandates, a willingness to exceed mandates, client advocacy, informal mechanisms of communication and collaboration, scarce resources, and a perceived need to collaborate. Collaboration was reined by the problems associated with collaborating with schools, such as having highly efficient private service providers, excessive paperwork, problems in interagency relations, the difficulty in getting parent consent for collaboration, and a history of poorly implemented collaborative efforts. The grease for putting collaboration into practice included the existence of formal procedures coupled with informal friendships across agencies, the physical location of agencies, and good access to records. The gravel in the process of collaboration involved differing agency ideologies, insufficient communication between agencies, the intransigence of schools to become part of the process, agency stigma, unclear procedures, inadequate transportation, unrealistic expectations, and meeting overload, leading to duplication of services.

Holderness County

The schools are not the only element of the services network prone to "distancing," as we discovered in Holderness County. To some extent every agency maintains a sense of autonomy that counteracts impulses to collaborate. Holderness has many of the surface features of a nicely collaborating system— multiple teams, task forces, and committees, which have had such tangible effects as the establishment of a safe-house for children in danger, and procedures for bringing new staff into the network and sharing news of changes among agencies. In the vignettes presented, however, these bodies and programs were only rarely mentioned having any possible impact on the described child's case. Instead, agencies, schools, and even offices within agencies seemed unaware of the work of others. In one extreme case, a Child Protective Services (CPS) investigator must ask the child's mother if she is receiving services such as food stamps, although both programs are under the aegis of DSS.

This autonomy has side effects for both agency personnel and clients. The phenomenon described for schools in Secord County—distancing other agencies by attempting to meet all the child's needs in-house—can also happen in any other agency. The Holderness clinic to which Jerome is referred indicated that the Health Department physician could evaluate learning and behavioral problems, which, although it may occur, seems an unusual use of resources. Some workers develop strategies of service delivery that accept the improbability of interagency cooperation: the same CPS investigator would encourage the school to include a child in one of the in-school programs described earlier. Many contacts indicated that they would allow the referring agency to set the direction and maintain control of the case while the contact provided support. Other interviewees instead focused on their part of the problem exclusively, and did not attempt to get the "big picture" on a client. Both trying to be comprehensive and trying to be specific in services may be responses to the same condition: agencies are sometimes simply reluctant to work together.

The spurs for Holderness County to collaborate across agencies include mandates for collaboration, good information, funding incentives, a willingness to advocate for clients and to go beyond what was formally required, existing cross-agency relationships, and positive cross-agency experiences. Insufficient staff and funds, work overload, mandated time constraints, problems in interagency relations, and reliance on private and volunteer service providers all serve to rein collaboration. Greasing the process of collaboration, once it has been initiated, were good relationships, formal procedures, universalized paperwork, willingness to use available coercive mechanisms to insure client participation, and phone access. There was less gravel in Holderness County because few people were trying to collaborate. The gravel reported, however, included inconsistent reporting, insufficient staff, conflicts between the needs of parents and children, differential power of agencies, and other interagency relations problems.

AGENCY DECISION LOGICS

One of the constraints (reins and/or gravel) of interagency collaboration is agencies not understanding how each other operates. Further, even when there is cross-agency understanding, agencies sometimes do not respect or agree with the system of operation of another. In accordance with this factor, the data were analyzed further, by looking at "typical" agency referral paths. Some caution is in order here, as with any generalization or synthesis. These referral paths do not fully characterize any particular type of agency because all of the agencies had much more complex and idiosyncratic paths than represented here. The best use of these paths is for comparing different kinds of agencies, as is the purpose in this section. Viewed this way, these referral paths indicate one source of the misunderstanding and lack of respect for other agencies' ways of doing things.

Figure 2 contains a rendition of how schools refer their clients. Although schools are perceived as basically hierarchical systems (e.g., teachers refer problems to middle-level personnel, who receive authorization from the principal to act), the researchers observed a more complicated path for students in crisis. Teachers are clearly sources of referrals; however, sometimes referrals come directly from the principal. The principal then may refer the case to one of the school specialists formally charged with handling such cases or to the school's informal resources (especially typical in perceived low-risk situations). If the case is referred to an outside agency (and this is, we found, somewhat unusual) it will be through the school specialists, who have more ready access to such programs. One problem frequently cited by school personnel in this system is that many school nurses, psychologists, and social workers are part-time in any one school, and therefore rarely available and often unfamiliar with the students. Another problem is that the teacher is seldom notified about the progress of a student referral if it leaves the school. One reason is that agencies have little contact with teachers, due in large part because teachers lack a telephone in the classrooms, the fundamental tool of collaboration. Therefore, the teacher, one of the key resources to give direct and daily assistance to the child, is often left out of the information loop because of his or her inaccessibility.

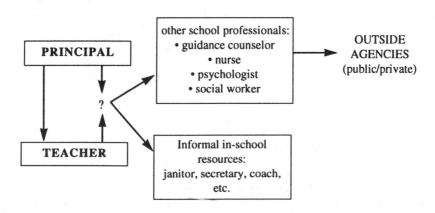

Figure 2. Schools.

Special education cases were seen in several instances to follow a completely different decision-making logic, usually through district-level exceptional children's programs. In these cases, the Exceptional Children's teacher was more involved in the ongoing intervention process, and the "regular" school staff and resources were rarely called on to contribute.

   Figure 3 contains the "typical" referral path for the Department of Social Services (DSS). A case reported to DSS' Child Protective Services appears to move through three phases: intake, investigation, and casework. At the intake step, the case details are recorded. This report is forwarded to an investigator, who has a limited time to determine whether the case meets the statutory eligibility criteria. During this part of the process, the investigator may not discuss the case with others at DSS (thus it is shown with a double box). If the investigation establishes that the case meets eligibility criteria, a caseworker is assigned (sometimes based on professional expertise, sometimes based on workload). At this point the case worker may refer the child to other DSS programs, for financial assistance or transportation, for example. The caseworker also may refer the case to outside agencies such as school programs, clinics, therapists, or private funds. In many cases, it was reported that caseworkers preferred to retain "control" of the case even when the child was served by other agencies. It should be noted that DSS is widely perceived to have heavy caseloads and more legal liability for those cases than other agencies. These factors likely contribute to the carefully regulated "assembly-line" process. Other agencies also see DSS as slow to respond and clients feel stigmatized by the investigation that determines eligibility for services.

   Figure 4 presents the referral path for Juvenile Services. This path was especially difficult to reconstruct given the hypothetical case vignette for Cal, because it begins at the end of the stream, as the teen leaves training school. Most agency personnel pointed this out to the researchers when shown the case

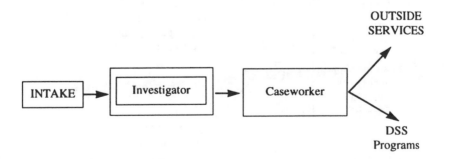

Figure 3. DSS

vignette, and they told a consistent story of what likely would precede Cal's commitment to training school. When young people are referred to Juvenile Services, they are assigned a counselor. It is mandated that this counselor exhaust every alternative before a juvenile offender is sent to training school. Thus most of the interagency contact involving Juvenile Services is initiated by mandate at this stage. If the youth is sent to training school, therefore, it is because interagency efforts have not solved the problem. After completing the required time in training school, the teen is again assigned a court counselor, who is almost never the original court counselor. This person must then seek the help of other agencies to place the teen at home, in school, and perhaps in the job market, in an effort to prevent further legal offenses by the teen. It was striking that many of the programs mentioned as possibilities for Cal were either

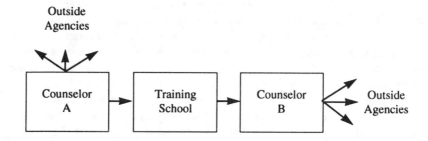

Figure 4. Juvenile Services

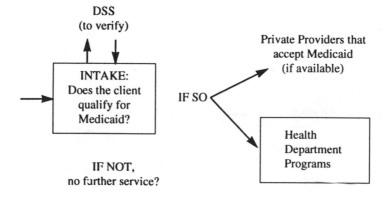

Figure 5. Health

volunteer (e.g., mentoring programs) or small, selective, private programs (e.g., wilderness experiences). Both alternatives offered limited openings for enroll-ment of people in Cal's life circumstances.

Health Departments were fairly self-contained in most of the researchers' observations (see Figure 5). Their ability to serve clients is deter-mined primarily on the clients' eligibility for Medicaid. At that point the client would be considered for Health Department programs such as Maternity Care Coordination; Women, Infants, and Children; Outreach; and Children's Clinic. These programs eliminate the need to seek such expertise in other agencies. The Health Department can also refer the qualified child to private providers who accept Medicaid. When private referrals are made, the client may be sent out of the county and may be subject to long waiting periods for services because pri-vate practitioners who accept Medicaid cases are scarce and usually accept a limited number of such patients. Only at the initial intake was another agency involved in referrals to Health Departments. At intake, DSS is contacted to con-firm information on the client's Medicaid application.

If a child or a family does not qualify for Medicaid, it appeared that there was little offered through the Health Department. It was assumed that all the case vignettes used in this research were eligible for Health Department services.

Based on the research, there simply is no "typical" referral path for Mental Health. Unlike the other agencies studied in this research, Mental Health did not have a uniform decision-making logic across counties. In at least one county, mental health services were the responsibility of one part-time worker who visited the county several times a week. In other counties, mental health services were provided comprehensively through semiprivate agencies or in independent programs, often with scattered locations. In at least two counties, the mental health centers had made recent changes that impressed personnel at other agencies as a step toward easier access. It is likely that mental health pro-grams need to educate other service agencies about their organization and pro-cedures because these seem to vary greatly from place to place.

WHAT HAPPENS TO CLIENTS?

The previous analyses reveal the state of interagency collaboration in the six counties. At best, this is a mixed picture. Interagency collaboration is essentially limited, even though each county can point to some initiatives and to dedicated professionals who use informal mechanisms to approach collaboration. However, it must be remembered that the data for these syntheses concern orga-nizational arrangements. These arrangements are judged according to how much interagency collaboration they sponsor or inhibit. Interagency collabora-tion, however, is not the ultimate goal, in and of itself. It is rather the means to serve the needs of children and families more effectively.

The final analysis examines the impact of the existing systems of service delivery in the six counties on the people these services are designed to serve. In doing this, it must be remembered that the clients used in the studies of current practice are fictional, and professionals faced with real people in need may act differently than they reported in response to the fictional client vignettes; yet it is also true that there is remarkable consistency across the counties. Therefore, the research team believes that the treatment of these fictional clients is not too far from what normally would happen to real people. Finally, if there is a systematic bias to the results, it is likely to be in the direction of prompting more reporting of collaboration than would normally be the case. Therefore, the effects on clients reported here may be best case scenarios, and, as shown, this is indeed distressing.

The results are analyzed for each of the fictional clients used in the studies of current practice and are reported systematically in the order of the agencies presented (schools, Social Services, Juvenile Services, Health, and Mental Health).

Tina

Tina is a physically handicapped child. She has a history of physical abuse and exhibits severe outbursts of anger. Her referral was initiated by the schools, where it was considered unlikely for such a case to result in any interagency collaboration (although a case such as hers would probably receive comprehensive services, they would not likely be delivered collaboratively) for two reasons. First, schools tend to try to meet the needs of children in-house. If this fails, they will seek assistance outside the school organization. Second, schools have a categorical system to deal with Tina's case. She is eligible for placement in a program for exceptional children and thus would be referred to the School Based Committee if a regular classroom assignment was not working out. Reportedly, the most likely result would be that Tina would be placed in a resource classroom for students with behavioral and emotional problems.

School personnel agreed that involving other agencies, especially Mental Health and Social Services, would be helpful. They also indicated, however, that any such referrals would have to be informal, relying on parents to make it happen. Further, Mental Health was seen as not particularly oriented toward serving children. DSS was seen as too bound by confidentiality requirements and other regulations to collaborate effectively or to provide timely services. Private agencies seemed better resources to school personnel but these agencies also offer limited ranges of services and are expensive.

The result is that she likely would receive school-related services. Her need for mental health treatment and services from DSS may not be a first priority. In other words, Tina likely would have received *within-agency collaboration* but not between-agency collaboration. Any services beyond those provided by the schools likely would come about from informal relationships and not from the normal operations of county agencies.

Tommy

Tommy is poor, lacks adequate food and clothing, has minor medical problems, and attends school irregularly. He also has difficulty with writing. His referral was initiated by the schools and, like Tina's, was not referred to outside agencies. As with Tina, any referral to outside agencies was seen to depend on the willingness of parents to request services, especially those of Public Health. Further, Public Health was perceived to have limited resources to help the child. The schools likely would ask private agencies for help in getting clothes. The schools probably would initiate an evaluation of Tommy's learning difficulties. The evaluation would likely result in special education programming, yet this, too, is dependent on the cooperation of the parents. As with Tina, the schools would probably "keep it in the building," seeking out a private agency and, if available, use informal relationships to try to involve other public agencies.

In sum, Tommy likely would not receive many services beyond the school, unless the parents sought help themselves from other agencies. This also means that whatever special assistance Tommy receives, the schools likely would position them as educational problems (e.g., although he would receive assistance with clothing, food, and possibly some medical attention, they are couched in terms of improving "the conditions of the learner").

Jerome

Jerome is the eldest child in a family headed by an unemployed, alcoholic, single mother. He is frequently absent from school, is learning disabled, and has repeated two grades in elementary school. He also has behavioral problems and has been caught stealing the lunches of teachers. Jerome's case began in DSS.

DSS began by establishing the eligibility of the mother and family for services within DSS, including Aid to Families with Dependent Children, Medicaid, and Food Stamps. At that time the mother also would have been informed of private agencies that could help, but the mother would have to initiate them. Jerome's mother would likely have been encouraged to seek treatment for substance abuse. The schools may have been contacted by phone, but the teacher probably would not have had direct contact with DSS. Any other contacts by agency workers would have been based on informal relationships rather than official procedures.

Jerome likely would have received services resulting from *within-agency collaboration* and much less from between-agency collaboration. Private agencies and informal relationships may have provided additional services, but it is not likely that Jerome or his mother would have received the services needed to address the problems of poverty, alcoholism, and educational failure.

Cal

Cal is a high school student who was convicted for selling drugs and possession of a weapon. As a result he was sent to training school. He idolizes his father, who probably abuses drugs. After training school, he is returning to his family, which consists of his mother, stepfather, siblings, and cousins. Cal is responsible for the other children while his mother works at night. He is academically able, according to test results, but he is behind in academic credits for graduation in school. Cal's case originated in Juvenile Services.

Juvenile Services personnel assumed that Cal would have been in their caseload prior to going to training school, and they would now be supervising his "conditional release"—a form of parole. Juvenile Services would focus on monitoring and supporting Cal's compliance with school attendance, making no other violations, and living at home. Juvenile Services would work with the schools to facilitate his reentry and would probably rely on private agencies for other support services. They would also try to help the mother improve the family situation. The net result, however, would be that Cal would receive limited services, and even those would be geared to fulfill the mandates of Juvenile Services. The services would be unlikely to fundamentally alter the conditions that promoted Cal's initial delinquency. Further, it should be noted that, in Cal's case, being sent to training school was seen by the professionals as an indication that the existing collaborative mechanism, from Community Based Alternatives to incarceration, had failed. Apparently, this means that Cal would not benefit further from interagency collaboration beyond that required by his conditional release from training school. Cal is likely to repeatedly fall back into criminal behaviors. As one professional put it, Cal "needs a miracle" that existing services are unable to provide.

Maureen

Maureen is a popular and successful junior in high school who was pressured by her boyfriend into having sex. She believes she may be pregnant, which would result in her being kicked out of the house by her parents. Further, her boyfriend has had homosexual experiences in the past and is suffering currently from pneumonia. A concerned teacher persuaded Maureen to go the Health Department.

At the Health Department, Maureen would be tested for both pregnancy and HIV. Negative tests would result in her being sent to a family planning clinic for counseling and contraceptives. If pregnant, Maureen would be referred to DSS and Child Protective Services. If she was determined to be eligible for services, Medicaid would be available to pay for her prenatal care. Her parents, however, would have to give their consent for all this to occur. A further complication is that few private practitioners are accepting new Medicaid clients. If Maureen tested positive for HIV, the Health Department would assign her to the HIV clinic for treatment and counseling.

Maureen would receive basic medical screenings. With parental permission and a DSS determination of eligibility, she could eventually receive social services benefits and limited public health treatment. However, once Maureen's parents are informed that she may be pregnant in order to obtain permission for her needed health screenings, her parents may insist she leave home. At her age alternative living arrangements would be a need that community agencies, as a rule, are not equipped to handle. Maureen would not have these services expedited by existing interagency collaborative relationships, nor would other services be sought that would help her deal with her emotional and educational needs. As a result, Maureen would become increasingly dependent on public services.

Justin

Justin is homeless, abused, and not performing well in kindergarten. He lives in a shelter with his sister and his mother, a recovering alcoholic who was abused by her husband. He is easily frustrated and quickly angered in school. He is being considered for special education placement, and the school recommended that he see a counselor at the mental health clinic.

As noted earlier, mental health processes vary widely, and thus it is difficult to identify any generalizable process that Justin might experience. However, his mother would have to consent to services. Additionally, she would have to sign a release to allow Mental Health to seek additional information on the services Justin was receiving at school so that a treatment plan could be designed. Through Mental Health services Justin likely would be referred to a diagnostic clinic, which may or may not be available in the county. The specific diagnosis would determine the treatment plan. The timeliness and extent of treatment, however, would be limited by the heavy caseload of Mental Health agencies. Service providers in Mental Health also would offer services to Justin's mother regarding her alcoholism and abuse. She would also be informed of services available to her from DSS. Interagency collaboration, however, would likely result from informal networks and from information sharing rather than resource pooling. It is likely that Mental Health and the school would be in communication about the diagnosis and treatment plans.

WHERE TO GO FROM HERE

Working together to improve services for children and families has never been more needed. Testimony to its importance is the development, among many districts, of informal collaborative processes in the absence of formal structures. The existing formal structures are limited to specific target groups and better insure the provision of usual services than lead to services that are more appropriate for the needs of the individual client. This research and the related literature, however, demonstrate that extensive, "practical" knowledge to change current practice exists, especially among service providers. Although ongoing research is necessary to inform policy makers of issues as they emerge, it is possible to anticipate conditions that might help and hinder new initiatives. There are many ways to go from here, but those directions depend on local and regional circumstances. It is important to address here the ways in which states and local communities may take advantage of what is understood about interagency collaboration and current practices in service delivery.

STATE AGENCIES

State agencies are often perceived as inhibiting interagency collaboration. At a minimum, states may wish to:

1. examine their own policies to see how they help or hinder interagency collaboration. Such a review also may be used to clarify the priority of collaboration;
2. educate state and local personnel to the requirements of collaboration, for collaborative measures are neither easily undertaken nor easily maintained;
3. expand funding and support for collaborative efforts that are necessarily more expensive than noncollaborative efforts;
4. redefine the goals of services to meet the actual needs of the clients;
5. foster state and local agencies working together more broadly to overcome the stigma associated with some agencies and the predilection to handle cases within a single agency; and
6. document and disseminate effective practice statewide in implementing and institutionalizing interagency collaboration; local groups need access to information about other groups so that each can continually learn and adapt to new circumstances.

Addressing each of these will take substantial effort and resources, but more importantly all these need to occur in the context of a systematic statewide initiative.

LOCAL COMMUNITIES

This research also has implications for local communities. Much of what impedes or enhances interagency collaboration is perception: about other agencies, about the right way to do things, about the primacy of client needs. Perceptions can be changed through experience and dialogue. Local communities can begin immediately to work on changing these perceptions by giving personnel cross-agency experience and beginning a community dialogue on collaboration. Local communities can also communicate the priority of interagency collaboration by accommodating its demands within work loads and by promoting the view of service providers as client advocates. Indeed, these are the bases of any further collaborative effort.

Only local communities can create the context necessary to successful implementation of interagency collaboration. They need to establish a context that values creativity and encourages some risk taking. Local communities can act in the absence of state initiatives, as they have demonstrated here. There is a sufficient literature for local communities to begin to educate themselves, and Melaville and Blank (1993) have provided a helpful guidebook for communities. Indeed, local communities can help the state by identifying areas in which state policy impedes local initiatives and by providing examples of effective collaboration.

Wherever state and local agencies go from the research reported, they should embrace Schorr's (1988) conviction:

> more Americans must become aware of the high stake that all of us have in what happens to these children, and more Americans must become convinced that we know what needs to be done and how to do it. (p. xix)

State and local governments need to exercise leadership by acknowledging that they do know how to better serve children and families and by communicating our common interest in improving the lives of our children. The challenge is to create a system of interagency collaboration that provides services that are tailored to the specific and individual needs of clients and that are adequate to restore clients to self-sufficiency. For this to happen all involved must be dedicated to overcoming the barriers to interagency collaboration: to create the conditions that spur collaboration and grease its implementation.

PART II
From the Other Side of the Desk: Client Perspectives on Collaboration

Penny L. Richards

It would seem logical that the design of human services should take into account the needs of the people served. However, the literature on interagency collaboration—the design paradigm currently held up as the ideal for service delivery—is silent on what features the clients might prefer in their service system. As recently as 1994, Wells and Freer noted, "we have little systematically collected information about how family members experience programs" (p. 399). Most often, their needs are assumed. Surely, the reasoning goes, clients want an efficient, effective, streamlined arrangement, just like the agencies. Other research assumes that clients cannot evaluate the services they receive adequately:

> Many clients of human service agencies receive "service" involuntarily, as in delinquency or child abuse cases. Others are functionally unable to evaluate the services they receive, e.g., the mentally disturbed or handicapped, the seriously ill or senile, etc. Many, if not most, are unlikely to distinguish between the "true quality" of the service received (e.g., counseling or an operation for cancer) and the quality of the interpersonal relationship with the service provider. (Martin et al., 1983, p. 747)

That last point is interesting. It says that clients cannot judge the services they receive, because they attach such judgment to the personal relationship which develops. As we see later, a system that deals with people in times of crisis, that wants to encourage and empower people, cannot afford to consider services and relationships to be entirely unrelated.

CLIENT NARRATIVES

What follows are the stories of 12 women—young and old, Black and White, married and single, high school dropouts and college graduates—who have found themselves in need of services from government social service agencies in North Carolina. Some of their experiences are heartbreaking, some are encouraging, and some are just bewildering. All of them offer insights into the needs of clients—insights that no reform plan should lightly ignore.

These client narratives were elicited in single interviews by representatives of the North Carolina Child Advocacy Institute. Interviewers followed a semistructured interview guide designed to prompt subjects to describe in detail their encounters with agencies and their personal feelings about the services received, rather than just the bare facts of the case. (It should be noted that subjects were selected by local interviewers in four counties, and that the result of only women as subjects was never specifically sought.) The narratives that follow were composed from the taped interviews and the interviewers' notes. In no case were agency materials (case histories, medical records, school files) sought for corroboration or refutation of the "facts" involved—these are perceptions, beliefs, emotions, and memories from the other side of the desk.

The resulting stories are arranged in three sets of four. The first four (Michelle, Lynn, LaShawn, and Alice) are women who have felt overwhelmed, defeated, or cheated by the multiple agencies whose help they have sought, some for many years. The next four (Betty, Meg, Sharon, and Wanda) may appear to be less entangled in the worst snares of government services, but still find such dealings exhausting and difficult. Finally, the last set (Cheryl, Ruth, Edith, and Susan) share the successes they have achieved both because of and in spite of agency involvement in their lives. For each client, we provide a brief life history, outline experiences with services, and summarize client needs and prospects. These women's stories are powerful individually. Together, they gain force, giving context and contrast to each other. As readers follow the 12 stories, common threads appear throughout: issues of trust and control, or desperation and deceit, for example. These common themes are discussed in a final section on the implications of these stories for policymakers in a position to make changes in the service delivery system.

6

Michelle, Lynn, LaShawn, and Alice: Narratives of Increasing Dependency

Penny L. Richards
Brian McCadden

The following narratives of increasing dependency on human services are compelling in their complexity. Michelle, Lynn, LaShawn, and Alice tell stories in
which they acknowledge, sometimes beg, for a system of support that takes into
account all of their needs (from childcare to vocational training to monthly
expenses) from a proactive stance; at the same time, they all share experiences
when they felt "burned" by the same system to which they appeal for help, leaving them suspicious and hostile. All four women present substantial needs to be
resolved before they can ever expect to become independent, yet they each perceive that their independence is not the operative goal as they check in with
their case workers; rather, they sense that it is maintenance- and crisis-oriented.

These four women subtly predict the future directions of their own
dependency. Alice, for example, can already see the signs in her daughter's truancy and discipline problems. They also offer suggestions for the kinds of services they need to improve their situations and head these nascent problems off.
This, of course, happens within the confines of the interviews. Their histories
with human services, including the humiliation and hostility they so often
include, reveal few opportunities for them to make demands of "the system."
Instead, they have learned to expect the system to make demands on them; they
have learned as well to resist these demands, whether or not such resistance is
counterproductive to the well-being of their families.

One last note to introduce these four women. Compared to the women in chapters 6 and 7, Michelle, Lynn, LaShawn, and Alice appear to be extremely passive with their dealings with human services. They sometimes strongly demand improved services, but, essentially, they make demands that the system "do" more for them. Such an orientation poses its own challenges to an overburdened system, because to promote clients with this view to a position of self-sufficiency requires a special commitment from service providers.

MICHELLE

Michelle, 24, was interviewed in the apartment she shares with her 1-year-old younger son. The interviewer commented that Michelle "was completely broke and needed money for gas—and this is only the 8th" of the month. There were no toys or baby products that the interviewer could see. Michelle has received public assistance (housing, AFDC, Food Stamps, and Medicaid) intermittently for the past 5 years, with a 2-1/2-year break when she was working part-time.

Life History

Michelle was born and grew up in a North Carolina city with her mother, father, and elder half-brother. She describes a home life that "was just so much arguing, and so much pressure . . . it was just an argument every day" with her mother. Sometimes, her mother would abuse Michelle physically, especially when she suspected that her marriage was threatened. Michelle summarizes life with her mother by saying, "It was just a lot of conflict, and my nerves, she messed my nerves up. My nerves are wrecked. I have real bad nerves." When things became very difficult, Michelle would go to stay with her grandmother. At school Michelle says she often talked to the guidance counselor: "I wouldn't tell her specifically what my mother was doing to me. I would just tell her I was having a lot of problems getting along with my mother at home." Michelle and her mother also consulted with their pastor, but without avail.

Beyond a temporary safe haven and sounding boards, Michelle did not find relief from her relationship with her mother until she turned 18. Michelle graduated from high school, worked as an intern clerical assistant with the Board of Education, and held a part-time job in a local retail outlet before she decided to live with her aunt. That arrangement was short-lived, because the manager of the Housing Authority unit where she and her aunt lived ordered Michelle out, saying he would otherwise have to evict them both.

Michelle became pregnant with her first child at 20, and she applied for the first time for government assistance (i.e., AFDC, Medicaid, and Food Stamps). Her application was denied because she had no permanent residence;

instead, Michelle says, "I was like here to there, like a place to stay, not a permanent home or anything, so I couldn't get it." For a time after her son was born, the Department of Social Services informed Michelle "that they were going to take my child because I didn't have a permanent home." A cousin then offered to let her move in, which counted as a stable residence, qualified her for public assistance, and enabled her to keep custody of her child.

She soon obtained her own apartment through the Housing Authority. When her son was almost 6 months old, Michelle left him with her mother while she and a friend took a trip. Transportation being difficult when she got back, Michelle never managed to meet her mother to bring her child home. She also never informed DSS, who, when they caught up with her months later, gave notice that she owed them over $1,000; around the same time, her landlord evicted her. Michelle's older son remains with his grandmother today.

For the next 2-1/2 years, Michelle received no public assistance, and she supported herself by working in various retail and fast food outlets. She worked at her last job, in a restaurant, until she was 5 months pregnant with her second child. When a doctor "took [her] out of work" because of back stress, Michelle was again unemployed, and filed for government services. Michelle and her son remain recipients of AFDC, Food Stamps, Medicaid, and public housing assistance. Regarding her plans for the future, she says, "I want to become a secretary. That's always been my goal."

Experiences with Services

To understand Michelle's experiences with government services, an appropriate metaphor is found in the layout of her county, her apartment, and DSS offices. The county is long and narrow, with a major township at each end. Almost all the government services offices are located in one town, Stroud. Michelle lives in the other town, Lowndes City, in a Housing Authority development. The two cities are roughly 10 miles apart, and there is no public transportation system in the county. Michelle is as far removed as possible from helping herself through public assistance, with no means of getting closer on her own.

During both of her pregnancies, Michelle needed financial and material assistance. She had, quite literally, nothing and no place to live. Hers was the classic Catch-22—she needed money for a place to live, but she could not receive money unless she had a permanent residence. When her son was born, the Catch-22 expanded because without a permanent residence, DSS would take custody of her son, but she could not rent an apartment without financial assistance, and so on. Not even Michelle articulates this loop, nor does she indicate the irony of it. Coupling her experiences with the broader context of her interview, however, it becomes apparent that she is passive in a system that asks clients to act or remain dependent. Someone needs to start the ball rolling if Michelle is ever going to leave the agencies' care.

Along with that critical first move, in order to escape total dependency, Michelle must see self-sufficiency as attainable. Three times during her interview, Michelle uses the expression "meet . . . halfway." Speaking about the physical location of services offices: "I'd say instead of it being located all the way in Stroud, it could meet Stroud and Lowndes City halfway. Then both Lowndes and Stroud would have to go the same length of miles to get where they had to go." Suggesting what people need from DSS: "You're first starting off, you got to buy everything your child needs. If Social Services could stand by you and maybe help you halfway." Describing her difficulty looking for a job: "More daycares or something, like if you've got to go out and you have to pay for someone to baby-sit, they could help you halfway." Michelle sees herself hopelessly distanced from any constructive activity. She has so little, materially and emotionally, that it is extremely intimidating to bridge the gap. Her words ask for guidance and for meaningful assistance and for someone to show her a way through the maze.

The interviewer picks up another theme in Michelle's interview. She writes, "This person is unable to fight the system to make her needs known." Michelle knows about the JOBS (Job Opportunities and Basic Skills Training Program) program, and, she says, "Maybe if I would really put my foot down and say to them, 'Can you please help me get this job that I want?'" However, she finds asserting herself difficult. Michelle has heard of various programs and requirements, but she does not seem to fully understand any of them; most of her comments end with "but they haven't explained it to me." Many, on considering Michelle's case, would be moved to ask, "So why didn't she put her foot down?" or "Why doesn't she ask for more details?" The answer to those questions is, "She didn't and she doesn't. She may not even know how to start."

Michelle's is a situation that begs for someone to treat her individually. She is both overwhelmed by the scope of her own needs, and, at the same time, has no inkling how to do anything about them. Her first experience with an eligibility worker was, to Michelle:

> very ugly. . . . She started questioning me [about] who the father is. . . . It's a whole lot behind my experience with my first child, and she was like, "You don't even know who the father is?" and all this and that. She was kind of upsetting me, plus hurting my feelings in a way, because I went for help, not for someone to just put me down and just throw a lot of questions in my face.

Michelle suggests as an alternative, "They could just stand behind you and help you make those steps for yourself."

Summary of Client Needs

Michelle needs someone to educate her about how social services are designed, so that she has a better grasp of what her caseworkers are able to do for and with her, and a sense of what she needs to do for herself. She also needs someone to "meet halfway" on the road between judgment and helpful service, between humiliation and self-esteem. These two issues encompass many of the challenges that face Michelle in seeking and receiving all agency assistance.

Finally, it is not accidental that more of Michelle's story is told in the author's and the interviewer's words than is found in most of the other narratives in this study. Much of what Michelle has to say about government services, she does not articulate. Instead, she expresses herself more subtly in the stories she chooses to tell and the way she chooses to tell them. That in itself—that she shares her experiences, but needs both an interviewer and an author to convey the situation explicitly—is Michelle's story.

LYNN

Lynn, 33, is the divorced mother of seven children ranging in age from 6 months to 14 years. One son is mentally handicapped and lives in a group home; the rest of the children live in an apartment with Lynn. In a life of abuse, desperation, and heartbreak, government services have only occasionally offered relief.

Life History

Lynn has lived in the same town all of her life. In the 11th grade, she dropped out of high school to marry. She worked briefly in a department store, but says she was "let go" because she was pregnant. "They saw me going to the bathroom all the time, and they said, 'We can't have you throwing up.'" Lynn has not worked outside the home since then. "Believe me, I want to go to work. I want to be independent, but when it's just one parent, trying to raise kids by yourself, it's kind of hard."

For 10 years, Lynn remained in an abusive marriage. When Lynn was pregnant with her second son, her husband threw her against a wall. That son, Andy, is mentally handicapped, and Lynn blames that incident. She also says her husband verbally assaulted her: "He was always putting me down." One day, Lynn's husband walked out on her. "He said, 'I can't take it any more. I've got to have my freedom . . . too many kids.'" Lynn divorced him, and child support is now taken from his paychecks. He does not visit the children regularly, and when he does, according to Lynn, he is drunk. Lynn says her ex-husband's relationship with the kids is strange. "One of my girls, she won't go with him because she's shaken up so much. She doesn't want to leave." This may be an allusion to child abuse, but Lynn does not elaborate.

The ideal of the traditional two-parent family appeals to Lynn. Her own parents are still married. "My parents have never separated, never divorced, and really, I don't believe in it. I thought two people were supposed to be together." By her own admission, however, Lynn harbors some bitterness about men. Her seventh child is the son of an ex-boyfriend who had told her he was unable to have children. When Lynn became pregnant, he left her. "I'm not crazy about men. I was hurt by the first one and the second one." Family, however, remains a support in her life. Her parents and her two sisters live in the same town as Lynn, and Lynn says they assist her financially when they can. Of her mother, Lynn says, "She loves her grandkids. She loves them."

Experiences with Services

Lynn's son Andy is 11, mentally handicapped, and lives in a group home. Andy's social worker persuaded Lynn to place him in the group home, saying he would get help there. Wanting to care for Andy herself, Lynn resisted at first but changed her mind when Andy was found playing with Clorox jugs in a neighbor's cleaning supply cabinet. "That was a real bad experience . . . the law brought him home to me. They were upset. I hated to put him in a group home like that but, you know, you need help. I couldn't do it myself because I wasn't trained." The first visit to the group home was a negative experience. There were no fathers visible. "I first walked in there. I didn't see any fathers around, just mama and the kids." Also, the staff at the home—many large men—intimidated Lynn initially. "I didn't like the place when I went in . . . I said to myself, 'Why are there so many big men here?' I said, 'This man's too big . . . he might be kind of rough." Lynn's fears have since been alleviated, and she appreciates the staff and their work. Andy is no longer obese, and Lynn believes he is better behaved. "He's minding better. They communicate with him. . . . They are nice people. They do try to help my son."

Lynn visits Andy regularly. Her mother drives because Lynn cannot afford a car, and there is no public transportation to the group home. As Lynn speaks about transportation, she indicates a reluctance to receive public services. "I don't want all the help I can get. I don't want that. My mother takes me to visit Andy or I walk. They say walking is good for you." Lynn says that sometimes she is embarrassed about receiving government assistance such as Food Stamps and Medicaid. She wishes people would not act "stuck up" or as if government assistance was "coming out of their pockets."

When food stamps do not stretch far enough, she and her children must walk to a nearby soup kitchen. Lynn stresses that her AFDC check should be larger. "Raise the money. Raise the AFDC for the people around here. It's not enough! Stuff is too high for us. If they'd raise the AFDC check, I could afford to pay my rent. That little bit of money doesn't help! It's good to have, but it's not enough to help." Speaking of herself and her friends living in poverty, Lynn says, "We're not out there selling our bodies. We don't do things like that. We're trying to make ends meet and it's hard."

Lynn's stories intertwine themes of the desperation of poverty and her own impulses to generosity. She tells of a neighbor who begged her for food. "I had this girl come to my house. She had four little kids, and I had six of my own. She said, 'Lynn, I hardly get enough AFDC to buy food. I get stamps, but I just cannot make it.' She asked if I had any food to give her." Despite her own family's hunger, Lynn gave food away. "'All I had in my refrigerator,' I said, 'you take.'" In another incident, she bought her daughter new shorts. The mother and teen girls next door were envious. Lynn said:

> I didn't want to show them off but my daughter showed them to the woman and her kids. Her girls are about 14 and 12 too. It made them cross because their mama can't afford new clothes. If I had enough money I would have bought those girls some shorts. It makes me feel bad when I have stuff and they don't. . . . Her kids want stuff just like other kids have.

Her own life has been difficult, yet she says, "I feel sorry for my neighbor because she's had a rough life."

Lynn's own desperation has led to crime, deceit, and humiliation. She spent 10 days in jail for writing bad checks. Hoping for money, she has also resorted to lying. Lynn admits she went to the Housing Authority and lied about having been robbed. "I don't know why I did that. I don't know why, but the kids needed clothes, needed Pampers and milk, baby milk." A housing authority official visited Lynn to verify the report, but she has not been prosecuted. The official humiliated Lynn. "He asked if I drank, did drugs, or messed around. He asked if I threw away my money on any of that stuff. I said, 'No, I threw it on my kids, put food in their mouths.'" The official also frightened Lynn. She called the Housing Authority manager and admitted she lied. "I called the manager and told her I was sorry that I lied. All she asked was that I try to get the money to pay the rent so I won't get thrown out." Lynn's advice to someone seeking government assistance: "Don't lie because you'll always get caught. They (government agencies) will help you, but if they think you're false, they'll terminate you. Always tell the truth."

The Department of Social Services waiting room is still an uncomfortable place to Lynn, because she anticipates further, less severe, humiliation and intimidation. She says waiting for someone to call her name, take her into a room, and ask if she has a husband or boyfriend is an intimidating process. Lynn knows of one woman who lives with her husband yet receives welfare, another act of desperation to maintain a reasonable living standard. Based on her own experience with trying to "dupe" DSS officials, Lynn worries about the day they catch up with this woman. There are teenagers getting pregnant just to increase their welfare checks, observes Lynn. "I see a lot of them getting pregnant just to get a check. . . . They're going to go out there and do it again." Almost apologetically, Lynn says, "I have a lot of children. I love them."

Summary of Client Needs

Lynn hopes that her story will help to improve services in the state. At the end of the taped interview, she is reassured of confidentiality. She says, "I don't care because I believe in telling the truth. I hope that whoever hears this, that they can help people." Lynn has suffered sexual discrimination at work and abuse at home. She was not helped by services in either of those situations. Agencies have helped Lynn care for her children—especially Andy—but she does not think they have done enough. Attempting to provide for her children, Lynn has committed crimes that go against her good nature. With inadequate education, no transportation, a criminal record, many dependents, and little assistance, Lynn is far from being self-sufficient.

LASHAWN

LaShawn, 27, lives with her husband and her school-age son, Simon. Her background as a victim of physical abuse, neglect, and anger contributes to her biggest fear: that her child will be taken away from her because of his psychiatric and educational needs. She had been told (by whom is unclear) to give the Mental Health agency a good report, but over the weekend she made the decision to speak her mind. The first words she says in the interview are, "Before we turn that thing [tape recorder] on, if you are here to get a rosy picture of the Mental Health Center, you might as well leave now."

Life History

When LaShawn was a small child her parents divorced, and her mother remarried a few years later. LaShawn remembers a very traumatic childhood, filled with profound feelings of being unwanted and unloved. When she was 16, LaShawn dropped out of school, having long been marked as a discipline problem. She describes herself then as a "16-year-old know-it-all." She later earned a GED and an associate's degree in business from a community college. These helped her obtain her present job as a supervisor in a factory. She loves her new job, and she explains that her appreciation for education is a value she wants to instill in her son. "An education, a good education, [is] the key to anyone's success," she states.

Whereas LaShawn's is a full-time night position, her husband holds a full-time day job. This arrangement allows them to care for Simon. Although LaShawn mentions only attention deficit disorder (ADD) and hyperactivity in connection with her son, the history she recounts suggests that his condition is far more complicated and serious. He has been medicated since kindergarten and in psychiatric treatment since third grade. LaShawn indicates that schools insist his behavior be controlled medically. The Mental Health Center has gone further, threatening to report that Simon is being neglected if he is not rehospitalized. LaShawn's struggle for control of her son's treatment is the focus of her most recent dealings with government services.

Experiences with Services

The Mental Health Center is the first agency LaShawn recalls as working with her when she was younger, perhaps from about fourth grade. She got involved through the school because she was a "real problem child," with recurrent disciplinary problems. She thinks her school dealt with her pretty well until she finished her first year of high school. During the second week of tenth grade, LaShawn was suspended for fighting, and she never returned. At 15 she packed her clothes and left home. The rest of her family were unsupportive of the assistance that she was supposed to be receiving from the Mental Health Center. LaShawn described her experience with the Mental Health Center as worthless. She tried several times to get them to take her out of her home when she was younger. She tried to explain the situation to them, but, she recounts, the only result that brought was a beating when she got home. The Mental Health Center was, for LaShawn, a dead end. The counseling at school never helped much either, because it addressed only the symptoms, never the source, of her problem.

Her frustrations with government services, particularly mental health, have continued into adulthood. LaShawn remembers the first time she contacted Mental Health about Simon, on a pediatrician's suggestion after Ritalin alone was not working (the child was then in kindergarten). She did not trust them, and, in her opinion, her suspicion was well-founded. Everything she has told them has been reported to Social Services without her consent. By the time they actually started Simon's treatment program, he was in third grade. Most recently, she was threatened by officials from the Mental Health agency that if she did not put her child in a psychiatric hospital in December, they were going to file neglect reports against her at the Department of Social Services. Four days after Christmas she sent him to a hospital. He was released a month later, and LaShawn and her husband were preparing to cut off his medication.

At that point, the family's needs and decisions came into direct conflict with those of Simon's school, doctors, and caseworkers. The school would insist that Simon be medicated and that the family participate in therapy, which were the hospital's recommendations. Failure to comply would mean Simon could not be readmitted to school. However, Mental Health does not provide these services when LaShawn and her husband are available. LaShawn tried several times to rearrange work schedules for herself and her husband, but when she finally got their bosses to grant them enough time off for the family counseling sessions, it took her more than a week to make contact with someone at the agency:

> I've been pushed and pushed and pushed and pushed by this agency—especially this agency. And it's getting to the point that I'm gonna sue 'em. But there are regulations about suing the government, so . . . either way, we're getting screwed. Practically. And I'm to the point that violence is gonna intervene if they don't do something.

The situation remains at this impasse.

Mental Health personnel have tried to remove Simon from his home. LaShawn and her husband bitterly refer to his first out-of-town placement as "Motel Hell," and describe it as a prison for children:

> When they couldn't control them by time-out or telling them, they just stick a needle of Thorazine in them and zombie them out on the floor. I'd just been in court letting them have him for 15 more days, already agreed to it, and walked in and found Simon zombie-like on the floor.

Her son could not even hold his head up. They had medicated him twice within 30 minutes—first they medicated him orally, and then they injected him. Seeing this, LaShawn removed him immediately. LaShawn was advised to send him to another hospital and she refused. The Department of Social Services then threatened her with a neglect charge. When she found out that her continued refusal could land her in court and Simon would be removed anyway, she agreed.

LaShawn says one facility where Simon was treated for a short time was a wonderful hospital. They offer no outpatient treatment, however, which conflicted with LaShawn's commitment to keeping Simon at home. Despite this, hospital personnel helped her "play the system" to pay for his medical needs by having Simon certified as disabled. This enabled him to receive Medicaid with Social Security Insurance. This, however, opened new areas of frustration for LaShawn. She now believes that money is being wasted because the services are not set up to accommodate all of her son's special needs:

> You know, we can't get a pediatrician to monitor Simon's medications because he's on so many medications. And it's just a continual circle all the time. And, you know, I hate to see my child suffer, because they don't want to get off their butts and do something.

She feels that her child is falling through the cracks of the system. "And I'm not the type of parent that sits quietly by and lets that happen. I raise hell the whole way down. We may still fall through the cracks, but I'll raise hell all the way down."

LaShawn asks for some reasonable cooperation and consideration in dealing with the agencies. When she calls to make appointments, the people she needs to talk to are difficult to reach; as for those she manages to contact, she said they are not helpful. For example, rather than telling her that the person she needed was on vacation, agency personnel let LaShawn call back several days before telling her why that person was unavailable. An ongoing struggle that frustrates LaShawn and her caseworkers at Mental Health is the contrast between her choices for Simon and their recommendation for his treatment. Caseworkers want to send him either to a residential camp or hospital, but LaShawn disagrees. If there were a day program, or if Mental Health officials could work with LaShawn and their family together, she would consent to treatment. LaShawn remains adamant that no one take her child out of her home again.

LaShawn offers some general observations about social service agencies. She describes the paperwork involved in receiving government services as detailed, thorough, and not difficult. She does not think any of it is unreasonable—just somewhat personal. She feels the paperwork tried to get to the bottom of the problem. They want to know the underlying reasons for everything, which seems reasonable to her. LaShawn also comments on the general "atmosphere" of service delivery in various agencies. The Social Security Administration is the only agency that has given her no difficulty. LaShawn notes that they were very prompt; she sent her son's birth certificate, and 2 days later it was back. However, in general, LaShawn advises anyone who is about to seek assistance from government service agencies to stay away. She has lost all hope in the system functioning in a beneficial manner. In particular, for LaShawn, the system needs some type of counseling program that is not limited to 8-to-5 operating hours, and one that is more compassionate, more understanding. "These people don't care if I work or not. They just want me there when they can get me there."

LaShawn talks of her dilemma despairingly, as though she cannot think of a reasonable way to resolve her family's need for help and the brick wall she confronts at Mental Health:

> I feel like a couple or 3 months in family counseling would do 100% good. But if we have to work with this agency, which we have no other choice, we're not going to get anywhere. People on Medicaid just get what they can get. And they're supposed to be satisfied with that. I'm not. Nobody wants to work with us, nobody, because it's just too much trouble. To me, that's the message that I've been handed: It's too much trouble for them. I am trying to do the best I can do with the resources that I've got. And if they don't want to help me...

Summary of Client Needs

LaShawn summarizes her own needs in an impassioned plea:

> If I could talk to these people directly, I'd just tell 'em. These kids are
> being abused by the system just like some of them are being abused by their
> parents. They've got the law out here trying to stop the child abuse, but I
> don't see any laws protecting my child from the abuse he's getting from the
> system. We don't have anybody to fight for the kids except us. And for a
> lot of people it's just a job to them. But when you're having to live with a
> child like this, and see what it's doing to this child, it's not just a job. I feel
> like these people need to take a little more pride in their work if it's just a
> job to them. And that's just the way I feel. Maybe this will help.

ALICE

Alice, 32, has seven children by six different men; she has never been married.
From childhood, Alice has depended on government programs for necessities
like food, housing, and help with family management. Her dependency on public support is deeply entrenched, fraught with frustrations, and without obvious
resolution.

Life History

Alice is the oldest of five children raised by her mother, an alcoholic who
depended on assistance from AFDC. Alice started having trouble at about 13.
She attended three different junior high schools, failed eighth grade, and was
sent to training school for 5 months. Because her mother "started having problems again" after her release, Alice remembers returning to a group-living environment, which she also calls "training school." This second experience lasted a
year and a half, during which time her mother never visited because of her
"problems."

Alice returned to a public high school at 16, but a year later became
pregnant and dropped out of school. Alice has been "on her own" since then. She
now has seven children (ages 14, 13, 10, 8, 6, 5, and 3) "by six different men."
She receives AFDC, Medicaid, subsidized housing, and Food Stamps, and she
has been involved with DSS Protective Services, juvenile courts, various job
training programs, counseling programs, and family mediation programs. She
lives in public housing and has no telephone or means of transportation.

Experiences with Services

Because Alice has had a vast array of social services experiences, they will be broken down here into four categories: Counseling and support, Financial assistance, Protective Services, and Schools.

Counseling and support. Alice seems to have had little emotional support or adult guidance as a youth. Alice "never got along" with her mother. A grandmother took care of the family, but she too was an alcoholic who left the children alone after dinner. When Alice was 13 and doing poorly in school, she began following her mother's and grandmother's example and spending her time out late at night. She says, "Nobody really ever sat down and talked to us and told us, you know, 'At your age, you shouldn't do this or that.' It was like, they really didn't care."

Alice's mother knew that she did not want her daughter to have the same life as her. According to Alice, she said, "'You really wouldn't like this boat.' She wanted me to stay in school and graduate, and get a job so I could do better. She didn't want any of us on social services." After Alice dropped out of school to have her first child, she attempted to finish her GED at a local community college. She wanted a degree in education so she could teach preschool or kindergarten, as her mother had done. Due to the difficulty of managing her growing family, however, she never completed her degree. She still speaks of being a teacher, but her hopes are phrased as conditional statements: "If only I could get some daycare for my youngest son; . . . If only I didn't have to go to court so much; . . . If only I could find the right program; . . . If only I could get some good counseling."

Alice remembers she "never had a person that I could really talk to and get problems off my mind, like responsibilities, you know." She considers the second training school she attended to be the first place she felt any sense of belonging. In her words, "I got to know the people there. . . . I didn't even want to come home." All the positive experiences Alice has had with services are related to such feelings of belonging, guidance, and personal attention. For example, Alice describes one case worker in this way:

> She helped me a lot. She got me beds for the house, tables, and stuff that I needed. She helped me get an account started so I could get a washing machine, kitchen table, and stuff. And I did. She was really nice. Clothes for the children when I needed them and stuff.

One program that Alice found especially helpful dealt with issues of parenting. Alice says the biggest benefit from attending the program was:

child discipline. Because I never could discipline my children. I just let them do mostly what they wanted to do. And it helped me sit down, get them in a group . . . they told me if we all do it together, it would be easier than talking to them one at a time. So now I know how to sit down and talk to them as a family. You know, sit down, do that, go to different places together, sometimes we take walks in the park.

Financial services. Alice characterizes the process of applying for financial assistance as a "hassle" that yields inadequate support. She says the main problems are that :

every 6 months you go through the same routine of asking where the fathers are, and if anybody gives you any money, and all the paperwork you've got to have—your social security card, your birth certificate . . . but this stuff has been on file ever since you started getting assistance. But you have to bring it all with you, every time.

She prefers the system of the Food Stamps program, which only requires that she bring identification with her to receive them. Finally, she notes that AFDC used to fill out her paperwork for her, but now "they don't even do that anymore." She says that it takes her more than an hour to fill out all the paperwork. The "300 and some" dollars she receives through AFDC are not enough for her family, she says. She has enough food, but she has difficulty paying her bills and often cannot come up with the required deposits for services such as the telephone. Finally, she reports having trouble keeping her growing children clothed, let alone buying them games or books.

Alice has tried to collect child support from her children's fathers, although this too has proved to be a struggle. From the six fathers involved, she estimated that she has received a total of $35 in child support. Periodically she has attempted to contact a child support worker, but has only received one letter, 4 years ago. It was some sort of invoice stating that the father of one of her daughters had sent $750. Of this she received the aforementioned $35. The father of one of her sons has two other children by another woman. Alice says:

He pays child support for them, and my son has never seen anything at all. Isn't that awful? I think that, even if a man does have more than one child, I think that his folder should have all these children's names in it, so when they contact one mother they contact the others. Because I'm losing money, but this other lady, she's getting money for her two children, and my son hasn't seen anything at all.

She also thinks that fathers should be tracked by their social security cards, their bosses should be notified, their paychecks should be attached, and, if all else fails, they should be taken to court.

Protective Services. Alice has had her most frequent and her most bitter government services contact through the DSS Child Protective Services (CPS) division. It began when her mother petitioned to have Alice's first child taken away soon after birth. Alice had broken probation following her release from training school. The child, 3 months old, was placed in foster care, but Alice's mother arranged to have the child transferred to her. She still retains custody of the child 14 years later. Alice has been in and out of court fighting her mother to regain custody or, at least, visitation rights. Although legally Alice was granted visitation rights, her mother has refused to cooperate, and the litigation continues.

She characterizes this as the time when "Protective Services became involved with me." In her eyes, CPS acts mainly as a threat, trying to control her life and constrain her. They keep her prisoner in her home, afraid to do anything for fear of losing her children. They always take another's word over hers, judge her harshly, and "do things" to her and her children without her consent, or, at times, even without her knowledge. In her own words:

> They [CPS] expect you to do too much. They're always looking for fault in
> a parent. The least little thing that you do . . . you're so scared that you're
> going to do something and they're going to come and take your children,
> that you don't do anything at all. Everything you say, they go to their super-
> visor, they have these meetings and stuff, but we can't even come. For the
> past 3 months I've asked for a meeting with my protective services worker,
> her supervisor, and hers, because there's so much stuff involved with my
> case. I haven't even gotten a meeting yet. They haven't even set up a date
> or a time or anything.

Alice's most recent upsetting experience with CPS occurred when four of her children came home from elementary school saying "a lady came to talk to us in school today." The "lady" was an investigator from CPS. Alice was upset because she thought the woman was trying to get the children to indict her. She believes that any bad thing the children might say will be taken as truth over anything she might have to say. Mostly, however, she is upset that the worker received a complaint about her and went to her children to investigate instead of asking Alice. Although Alice believes that CPS serves a necessary function, she says that their investigative method is flawed. She dislikes the way she was placed in limbo: "When they get calls, they should come out and see if its true. If it's not, they should say everything is over. But you're still uncertain for another 3 or 4 months."

To illustrate the threat of CPS' procedures, Alice cites an incident when one of her sons broke his elbow and someone complained that he was not receiving any treatment. A CPS case worker came to Alice's house after the boy's cast was removed and took him into protective custody until the injury could be medically examined. When it was found that the boy had received treatment, the case worker agreed that Alice was not at fault but nonetheless insisted on "therapy" before returning the son. The therapy turned out to involve questions about a sexual abuse incident between the boy's natural father and one of Alice's daughters. Alice is uncertain about exactly why the boy is being kept from her, saying, "I don't know why I'm still on Protective Services now. I never got a letter stating, 'Well, this is why you're on Protective Services.'" She feels that she was vindicated on the initial cause of the investigation, the broken arm, but that CPS wanted her son and found an excuse to keep him. "That's why I'm really scared now because, I mean, you have to be so careful with Protective Services."

Schools. Alice's luck with the school system has been no better than her luck with CPS. She has had particular trouble with her daughter Jane, 13, who was suspended from school at the time of the interview, apparently for being disruptive. Jane was starting to stay out late at night, "drinking, having sex." Before the suspension, Alice was in the process of "taking [Jane] to court because she used to stay out a lot at night, and, well, now she's on a year's protective supervision from juvenile courts." Alice feels that her daughter should have been put in a training school to "settle down," rather than undergo a year's protective supervision. Alice wants to send Jane to camp for the summer, but has been waitlisted. She fears that her daughter will just be "running wild" for the summer, "doing what she wants to do."

Jane's recent suspension was not her first major disciplinary encounter. In fact, this is her third suspension from her second middle school. She was transferred from the first school because one of her teachers was unwilling to deal with her anymore. The transfer was initiated by a teacher who had Jane for "four or five classes." Alice and her CPS worker called the principal, who said he knew nothing about it. "She [Jane] called me from the new school that next day: 'I've been transferred.'" Alice never talked with any school representative besides the principal about this. Before the transfer occurred, she and her CPS worker had scheduled "four or five" conferences with the teacher who was having problems with Jane, but the teacher "never showed up to any of them." Alice's younger children are having discipline, learning, and behavior problems at school as well.

Summary of Client Needs

Alice's needs are many, and she demands even more from social service agencies. Lifelong dependency has left her expecting public assistance in the most private of decisions and relationships. "If I can find the right program" is her prayer. Alice's case begs for an integrated approach, but agencies address her needs in bits and pieces. She knows she needs integrated, nonjudgmental help, and she has even asked for such a meeting:

I mean everybody, Protective Services, the counselors, the foster care, everybody, but that never happened. But I think that if we all could get together, to talk about things, I think that might help because then everybody knows what everybody is doing, like Protective Services can tell the counselors what they're doing, and the counselors can tell the Protective Service workers what areas I need to work on. He might know something that she doesn't know, and she might know something that he doesn't know, and they can all work together.

SUMMARY

Michelle, Lynn, LaShawn, and Alice reveal the many different ways people can become dependent on public services. Michelle's is a story of a girl cut loose from family and who, with the birth of a child, has become dependent on services. She is in despair and cannot see a way out of her predicament. After a couple of bouts with defying regulations of public assistance, Michelle has learned the best course is to be passive. The result is that her child may well slip through the cracks—not getting appropriate services and potentially perpetuating another generation of dependency on public services. Lynn's escaping an abusive marriage led to her involvement with services. She has a helpful family and a large number of children to support. Public assistance, however, is not sufficient for her children, leading her to live in desperation. This, in turn, led to a criminal record and repeated humiliations in negotiating public services. She does not seek all the benefits to which she could be entitled. Ironically, she sees this as her accommodation to life of dependency on public services. LaShawn reveals how simply having a child who needs and is eligible for special services can lead to an expansion of agency involvement in the lives of family and children. Because she will not submit to drugging her child, she has run afoul of the schools and Mental Health. Her child may also "fall through the cracks," albeit in a different way from Michelle's. She is entangled in a dispute and has given up hope of finding an adequate resolution. Alice has been dependent on services since childhood. They define her life. On the one hand, she has found services helpful in her learning how to parent, but Child Protective Services has become a threat in her life. She expects that her most private life is subject to government scrutiny. Alice hopes to find the right program rather than to escape public services.

These narratives attest to the fact that there are many ways to become dependent on services. In all cases, however, these women have found the experience humiliating and intrusive. LaShawn's case is instructive because she is not dependent on services first because of poverty. Her son needed services and qualified for them, but her insistence on involvement in treatment decisions has spiraled into an inescapable mire of agency entanglements. Agencies then contribute to the dependency by their very logics. Moreover, the interagency collaboration these clients have experienced seems to spiral into increasing dependency, not increased self-sufficiency.

7

Betty, Meg, Sharon, and Wanda: Narratives of Maintenance

Penny L. Richards
Mary Nix

We grouped the stories of Betty, Meg, Sharon, and Wanda under the moniker of "maintenance" because they appear neither likely to become increasingly dependent on services nor do they hold much hope for gaining complete independence from the human services system. For the most part, their experiences with services are less dramatic than the preceding women, but their critiques of human service delivery, both explicit and implicit, are no less demanding. Because they pose fewer crises to their caseworkers, they tend not to stand out; thus, it falls to them to secure rehabilitative or compensatory services for themselves (or not, in Sharon's case). In the end, Betty, Meg, Sharon, and Wanda look to social services to keep them above water and to get them through whatever issues they happen to face at the time. Maintenance, for these women, takes on a double meaning. On the one hand, the human services system maintains them, providing the support to keep them going but not enough to boost them to self-sufficiency; on the other, these women have learned how to use the system to maintain themselves, but none of them appear adept enough to use it to gain their independence.

BETTY

Betty, 52, has been married for almost 30 years and has three children: a son and a daughter in their late 20s and 17-year-old Eric, who is adopted. Although Betty's whole family is not in need of government services, they have had a long relationship with the system in seeking educational and psychiatric help for Eric, who remains in danger of "falling through the cracks."

Life History

Betty, the oldest of three children, grew up in a typical small town in North Carolina. Her childhood could be described as idyllic. It was a supportive, close-knit community unscarred by substantial crime or drug abuse. Betty and her friends were in Brownies and Girl Scouts, and they had strong relationships with family, school, and church. She remembers a couple in town that owned a shoe store who adopted a child, an act that made a lasting impression on Betty. Her only goals growing up were to go to college, raise a family, and, hopefully, to send her children to college as well. She has met those goals; she graduated from college, married a college-educated man, bought a house, and set about raising a family. Her two children by birth grew up well-adjusted and went on to become college-educated. Everything seemed ideal, until Betty and her husband, once Eric's foster parents, adopted him. They have no regrets about their decision, saying it was the right thing for them to do. When they were making the decision, however, Betty says, "I don't think anyone could have prepared us for the experience to come."

Experiences with Services

Eric was about 5 when he came to live with Betty and her husband. They knew Eric's mother. She had divorced her husband and, Betty mentions, it was a messy one involving "charges." When Eric was in preschool, it was decided that his emotional problems were so severe that he could not remain in a normal school setting. Eric's mother was not equipped to handle him, so Betty and her husband agreed to take him. They were not yet officially foster parents, so they had to go through that process while he was already living with them. This and the adoption process took 2 years. It was done through the Department of Social Services, and Betty has no specific complaints about the process, although she calls it "a bear." Since he has been with Betty's family, Eric has received little help from their county's government services. He has had some contact with them, but little help has resulted from that contact.

The only clinical information Betty offers about Eric is that he has been diagnosed as having Attention Deficit Disorder, yet his problems sound much more severe. He has serious behavioral problems—to the point that a Department of Mental Health psychiatrist, who evaluated him following his adoption, offered some medication, saying, "If it works, you do what you want to; if not, then there's nothing else." This sort of diagnosis followed Eric through most of his life. Doctor after doctor, primarily in private practice, tested him, talked with him, and worked with him. Most specialists come to the same conclusion—that there is not much that can be done for Eric. In one instance, a woman who tested him said she "had never tested a child that was as bad as he was. I guess he was institutional-level." Betty does not explain the origin of Eric's problems nor their development; she discusses his status more as a fact of life to which she has grown accustomed, although not resigned.

Betty was unable to get any help from DSS' foster care or adoptive services departments because they did not then have structures in place to offer help to someone with Eric's problems. Most of the struggles Betty talks about revolve around keeping Eric in the public schools. Because she maintains her belief that Eric can learn, she wants him to attend "regular" classes rather than special education classes. She has often run into resistance from the schools, as they try to move him to special classes for more individual attention. Betty complains that special education classes are not challenging academically, that they often only sing songs or color in books in those classes. She wants Eric to go to college, and to do that he has to push and be pushed.

Finding that help for Eric within the public school system has been difficult. Until second grade he was in a private school "where children could get the things they needed" but "he got kicked out." Eric bounced from school to school, from summer program to summer program, some private and some public. He was mostly placed in BEH classes, which Betty comments "spent more time trying to get the children to behave than they did on academics." Progress came only when particular teachers took special interest in Eric. Betty describes one such teacher: "She just understood him. Did not react to him. She knew how to work with him; she knew how to go in; she knew what to do; she knew how to work with me and my husband." Teachers and schools that have helped Eric are marked by flexibility, specialized attention, and acceptance. Unfortunately, what Betty more often encounters with Eric are people who quickly label him unable to learn.

In fifth grade, Eric was taken to court on a charge that was later reduced to simple assault, for an incident that occurred at school. He was given 2 years probation after being "declared the most dangerous child to ever come through the court." Although he spent most of those 2 years in private mental health facilities, Betty remarks that Eric's juvenile court counselor was very good, very helpful. She was "always looking for the best," and was "more on [Betty's] side than anybody else had been." The court process itself was not so friendly. Six months passed between the incident and the trial, during which time Eric was taken away from Betty and her husband. They "were no longer in control of him" then, and they were "excluded from the whole process," which was "very frustrating." The probationary period when he was in a private mental health facility was also marked by a feeling of lack of control on Betty's part: "Their objective was to eliminate everything in his life to try to see what was wrong (including us)."

As Eric's probation was ending, Betty encountered another exceptional person. The director of a private school offered to help with Eric's transition from the mental health facility to her school. "So she picked him up. She set some goals and in 6 months she met all those goals. And he was out of the school in 6 months." At the end of the 6 months Eric went back to his home county. It should be noted that in the years of his probation Eric had no contact with county social services, mental health services, or the courts. What Betty needed most from the county was financial assistance for Eric's treatment and schooling, yet she received none. To get the help Eric needed, Betty went outside the county, but her local agencies would not pay for outside services. All of Eric's private services were paid for by Betty and her husband.

When he came home, Eric re-enrolled in public school, but again, he lasted less than a year. The cycle of revolving schools continued. None of the schools' teachers could help Eric. Betty's family was assigned various counselors from the Department of Mental Health and DSS foster care, but neither proved helpful. According to Betty, they just shuffled the family back and forth and finally out. Eric is now in the 11th grade at public school. He has made it through the 4 years since the end of his probation with intensive private instruction. His behavioral problems remain, driving him from school to school, and he is now far behind his peers academically. In fact, he most likely will not gain admission to any college. Betty's earlier fears about the nonacademic stigma of special education have come true.

Summary of Client Needs

Betty wants Eric to be a "normal" child, especially in school. She wants him to receive the same education as "normal" children and to be able to reach goals like "normal" children. Betty believes that the public schools are not equipped to integrate children like Eric with special needs into regular classrooms, and that their special education and BEH classes do not teach a challenging academic curriculum. Betty had to turn to private schools to find the kind of individualized and academically directed instruction she wanted for Eric. The compassion and talents of the few public school teachers who were willing and able to work with Eric were the exception. Betty and her husband had to help Eric themselves, both emotionally and financially. The county allowed them to adopt Eric, but they either could not or would not provide assistance afterwards. Eric did not fit into any of the resource categories. Betty fears losing Eric, losing control over his life. She cannot entrust him to people who do not know him or understand his needs.

MEG

Meg, 29, was interviewed in the trailer where she lives with Jerome, her common-law husband, and her three children by a previous marriage. She and her family receive monthly child support and Aid to Families with Dependent Children (AFDC). They are also enrolled in Medicaid. Jerome is employed, and Meg worked at a local fast food restaurant until about 7 months ago, when her car "blew up" and left her unable to get to and from work.

Life History

Meg was born and raised in Alabama. Until she was in seventh grade, she and her mother, who was young and single, lived with her grandparents. Meg says, "I was mostly raised by my grandparents." When she was in seventh grade, her mother married Meg's stepfather. "He was fine then, but when we moved up here [to North Carolina] he became slowly an alcoholic. There was some beating and emotional abuse I guess you would call it." She lived with them for 2 years, but when she got pregnant, "got dropped out of school," and got married, she moved away from home. Meg tried to finish her senior year of high school, but, she says, "my son was very ill when he was born so I missed a lot of days and I was dropped out."

She and her husband soon sought help through DSS in the form of Food Stamps and heating assistance. Of life with her husband she says, "We moved quite a lot because he could not keep a job and didn't want me working because he didn't want to take care of the baby. So I was on and off [public assistance] for many, many years." Her husband eventually was sent to prison, "for all the crime he'd been into," so Meg shuffled residences, living in turns with her mother, his parents, and, ultimately, out on her own, with her own children and another husband. When Meg was 23, she enrolled in an adult basic education program run by the local community college and received her high school equivalency degree. Then 2 years later, Meg made the decision to return to school, in addition to working part-time, to pursue an associate's degree in general clerical skills. She has finished the course requirements and is awaiting graduation.

Recent months have offered both difficulty and hope for Meg. As noted, her car "blew up," which forced her to quit her job. Also, personnel at her daughter's school became concerned that the child was being emotionally abused at home. They reported Meg to Child Protective Services (CPS), and, although the investigator did not substantiate the charges, CPS urged, perhaps forced, Meg to attend parenting classes at the area Mental Health agency. However, the program has turned out to be a positive experience for her. Another positive experience has been the JOBS program. Since she began 6 months ago, she has worked at the same work site, in an administrative office at the college. She hopes to become independent of government services, find an office job, and perhaps eventually to move into "paralegalism," which, she says, would let "me be home with my children in the evenings and on weekends, a secretary . . . that would offer me benefits and maybe full-time work."

Experiences with Services

These two events in Meg's life—confronting the impact of emotional abuse through parenting classes and opening career opportunities through the JOBS program—are the two themes that best capture her experiences with government services. Both of them are relatively recent hopeful developments in an otherwise monotonous 11 years of on-again, off-again service dependency. It is also worth noting that Meg almost accidentally "found out" about the appropriate government services. The JOBS program came to her attention because there was no more popular reading material in the waiting room at DSS, and the mental health counseling only came about because a concerned school teacher or counselor noticed her daughter's "nervousness."

One door opened for Meg by the parenting classes was the opportunity to confront her own childhood abuse and to seek new models of caregiving. The issue of emotional abuse had buried itself until the neglect allegation was made. "They interviewed my kids at school . . . they interviewed me. . . . It was scary for me. Then later on, they sent me to a center, and I talked to a child therapist. She was very helpful to me." This help was all the more crucial in light of Meg's isolation from family and others. "We don't have a lot of friends, so we don't get a lot of people calling needing help which is, in a way, a relief. You can't give them support because you've never had support, and you don't know how to give it." The poor parenting with which she grew up and her limited interaction with other parents left her needing the perspective that parenting classes offered. Of the parenting group she says, "I realized when I started going there how much help I needed to get back in shape, to understand how to deal with my children better."

To get that help, however, she first had to endure a frightening DSS investigation. Meg's voice takes on a tone between irritation and indignation: "I had to go through all that humiliation for one, scared to death they were going to take my children. I didn't know how to act, what to expect." Reflecting back, Meg indicates that had she known about the group, she probably would have taken advantage of it long before DSS became involved. As it happened, she was coerced into participating ("I was kind of roped into it") by Child Protective Services, which put her in a defensive, threatened position.

Similarly, the JOBS Program has been a welcome opening, but one to which she came only by chance. She found it while she was waiting for her AFDC eligibility worker:

My case worker never contacted me about it. From what I gathered, it's because the program has very limited space, limited funding. They can only take so many on at a time. But because I pushed them and they found out I had taken college classes, they pushed to get me in there. They wanted me to come into the program, but it had to be my initiative.

The JOBS Program has afforded Meg experience with preparing a resume, negotiating the application process, and collecting work experience, in addition to allowing her to complete the course credit she needed for her degree. This last benefit is particularly important to Meg from a practical and an emotional point:

They helped me get back into school when I could not keep going because my car had been demolished. . . . I had no transportation. I had no way to finish. It depressed me quite a bit. I had no way to finish my college degree, even start the goal that I wanted for myself. So they helped me, got me back into school, helped me with transportation.

Another detail she mentions as significant, although some might think it minor, is that her JOBS worker took her to discount and thrift stores to put together a small professional wardrobe. "We went to thrift stores. They helped me get a few dresses to wear so I could be in public, which helps your self-esteem."

Summary of Client Needs

Except for AFDC, the consistent pattern in Meg's story is one in which she locates services incidentally. She did not walk into the Department of Social Services and survey what was available to her, nor did a case worker array the possibilities for her. She incidentally discovered the JOBS Program, and it "had to be [her] initiative." She also incidentally discovered family therapy at the Mental Health agency, after her interaction with Child Protective Services. This is a client being served, but more through chance than competence; and chance is too uncertain a mechanism to know where government services will ultimately take Meg and her family.

SHARON

Sharon, 20, lives in a mobile home with her grandmother, mother, and younger sister. She is unmarried and 8 months pregnant with her first child. When the baby is born, four generations will live under the same roof. Physically uncomfortable during the interview, Sharon continually shifted about in her seat. It was a hot, humid June afternoon. The baby was kicking, and Sharon's legs ached. Sharon, a quiet woman, spoke softly and gave single-sentence answers. She revealed little about herself, and what she did reveal was elicited carefully by the interviewer. The only service agency Sharon has dealt with is the Health Department, and she voices no complaints.

Life History

In the ninth grade, Sharon quit school in order to work. She has thought about getting a GED, but has not pursued it. For the past 3 years, she has worked the graveyard shift, 12:00 a.m. to 8:00 a.m., at a local garment factory. Her job entails knitting and requires her to sit constantly. When Sharon was 4 months pregnant, she developed blood clots in her legs. Following a doctor's orders, Sharon quit her job in order to get more exercise but plans to return to work at the factory after the baby is born. Sharon is not excited about having a baby. Pregnancy disrupts her life and makes her uncomfortable. She repeatedly refers to "it," not "the baby." Nor is the baby's father—also a high school dropout— excited. He lives across the street and works as a waiter at a local steak house, but Sharon hopes he will be able to pay child support.

Having been relatively self-sufficient, Sharon says, "I don't look for too much help unless it is from my Mom. . . . I haven't ever really had much help (government assistance) except for now." She relies mostly on the women in her family and female friends for support. When asked about child care when she returns to work, Sharon says that a female friend "is willing to take care of it."

Experiences with Services

Sharon's experience with services is limited. For the past 8 months, she has been receiving prenatal care. She is not dissatisfied with the Health Department. The wait for care is long, 3 hours on average, but she does not seem bothered by it. "Once you see the doctor, you're out in no time." The many forms she must fill out and the numerous Health Department workers she must meet with, approximately five per visit, are not problems for Sharon. She considers the staff at the Health Department nice, especially the younger staff, to whom she relates better.

Sharon indicates that she values work and has been bored at home. She says, "I want to go back to work." Of people she knows who are receiving unemployment checks, Sharon says, "Most of them could work if they wanted to. I know that much. . . . Some people rely on too much help."

Summary of Client Needs

Sharon is young and seems aimless. She has not initiated obtaining a GED; she has not sought family-planning counseling; and she did not know if her place of employment will provide health care coverage for her child. Sharon made no conscious decision to receive Medicaid. "Someone at the Health Department must have signed me up because next thing I knew, they just started sending it to me." The results of this seeming aimlessness are that Sharon is undereducated, unmotivated, and uncertain about a future that holds the added responsibilities of motherhood. Her situation—in need, but never quite in crisis, undemanding and even resistant to help—presents a common, silent challenge to social service agencies across the state.

WANDA

Wanda, 50, has 5 married children and 12 grandchildren. Her granddaughter Tammy, 9, has been living with her since she was born. Wanda is a nursing assistant who aspires to be a registered nurse, and a renter who would like very much to own her own home. She has been involved with the Department of Social Services for about 4 years, although she also received assistance from government agencies as a child.

Life History

Wanda is a native of North Carolina. She once worked for 10 years as a migrant laborer traveling from state to state with seasonal work, before moving back 2 years ago. Her childhood home life was uncomfortable, due to domestic unrest, and to the family's financial and legal problems. There was a lady in the neighborhood who would take her in when things got rough at home. The YMCA and a local church were other sources of minimal support for her. Wanda dropped out of school in the 10th grade and got married. She returned to school and received her GED in 1979. She is currently working as a nursing assistant on a temporary, part-time basis at the county hospital. She recently finished training for this position through a nearby community college, and she hopes to go back to complete more courses to become a registered nurse.

Experiences with Services

Wanda's first involvement with government services came while her father was in prison. Someone at the prison facilitated the connection between her mother and the Department of Social Services. She remembers her mother getting a check once a month, but the family did not receive Food Stamps or any other types of assistance. "He was sentenced to 2 years and served about 9 months to a year. We got help while he was there, and financially we were a lot better while he was gone."

Wanda remembers the first time she had to ask for assistance in adult-hood as a humiliating experience. The first time she went she cried because she felt degraded to have to ask for help. She worries that she will never be able to stop receiving assistance from government agencies:

> Everybody talks about the system, the system, the system. It is so hard to get off of welfare. I've been on it; I've been off. I go back on it; I get off. If I lose this part-time, temporary job I have now, I don't want to go back on welfare, but what choice will I have? To put it bluntly, you make more money staying home on welfare than you do working. If you work part-time your Medicaid's gone, your Food Stamps are gone, your check's gone. And you end up bringing home less.

For Wanda, financial security is not the only frightening unknown to finding employment. She notes, "No one gets insurance on part-time work. Well, even the job I've got right now, I've got no insurance, nothing. Because it's temporary. Yeah, I can have a check coming in but my Medicaid stopped. And that's scary." Every time she finds a job, her Medicaid is revoked immediately despite the lag time before health insurance on any job goes into effect. The fact that she is working a temporary, part-time job does not affect the agency's decision: the Medicaid must stop when the job starts.

Wanda describes other problems she has with the system. Once she started receiving AFDC and Food Stamps, several conditions were imposed. She had to attend mandatory meetings, register with the employment office, and continuously look for work. As Wanda understands it, the Employment Security Commission requires one to look for a job twice a week, but one cannot look twice on the same day. This regulation makes the entire process more difficult. When Wanda was not working, money was too limited to spend on transportation looking for work on two separate occasions. She observes, "If you're already out there you should be able to do all your looking then." Neglectful duplication of services also annoys Wanda, who sees it as a sign that agencies are too busy to care about her time and trouble:

> The first time I went to apply for Food Stamps they gave me a piece a paper, and I went over to the Christian Ministry. I didn't like that. You go to Christian Ministry, and they send you back to Social Service, and you've got to get a paper saying you need Christian Ministry, and then you go back to Christian Ministry with the note. I didn't like that.

Wanda also complains about the repetitiveness, not of the forms, but of the speeches and information sessions she must attend in order to receive services. She does not like the meetings she had to go to because they kept repeating admonitions about attempts to defraud service programs:

They can tell you one time, and you ought to understand what fraud is. But to go 45 minutes to an hour on fraud, it makes you feel terrible. Because I thought, well you go and discuss one topic and then you go on to another topic, but no matter what topic was being discussed, she always went back to fraud. It makes you wonder, would they be talking to other people like this? It just makes you feel . . . like they don't trust you. I know a lot of people do abuse the system, but this is childish. It makes you feel like they think they are so much better than the people in that room are. I really feel belittled in there.

She found still further regulatory roadblocks on her way to the JOBS Program. When no jobs were available, Wanda returned to the agency that helped with her GED, but she did not qualify for their assistance because she had been on the program before. They advised her to sign up for AFDC again, so she could qualify for the JOBS Program. Next, she learned that the seasonal work she was doing made her ineligible for AFDC, Food Stamps, and Medicaid. As soon as the seasonal work was over she had to go back to sign up for AFDC and to get an appointment with a JOBS Program worker. The program paid for her tuition, her books, and even for Tammy's daycare. Wanda has nothing but praise for the JOBS Program's personal and convenient service:

My worker called me a couple of times to see how I was doing. I didn't have to go in. And when I go in and pick up my gas mileage check—you have to pick it up at the office—she would talk to me there and see how things were going. And see if they could help me with anything further.

The JOBS Program was successful; she went to work a couple of days after she got out of school.

Summary of Client Needs

Wanda asks in many ways for no-nonsense, straightforward, realistic services. She found that agency guidelines were not written for the real circumstances of the seasonal worker; rather she, not the agency, would have to adjust in order for her to be served. She found some guidelines arbitrary, and some workers careless, causing her unnecessary trouble and expense. The costly hassles of trying to improve one's lot in government programs, she believes, make many people just accept assistance without a struggle, knowing that as long as they ask for no more, they will continue to receive minimal funds. Her concerns boil down to two issues: how hard it is to get on assistance—"It never feels good to have to ask for help. I can't say anything good about that"—and how hard it is to get off—"It's cheaper for people to stay home."

SUMMARY

Betty, Meg, Sharon, and Wanda are not increasing dependency on services, but they also are not becoming more self-sufficient as result of their experiences with services. Rather, they are maintaining their current status. They go on and off the rolls of various public service agencies. Meg and Wanda have found the JOBS program to be helpful in getting employment. Betty's experience with her adopted son has included school system resistance to mainstreaming him and juvenile services' sending him to treatment. However, she never receives support from services to cover his needs when he is at home. She is walking a tightrope between getting her adopted son appropriate services as she defines them and risking having agencies take her son away. Meg has a history of being on and off of public services all of her life. Destitution led to her first involvement, and she has worked hard to get an education. The program that has benefited her most, JOBS, she found out on her own initiative, not from her caseworkers. Even with JOBS, however, she will likely be on and off services for a number of years. Sharon is having a baby, but is not excited by the prospect. She represents one more generation of single parenting in her family. She values work and wants to return to it. Sharon is using services selectively and may well continue to do so. Wanda demonstrates that services are unable to effectively respond to temporary, seasonal, and part-time work. Terminating services for such employment is a disincentive for seeking such work, and this creates repeated periods of desperation for the family until services kick in again. She shows that public services are hard to get and hard to get off of. Again, the JOBS program has helped her into a job and has treated her decently.

For these women, public assistance is necessary for periods of their lives. This involvement does not increase their dependency on services; rather, they use services to get them through difficult periods in their lives. They dislike their treatment by the agencies, but they need services to maintain themselves and their children. Betty, Meg, Sharon, and Wanda will likely maintain this pattern itself over much of their lives, using public services incidentally.

8

Cheryl, Ruth, Edith, and Susan: Narratives of Increasing Independence

Penny L. Richards
Rhonda Jeffries

This chapter presents the stories of four social services clients who, sometimes with the help of agencies and sometimes fighting agencies all the way, are moving toward increasing independence. Although each woman still foresees struggles and obstacles on the way to meeting her goals, the stories they tell are all to some extent success stories. They speak of social services agencies with mixed feelings, recognizing that they have been a crucial safety net during difficult periods but describing their experiences with agencies as sometimes frustrating and demeaning. Their experiences suggest ways in which agencies, separately and together, can facilitate the quest of clients for independence, as well as ways in which agencies may inadvertently stifle that quest.

One thing all of the women in this chapter have in common with the women whose stories were told in the previous two chapters is their emphasis on the high emotional costs of seeking help from public agencies. None of these women, as some political rhetoric might suggest, saw public assistance as a desirable "way of life." For all of them the decision to seek help from public agencies was a painful one, considered only as a last resort. All of them recalled feelings of fear or shame before their first visit to apply for social services. For some, these feelings resulted from a sense of public stigma attached to welfare recipients; others had even more serious concerns that if they approached public agencies for help they might have their children taken away. In some cases their worst fears were realized when they encountered agency personnel who they felt were judgmental or looked down on them. By contrast, they praised workers who listened to their stories in a patient and matter-of-fact way. In most cases walking in the door of a public agency is a daunting moment for clients; agency personnel can make the experience less traumatic by obtaining information in a respectful and nonthreatening way. The stories of these women make it clear that these initial encounters are crucial in establishing trust between agencies and clients and demonstrating to clients that agencies are "on their side."

In addition to the initial intake interview, certain other junctures stand out in these stories as critical to a successful agency-client relationship. For each of these women, timely and coordinated agency support made the difference at a crucial transition point. One recalled how a positive relationship she had established with a caseworker gave her the emotional and material support she needed to move out of an abusive situation. By providing encouragement and working with other agencies to secure housing and support for the client, this caseworker provided the client with an opportunity at a critical moment. The ability of this caseworker to pull together a complete package of support at just the right moment has proved crucial to the client's future success. It should be noted, however, that this client was making a transition into an established agency program. The transition away from public assistance is much more difficult to negotiate. These women noted that although the routes into public programs are clearly structured through regulations and paperwork, the paths out have to be forged by each client individually. Often, clients do not even have a clear roadmap of how regulations will change as they attain increasing independence. It seemed to them that public assistance was designed in an all-or-nothing fashion—they were either eligible for a comprehensive list of services or they were dropped from the rolls altogether. They spoke poignantly of their uncertainty about issues such as daycare and health coverage as they moved into jobs. It takes a great deal of confidence to make this leap; current programs and agency structures do not seem well designed to smooth the transition. This is one juncture where interagency collaboration could make a crucial difference by filling in some of the service gaps and providing clients the information and support they need to negotiate the transition.

When comparing the experiences of social services clients who have achieved increasing independence with those in the previous two chapters who are either becoming more dependent or running in place, it becomes clear that moving off of public assistance requires a great deal of individual initiative. There is a tremendous bias in the system toward inaction and the status quo. Once clients have jumped through all of the hoops necessary to get *on* social services, there are not many incentives to leave that safe haven. Each of the women in this chapter made an active decision to reject dependency; there is no indication that the system encouraged them to move toward independence. They present themselves as having to serve as their own advocate and aggressively pursue information and opportunities. Perhaps the most dramatic example is the woman who, after trying to obtain child support through normal channels for many years, went to the Pentagon personally to obtain the address of the children's father, who was serving abroad in the Army. This same woman, after failing to obtain appropriate services for her learning-disabled son from his school, took her case directly to the Office of Civil Rights. Given that not many individuals are likely to go to such heroic lengths, changes should be made in the system that reward and encourage rather than stifle initiative in social services recipients.

The bottom line for the women in this chapter was a need for consistency and respect from public agencies. To the extent that social service agencies have helped them to achieve independence, it was through providing information and services in a stable and nonthreatening way, working with them as partners. Their most positive experiences were when they felt themselves full participants in their own case rather than passive recipients of treatment. When clients perceived that rules and procedures were always in flux or that things were going on behind their backs, their relationship with agencies became adversarial and actually became an obstacle on their road to independence.

CHERYL

Twenty-six-year-old Cheryl lives with her son Paul, 11, in a government-subsidized apartment with all the furniture "bought and paid for." She was interviewed in the local hospital where, through the JOBS program, she is working in the clerical department. This summer she looks forward to "having fun" at a new job with a community center summer camp.

Life History

Cheryl begins describing her life with the note that it is "full of pain." She was born in New York's South Bronx to a family with three older brothers and two older sisters. Her father died before she was born, and her mother died when she was 7. When Cheryl was 5, her mother put her up for adoption while keeping her brother, who was a year older, at home. When her mother got sick, an older sister came to take care of her brother, and Cheryl's grandparents went to New York, "and they adopted me in order to bring me back here." Her grandparents made her recipient of their Social Security checks, and when they became too old to care for her and her mother died, "one aunt just finally decided, 'Okay, we'll take care of her.'" Her aunt brought a series of abusive men into their home. "None of her boyfriends ever touched us or anything like that," she says, except for one when she was 10. "I would always get beatings with like extension cords until I bled."

Cheryl describes her teen years with that aunt as "crappy": "At 15, she started putting me out, and then she realized that if I left, the money went to wherever it was that I was staying. So eventually, she kind of let me stay back, and I got pregnant." She had her son Paul during ninth grade, and, with the encouragement and help of her nephew, a college student, Cheryl remained in high school and graduated. In fact, she only missed about a week of school to have her baby, and afterwards, she found people to watch him during the day. Whether it was her nephew or someone else, Cheryl says:

> I was still in school, but I always ended up with somebody that would watch him, as long as I went to school. It was always, 'Well, if you go to school, I'll watch him, but if you don't, if you goof off or something like that—' These were just people I was living with . . . somebody, a friend of a friend, or something like that.

Cheryl got an apartment for herself and her son when she was 19. She "always did little odds and ends jobs . . .anything that made money that was legal, and, you know, acceptable." Such jobs did not pay enough for a single parent, however, and she applied for AFDC, Food Stamps, and Medicaid. She says she "decided that this is not what I want to do. I did not want to sit around at home and just wait for my son to come and go to school all day." Cheryl went to the Department of Social Services to push them for ways to help her. She found a couple of classes on job skills and the like, and then, about 3 years ago, she enrolled in the JOBS Program, which included a combination of college classes and volunteer work to gather work experience. Cheryl has taken "like fifty million" classes and has since earned a 2-year, associate's degree in general office technology. She has worked at JOBS sites in the Department of Social Services, the local hospital, and a community center. She gets along "great" with her son, and they hope to save money to buy a home.

Experiences with Services

Cheryl's involvement with government services has been limited to the Department of Social Services—Social Security; AFDC; Women, Infants, and Children (WIC); Food Stamps; Medicaid; and the JOBS program. She reports having to serve as her own advocate to get the services she needed, and she describes several instances of advising others on negotiating the system. Several themes emerge to characterize her experiences with DSS. In the beginning, her eligibility for services made her a "useful" addition to her aunt's home. During her pregnancy and her son's early years, she continually found services too late. Once she began the JOBS Program, however, she began mustering the confidence to take charge of her life, to reflect on her experiences, and to evaluate them.

One message of Cheryl's early years is the tricky position in which services place children who have uncertain family situations. According to Cheryl, her aunt decided to take her in "only because I was bringing in money being there." There was a constant tug-of-war between wanting her out of the house and wanting the benefits of Cheryl's Social Security payments. With Food Stamps, Cheryl was also literally a "meal ticket." "That was one reason that she wanted me to stay there, because that meant more Food Stamps." For Cheryl, whose youth was a series of displacements, this was yet another instance of not really being wanted. Her services eligibility—intended to help her—made her a useful tool, but not a part of a family.

Cheryl went through her pregnancy alone, only later to discover that agency help was available. Her aunt was not materially or emotionally supportive, and she did not describe any special attention from school personnel. Not even her doctor provided much support. Cheryl says that when she was admitted to the hospital:

> I had one doctor, and he was just nowhere to be found. So another doctor came in, and he was real upset, because I was underweight and I was undernourished. He was like, "Why didn't you apply for WIC or something like that?" And I was like, "I didn't know."

Cheryl did enlist in the WIC program after her son was born and remained a recipient until he was about 3 years old. Not only did she not know about WIC, but Cheryl was also unaware of Medicaid as a possible source for health insurance. She continues to pay the hospital costs incurred during her son's delivery. About 7% is deducted from her monthly AFDC checks for those payments. She says, 11 years later, "I'm still paying for it."

Cheryl's lack of knowledge about available services was sometimes treated as a moral failing by agency personnel. Of her first encounter with an AFDC worker, Cheryl recalls, "The lady I had to go see was evil. God, was she evil. She was like, 'Why don't you do this, and why don't you do that?' I was like, 'Well, I been going through. . . .'" During the course of the first visit, they both eventually relaxed a little, and the eligibility worker was able to direct Cheryl to the appropriate sources. All told, it took Cheryl almost 5 years to get the help for which she was eligible.

Her first encounter with the JOBS Program held more hope. The day Cheryl brought herself into DSS with the goal of doing something with her life, the JOBS Program director said, "Cheryl, fill out all these papers." "Gosh," Cheryl recollects, "I filled out a lot of papers, but I ended up in school." At first the program concentrated mostly on courses and workshops for service recipients. The classes "gave you this positive image of yourself and things that you could do, no matter how bad you felt about being on welfare or anything like that." She admits that it was taxing, but, "Every time they offered [a class] I would take it."

The JOBS Program expanded to provide opportunities for actual work experience. They found "JOBS sites" where participants could work, as volunteers, to get the experience that every employer seemed to expect. Although Cheryl clearly understood the importance of this, it was a serious challenge for her. "It had got to the point that I would come in in the morning and I was going to the JOB site for like 3 or 4 hours, then I was coming to school, and then I would go back to the JOB site, and then I would come back to school at nighttime." Despite the rigor of the JOBS program, it has brought Cheryl opportunities that she otherwise would not have had. She knows three or four other women who have "graduated" to paid employment and have pulled themselves out of social services, and their realization of that goal is a powerful example.

Sitting on the brink of virtual self-reliance for Cheryl is an exciting and insecure position. She wants to be independent, but she says, "The only thing that scares me is not getting the Medicaid and the Food Stamps. I could stand to get Food Stamps another month, and then I'll be situated. . . . The Medicaid I could stand to get for another year." Cheryl is uncertain about her eligibility for services during this transitional period. She believes DSS allows a "grace period," but she does not know how that applies specifically to AFDC, Food Stamps, and Medicaid. The transition from monthly to biweekly pay schedules is also a concern:

> I'm so used to getting paid once a month that it works for me. I would rather get paid once a month because getting paid every 2 weeks, I quickly learned that your money is gone. Then I'm like, "Gosh! What did I do with all this money?" Then you have to take that one paycheck and pay everything and get all the food and all that.

Cheryl remembers taking a budgeting class that was offered to help people manage their benefits. She suggests that may be a helpful addition to any program that brings people out of service dependency. "A lot of the girls, the two or three that I know that have gone off it, it seems to me and it seems to them I have less now than I did when I was on AFDC. They make more money and all, but it's only because we have no idea how to budget it."

Logistical frustrations with agency services remain. As explained earlier, several of the JOBS sites turned unexpectedly into temporary paid positions. The first time this happened, Cheryl called her AFDC caseworker to find out what to do. She did as the caseworker indicated and had no problems. The second time, however, she again sent in copies of her pay stub to her AFDC, Food Stamps, and Medicaid workers, but the AFDC worker called her back and told her she would be penalized through her checks. Later the case worker relented—apparently Cheryl's JOBS worker told her, "You've never had a problem out of Cheryl." Of this Cheryl says, "Everything they've asked for I've given to them. I've dealt with them, and I've been honest. It doesn't matter how honest you are. . . . There's always something that's not going to be right by their standards."

Summary of Client Needs

Cheryl came into the realm of social services a virtual pawn, but she leaves it a player. She has managed to act for herself since her teen years, but has not always realized the necessity of such a stance. When she sees friends now who helped her by watching her son while she finished high school, they say "I'm so proud of you!" Other people she sees, Cheryl says, "who knew me and knew my situation, they've said 'Cheryl, you've come a long way.'" This growing sense of self-efficacy has given her an air of confidence and experience, which in turn allows her to help other women. Several of the stories she tells involve classmates who look to her for advice. She encourages them to communicate their concerns to their own JOBS workers, and she answers them honestly about how to deal with the logistics of social services. In all of her stories, Cheryl expresses concern that others will miss the opportunity she has found to direct her own life.

RUTH

Ruth, 32, lives in a spare but clean apartment with her four children: a 12th-grader, a 9th-grader, a 1st-grader, and a toddler. She is a single mother and has dealt with various service agencies in the county. In these dealings she believes she has faced and fought racial prejudice against herself and her children.

Life History

Ruth has four siblings. She remembers her family taking trips, helping each other with homework, and attending church regularly. When Ruth was 15, she became pregnant and dropped out of school. Her second child was born 2 years later. She has since been a single mother and has tried to provide for her children without the support of the government. Ruth has spent some time at the local community college working toward completing her GED. Although she is not currently employed, she has worked most of her adult life: first at a convenience store, then at a knitting plant that closed not long ago. She is waiting to hear about a job for which she recently applied.

Ruth's children have brought her into contact (and conflict) with service agencies. Child support issues have taken years to resolve. Her son Joe, a ninth grader, has special educational and behavioral needs, and has recently found himself in trouble with the law. Her daughter Rose is considered an at-risk troublemaker at the same high school.

Experiences with Services

Ruth says that the Department of Social Services and the local school system have served her poorly in her "battles" to obtain child support and special educational services. Her child support problems have focused on the father of her older two children, who is in the army, stationed abroad. The Department of Social Services was unable to locate him. Ruth says angrily, "I can't believe they couldn't find a man in the United States Army!" Ruth finally went to the Pentagon herself to obtain his address. "That's how we got support started after 10 years."

For more than 2 years, Ruth has been at war with the local high school principal. The story is complicated. Ruth's son, Joe, has been suspended from school repeatedly. He has "cussed a teacher" and been generally disruptive. Ruth became actively involved in the dispute when a warrant was wrongfully issued for her arrest on the charge of failure to send Joe to school. Ruth had been told by the school's principal that Joe was expelled. She had asked if there were any special education programs available for students such as Joe with behavioral problems, and was told there were none. Despite having been told her son was expelled, Ruth was taken to court for failure to send her child to school. The warrant was issued because the records of the expulsion had been lost. The records were finally found in the school system's central office. Ruth eventually received a letter of apology from the school for the mistake.

While expelled, Joe got into further trouble. He was convicted of possessing a sawed-off shotgun. Joe was appointed a court counselor, who suspected that Joe was learning disabled. He arranged for Joe to be tested, and Joe was indeed found to have a learning disability. There are special classes for learning-disabled students at the local high school that Joe might have attended. Ruth was angry that Joe was not tested sooner. She contacted the Department of Education's Office of Civil Rights in Atlanta and filed a complaint. When the Office of Civil Rights became involved, Joe was admitted to the high school as a learning-disabled student. Ruth withdrew her complaint but she is still bitter toward the educational system. "The system just isn't fair. It's not right. They don't do what they're supposed to be doing. It took them that long to get him classified as LD."

Ruth's eldest child, Rose, was recently suspended for fighting in school. Her brother Joe believes Rose was just playing, not really fighting. To make matters worse, at the time of the suspension, a teacher stated she believed both Rose and her mother were on drugs. Ruth is indignant. "Those accusations about Rose and me—I don't think that's right without proof." Ruth is also upset she was not informed sooner of the teacher's suspicions. "When I asked 'Why haven't I heard about it until now?' [The principal] didn't say anything—no comment." Ruth says she plans to file another complaint with the Office of Civil Rights. The worst thing about her experiences with the school has been "their tirading against me, trying to get me out of the way because I'm asking for help for my child."

Her advice for child and family service providers is:

> Treat everyone equally as you're supposed to do. Make sure things get
> done in the way they're supposed to get done. When you're wrong, you're
> wrong. Admit it. When you're right, you're right. Take the time to listen
> instead of trying to judge. That's what I felt they were doing just because I
> was Black. They thought I didn't know anything. They thought I'd roll over
> and play dead.

She stresses that her complaint is more against specific individuals than the system itself. In fact, Ruth would like to be a counselor herself. Joe's court counselor and staff members in the Department of Education's Office of Civil Rights have been her allies. Ruth says, "I want to help people when they don't know their rights."

Summary of Client Needs

Ruth has faced obstacles in her contacts with social service agencies. She did not receive much-needed child support for at least 10 years. Her son did not receive special education when necessary. Ruth has been accused of being a drug user on little or no evidence. What is remarkable about Ruth is her courage and determination. When social services could not track down the father of two of her children, she went to Washington to track him down herself. She succeeded in proving to the local high school principal that her son was learning disabled and entitled to special education. She has enlisted the help of the Department of Education's Office of Civil Rights in self-defense. Ruth knows how to fight for her rights and obtain the quality services she and her family deserve. She needs only encouragement and fairness, not obstruction and suspicion, from the individuals she encounters.

EDITH

Edith, 32, has four children ranging in age from 11 to 2. She lives in an apartment near many members of her family, who are mostly on public assistance, as Edith has been most of her life. She has also sought government programs for help with reading, childcare, and domestic turmoil.

Life History

Edith was born to a single mother, so although she knows and has contact with her father, she grew up with a stepfather who made their home "turbulent." He made her leave home several times, and family relationships continue to be strained to this day. Her grandparents were a source of emotional support when she needed to talk. Another person to whom she turned for help was a local woman with whom she came in contact early in her life through a government agency. This woman took her to Head Start classes, and she remained a life long source of support to Edith.

Edith has positive memories of the helpful people she encountered as a child involved with the Department of Social Services. She says they always did a good job of supporting her family when they were in need. They provided Food Stamps for her family and funds to buy clothes and shoes and other necessities for school. Edith's impressions of the agencies are bad, although her memories of the services they provided were good. She remembers her mother being afraid that if she accepted assistance, she would invite the possibility of losing her children. "I mean they've done real good. I mean, by me now. Other people, I don't know. But by me, they've helped me out real good."

Edith quit school in the 11th grade and went to live with her uncle. She has recently done work in a literacy program, toward the goal of earning a GED. She believes this will enable her to get her driver's license, and, once her youngest son can enroll in Head Start, she hopes to begin working a full-time job. Edith has set these concrete objectives—which all rely on the availability of government help—as markers on the way to her dream: to move her children to a quiet country setting where they will have more room to run around and play outside, and to be independent of public assistance.

Experiences with Services

Edith talks about several DSS workers in particular who have been especially helpful:

> I really think the world of her. She was working with us, with me when I lived on Broad Street, and she knew how I had to live down there. My husband was working and making a good amount of money, and that just stopped all my help. Then he started drinking and hanging around bars, and then they came in and I talked to Mavis. She was the only one that I felt that I could talk to, and so, I talked to her and she told me, "I'll help you any way I can." So she has. She's the one that helped me get this apartment. If it hadn't been for her I wouldn't have anything. They have done a real good job for me. I don't know about other people, but now myself, what more could I ask for? I mean, I can't ask for more from them, because they've done good.

When Edith's husband began abusing her and the children, she found the strength to leave him with another agency worker's encouragement and the financial assistance of DSS. Her husband reinforced in Edith the same fear her mother had, that if she asked for assistance, DSS would take the children away from her. Edith says that he seemed to know that she could not afford to leave without asking for help, so he played on such insecurities to convince her to stay. The DSS worker, Cindy, made trips to Edith's house to work with her because Edith's husband had removed the telephone from the home. Cindy found an apartment for Edith in less than 1 week, opening a crucial opportunity for Edith to leave an oppressive situation with confidence. Cindy referred Edith's case to a local housing agency that is another big source of help for Edith. This organization pays the rent on her apartment and half of her electric bill. Edith does not, however, have full confidence in the housing agency's goodwill because she tried to get alternative living arrangements through them before, without DSS intervention, and was denied.

Overall, the workers Edith deals with are cooperative and make things easy for her. They initiated paperwork for her to begin receiving AFDC, Medicaid, Social Security, and Food Stamps. The workers are in contact regularly with Edith, and she seems to appreciate this attention when they come to visit her. The last time she went to DSS, she talked to a child support worker. "We were discussing my husband paying child support. And I told her if he started paying child support he wouldn't have anything left for himself. And she said if you could get some statements on his situation, and how he acted toward you and the kids, we'll just drop it. So I went ahead and did that." Visiting DSS was comfortable, says Edith, and even the paperwork presented little difficulty. "Well, see I'm so used to her, if I read something and I don't understand it, I'll go back and ask her what it's about, and she'll explain it." This entire process took about 2 or 3 hours, but Edith says that was not an overwhelming ordeal. Once all the paperwork was completed, she began receiving assistance within 60 days, as they had promised her.

Edith believes DSS is a good resource: "If they see you are trying, they'll help you." The worst part of dealing with the agencies for Edith is having to make the initial step of going in and asking for help. "Making the decision and walking in the front door was the most difficult thing to do." As she recalls, the best things about it were going in and fulfilling the requirements and actually receiving the assistance that can make such a difference in one's life. "They'll give you as much help as you need."

Summary of Client Needs

Edith expresses satisfaction with the services that she receives from governmental agencies. She envisions eventual independence through further services, in hopes that they will be as friendly and cooperative as the DSS workers on whom she has relied to date. Edith may not yet be a "success story," but her positive experiences with agencies offer insight into how government services can give personal as well as material benefits.

SUSAN

Susan, 26, is married and has a 3-year-old son. Her previously secure family has fallen on hard times and needs temporary help to get back on their feet. They have dealt with DSS, an agency Susan was raised to avoid, but has come to appreciate, with some reservations.

Life History

Susan's father was a tenant farmer, and her mother stayed home with the children when they were small. Although her father worked hard and made sure the family did too, they were, in Susan's words, "low income," but never relied on public assistance. Susan and her one sibling were brought up in a strongly religious household and were "invested with good moral values." Susan and her sibling both completed a public high school education, and Susan attended college, which she left for a job with an insurance company. She then got married and stopped working, as she became pregnant shortly after the marriage.

Her husband Mark was working in a middle-management position at the time of their marriage. He was laid off from his job in 1991 and started his own business, one that was "proven profitable." The family put all their money into a deal that completely fell through, causing what Susan calls a "devastating trauma" in the family. They had to sell their house and relied on the help of friends and family for a while. Then they turned to their county's social services agencies. Susan initially resisted her husband's suggestion that they seek such help, believing that it should be a "last resort." Her husband convinced her that, indeed, their options were few, and she grudgingly agreed to visit the Department of Social Services. She went, however, feeling "degraded."

Experiences with Services

Initially, Susan was pleasantly surprised with the treatment she and Mark received at the Department of Social Services (actually, the treatment Mark received because Susan did not accompany him for the first few visits). The intake worker with whom Mark initially met was very receptive to his needs and sympathetic with his situation. Susan and Mark believed, half jokingly, that it was due to the fact that he wore a suit to his DSS visits. Their case was processed quickly; Mark applied for AFDC, Medicaid, and Food Stamps, and they received their first AFDC payment and "food coupons" (Susan refused to call them food stamps) about 2 weeks after Mark's intake session. Susan was surprised with the efficiency of the system because they had heard many negative comments from friends who had dealt with DSS before. She remembers thinking, "They pulled through for us, you know. After a while we said, 'Well, it's not that bad, at least we're eating, you know, at least we have some money to put in the gas tank.'"

Then, during one of his visits, Mark talked with a woman who "threw everything off." She "entered something into the computer that just threw everything off." Because of that incident, Susan and Mark had to fill out a lot of paperwork—three or four rounds' worth. Once a report was sent in too early, was sent back, and more forms had to be filled out. As Mark's visits to DSS became more frequent, and the tension greater, he began to feel that, because he is Black, the DSS workers he talked with began "putting up a wall." Susan and Mark were doing what they thought they were supposed to do, yet they always had more forms to fill out, and no one would tell them just what was happening. Their case worker was "never in" and when she returned their calls, they were out. They would leave messages or talk with someone unfamiliar with their complicated situation.

After all these efforts, Susan and Mark had their AFDC payments discontinued. Although first claiming that she did not know the reason, Susan later divulges that her part-time job was the cause. She and Mark had participated in a job training program through DSS, and, as a result, Susan was offered work. She says that she found the program very rewarding, in that "we learned techniques we had never heard of before." Her job, however, put the family at too high an income level to receive AFDC, although they continued receiving Food Stamps. Although her working stopped the "free money," Susan remains motivated to continue her job because she is uncomfortable using food stamps at the grocery store. She says that experience:

> pushed me to the point where I said to myself, "Well, I'm going to get a job." And, you know, my husband has done everything within his powers to find employment also, and . . . nothing. I've always been the type person that, you know, if something comes up I will find a job somewhere. I needed to, and I did.

To Susan, having to ask for help in the first place was a very humbling experience. Even helpful, efficient processes left her emotionally weary. She feels that workers were fairly harsh, questioning everything on the couple's paperwork, and making them feel worse than they already did. She advises others who might seek public assistance to:

> be emotionally prepared (for) how you will be dealt with or talked to. I mean, if you're down at your last point when the last thing you need is to be stomped on some more, you know, you have to just prepare yourself for examinations of all questions that they can ask you.

Susan also has some advice for case workers, saying, "I know you hear these cases all day long, and when you hear the same thing over and over, you can become kind of resistant, you can become kind of hard. I think that was proba-bly what my husband ran into. I think someone had probably heard enough of what we're going through." She adds, "I would think that more training for workers [would help] . . . listening [to clients] and saying, 'Well, maybe this did happen,' or, not saying, 'Well, this didn't happen. They're just lying, they just want state money.'"

Summary of Client Needs

Susan is basically satisfied with the help she and Mark have received from DSS. Initially, people were receptive, and the job training program led to a job for Susan. On her husband's continued unemployment, she defends both Mark and the program, saying "they did all they could, and he did all he could." She believes that DSS is supposed to "help people to at least get back on their feet again and push them forward into society." Susan fears, however, that her family will become permanently dependent on public assistance. This worry is rooted both in her upbringing and in her recent frustrating experiences. She is especially wary after being caught working in violation of regulations. To others in her place, Susan warns, "Just tell them the truth because if you don't, something is going to unravel somewhere. You really have to be honest with them and with yourself. Because saying that you used to work for 'X' amount of dollars, of course they're going to do their research." When Susan asks for social services workers to be more sensitive, she may be asking for them to understand what might push ordinarily honest people to lie about things like income.

SUMMARY

The narratives of increasing independence are different from those of increasing dependency and maintenance. They are using services temporarily like many of those maintaining themselves with services, but they have found ways to use services for their own ends. Cheryl has had a hard life but is on the brink of self-reliance. She found she had to be her own advocate if she was to get appro-priate services, and she has done so effectively. This has resulted in her involve-ment in the JOBS program and an associate's degree. She is both excited and insecure about her future, but she has confidence she will be able to handle it. Ruth is also a self-advocate. She is clear about what her children need and fought to get appropriate services. She has been unfairly accused and subject to racial prejudice when dealing with agencies. When faced with an obstacle, Ruth confronts the agency and becomes the initiator. She takes responsibility for get-ting what she needs. Edith is not a self-advocate like Ruth and Cheryl; rather, she was fortunate to have found advocates on her behalf in DSS. She is pursuing her GED and envisions a future independent of public services. She has learned that agencies will help those who are trying to make a transition, as she and her family are attempting to do. Susan has found that agencies were receptive to their temporary needs but respond quickly when they perceive that the client is cheating. She believes that racism accounts for their treatment, yet still appreciates the services. She has entered the work force and is determined to return to self-sufficiency.

Cheryl, Ruth, Edith, and Susan all show a side of public services we had not seen in the other narratives. They have gotten much of what they needed from existing services, but they did so because of their own self-advocacy or the advocacy of a caseworker. They have had to push, some more than others, but they have found that they can make their way with determination. Increasing independence from public services seems to require more than the usual services; it requires someone to make something unusual happen. This is clearly an unfortunate story about public services.

PART II CONCLUSION:
Five Messages from the Other Side of the Desk

Penny L. Richards

Certainly, the stories resound with notes of anger, frustration, and fear about the current means of service delivery to children and their families in North Carolina. Gratitude, triumph, and hope also emerge from their stories, although perhaps less often. The strong emotions shared by these women indicate how important government services, integrated or discrete, have been in their lives. The experiences that prompted such emotions may point out opportunities for policy makers whose reforms are intended to benefit the clients as well as the agencies. In this section are five "messages" that emerge from the experiences of these 12 women. The messages roughly follow the client's experience from entry to exit. After a brief elaboration of each idea, specific policy options are listed which address that message.

UNDERSTAND THE DESPERATION THAT FIRST BRINGS CLIENTS TO ASK FOR HELP

When the clients described their first approach to an agency, they used words like "embarrassed," "afraid," "coerced," "degraded." The crises that precipitated their serious need were sometimes sudden—a job lost due to pregnancy or car problems, for example—whereas for others, their lives had long been difficult but had at last become unbearable. Most had previously tried to find help through family, neighbors, or their own resources before deciding to ask for government assistance. The responses they remember from that first intake, and many later, were being "stomped on," "judged," "given a hard time," "put down," and "intimidated." If first impressions are lasting, it is no surprise that such clients maintain a resentment toward agencies on which they must rely.

Several of the women described resorting to deceit as a consequence of their desperate situations. One admitted having written bad checks and making a false robbery report, when her children were literally without food or clothing; another remembered that a neighbor once wrote a bad check so that she could receive medical treatment after an accident; a third hinted that she and her husband bent the truth about their income to receive financial assistance. These women all regretted their dishonesties, but they shared them to illustrate the absolute need they felt when asking for government help. Further, they said that agency personnel rarely understood this desperation, offering little compassion even when material help was forthcoming.

Policy Options

- *Allow time for new clients just to talk and explain their whole situation.* It may not be information necessary to process the case, but it may meet the clients' need to tell their story to another human being; it may also help agency personnel think of their clients as unique people, and be more personal in their dealings. It could also build trust and a sense of being understood for wary, frustrated clients.
- *Examine intake protocols for judgmental signals.* Whether actually judgmental or not, agency personnel are often perceived as such by people already at a low point. Can questions be rephrased, voices softened, offices rearranged to project more acceptance? Will streamlining other procedures permit the client to make her difficult intake visit just once, for a range of services?

INCLUDE CLIENTS IN THE COLLABORATIVE PROCESS

Although their need for assistance was often great, the women emphasized that this definitely did not mean they were willing to surrender control of their lives or of their families to receive that help. Mothers in danger of losing their children were especially sensitive on this point. "No one takes my kid away from me!" was one woman's cry, whereas others expressed similar insistence that they retain final authority where their children are concerned and similar frustration with a system that they perceive as disinterested, disdainful, or dismissive of their wishes.

One of these unfulfilled wishes echoes a familiar policy goal: that agencies work together to meet client needs. Alice asked for meetings with all the various case workers she dealt with, and with their supervisors, to discuss her complicated case, but no such conference has been scheduled. Although clients may overestimate the amount of personnel time that can be devoted to any one case, they know that meetings among agencies already happen—but without including the client: "They have these meetings . . . but we can't come," Alice noted. Such "behind-the-scenes" contacts (which, incidentally, meet many professional definitions of successful collaboration) leave clients feeling isolated, ignored, and suspicious of agency personnel who share their secrets with others.

Policy Options

- *Consider including parents in decisions which involve their children.* Unless there are legal reasons to distance parents from their children's lives, medical, educational, and other decision makers should seek parental input beyond mere notification or consent. Parents from the community also could be invited to review general policy and to make suggestions.
- *Invite clients to collaborative meetings.* Certainly there are times when this may inhibit frank discussion, but meetings might also benefit from the client's further explanation of the situation. After all, only clients are in a position to identify all the gaps and overlaps in the current service system as it relates to them. Inviting clients to meetings would show the client that caseworkers are attending to their needs, and that the agencies cooperate to serve them. This may also encourage consistency in the details shared by the clients and providers at various offices. A sincere invitation can be an important gesture of respect toward the client, and can be a significant step toward empowering the client to take charge of her own affairs.
- *Accommodate clients' schedules.* A client with children, a day job, no car, and housing in a dangerous neighborhood cannot be summoned at a moment's notice to meet for counseling, conferences, or paperwork completion. Multiple, conflicting appointments can be hard to explain, and impossible to keep. The 8-to-5 workday at most agencies frustrated several of the women in their attempt to participate in recommended programs. Furthermore, inflexible schedules can send the message that programs are designed more for the convenience of the providers than for the clients.

REMEMBER THAT CLIENTS' BEST
EXPERIENCES ARE WITH INDIVIDUALS

Good people are more important than good programs, according to the client stories. Most of the positive experiences with government services were told in sen-
tences beginning something like, "There was one counselor who was very helpful," or "One teacher, I remember, really understood my child." Although the
Martin et al. (1983) quote in the introduction to this section dismisses clients'
evaluations of services for this very reason, the words of the clients themselves
should make clear why good services are, to some extent, good personal relationships. These special people are often described as "nice," yet they are more than
that—they get concrete results promptly, and they are flexible and accepting in
the face of realities. They are natural collaborators and advocates who provide a
human face for what can be a daunting bureaucratic system.

Policy Options

- *Seek client-contact workers who exhibit the characteristics of an
  advocate.* These might include, again, flexibility, persistence, openness, empathy, and creativity in problem solving. Additionally, personnel familiar with local culture and resources might be appreciated
  by clients and be able to make contact with little-known programs.
- *Create an environment that allows these characteristics to be exer-
  cised.* All the creativity in the world will not conjure a reliable phone
  where there is none. Support individual efforts with appropriate,
  compatible technologies, up-to-date information, and trust.
  Incentives to encourage low turnover will allow individuals to build
  the collaborative networks that make them more effective for clients.

MAKE INFORMATION ABOUT PROGRAMS
AND PROCEDURES ACCESSIBLE TO CLIENTS

A client cannot benefit from a program if she never hears about it. The stories
feature a number of instances when the client "accidentally" discovered a counseling group or educational opportunity that became an important step toward
the improvement of her situation. Women who grew up "on assistance" may
never seek newer programs; women new to a county may be unaware of local
offerings; women who cannot articulate their interests to a caseworker will recognize a program that suits their needs when it is presented. The story of a
client who only learned of the JOBS program because she wanted something to
read in a waiting room should be taken as a lesson to avoid missing such oppor-

tunities. Remember also that when a client has no correct information, she instead may believe misinformation—rumors, misinterpretations, and lies—which can further damage any chance of receiving appropriate services.

Once a client knows about a program, its procedures should be clearly explained to the client, from the start. "No one ever explains anything to me" may seem a poor excuse to some, but a recipient paralyzed by crisis or wearied by years of frustration may find actively seeking information impossible. Finally, it is only fair that a client be apprised early of her rights in the event of a dispute with the agency, and be given correct information about due process and the offices involved in making a formal complaint. A client armed with all the facts and details will be better able to make decisions, and she will appreciate the agency's openness in this respect.

Policy Options

- *Publicize agency programs and procedures widely and in various media.* Remember that non-English-speaking, sensory-impaired, and illiterate clients need information in a form they can access. Agencies should consider nontraditional locations for distributing pamphlets and displaying posters—keeping everything in the waiting room is "preaching to the converted."
- *Encourage other agencies to refer particularly suited clients to programs.* This might be a way to reach good candidates for small, limited-funds or short-term trial programs that cannot accept every interested client.
- *Give clients a tour of the agency offices.* There is a lot of mystery behind those space dividers. If the trail a client's file will take is demonstrated, rather than just explained verbally, it may be more readily understood. Anything that takes the mystery out of the process will give the client a more realistic picture, and it may avoid later confusion.
- *Get experienced clients together with new clients.* Agencies might pair long-time participants with new cases to share their experiences and offer advice and support. There might well be benefits for both sides in such a match.

PROVIDE A VISION OF THE CLIENT'S
EVENTUAL SELF-SUFFICIENCY

Finally, although information about getting into a program may be scarce, information about how one eventually exits the whole system of social services is far more elusive. The more successful cases recounted here point out this gap: When almost ready to go it alone, the women have no idea what that will mean. They ask, when will they cut off my food stamps? How do I manage monthly checks when I'm used to weekly installments? Especially for women who never saw their parents or friends live independent of government services, this can be a bewildering transition to make. This vision should be realistic as well as encouraging; a message that says, "Yes, it will be hard to make ends meet with the new job, and you may need to arrange for your children to be cared for after school, but we will prepare you to face these challenges and we believe you will succeed."

Policy Options

- *Make long-range plans with clients*. Agencies should help clients find goals they want to reach and the means to do so. These plans should be reviewed with the client periodically to discuss changes and to recognize progress made.
- *Record success stories of former clients*. These should not just sit in a file for personnel to read, but might be videotaped, or offered in whatever form will reach clients.
- *Do "exit polls" and study the answers*. Agencies can ask which specific features of programs successful clients believe led them to become self-sufficient. Clients may have ideas for improvement.
- *Follow up on former clients*. How are former clients doing a year after leaving the program? Five years? Ten years? This information might help present clients visualize what they may encounter, and achieve, in a given time frame.

These messages are not directed at individual agencies, because they can be adapted to the mission of any government service. A school, for example, might well try to provide a vision of life after graduation, or, for that matter, early withdrawal, through the mechanisms suggested. Similarly, a maternity care program might give new mothers-to-be a chance to talk and tell their stories to a compassionate listener before the first lab test or physical examination is performed. In fact, system-wide implementation of such measures, in a coordinated fashion, may bring benefits to all agencies' clients, images, and atmospheres. All of these ideas, synthesized from the stories of 12 women, are offered to improve overall government service delivery for the client. These ideas might prove to be welcome reforms for agency personnel as well, humanizing a process that often seems routine, impersonal, and adversarial from both sides of the desk.

PART III REALITIES OF COLLABORATION: Lessons Learned from Best Efforts

Catherine Awsumb

INTRODUCTION

The county case studies in Part I of this book document the difficulties of working across agency boundaries in counties that have made a few systematic attempts at integrated human services delivery. These case studies, along with the narratives describing services from the clients' point of view (part II), paint a portrait of the existing human services delivery system as fraught with gaps and overlaps in service, bureaucratic obstacles, and entrenched cultural attachments within agencies to narrow organizational mandates. Taken together, parts I and II of this book present a somewhat daunting view of the prospect for collaborative services. In order to capture a more comprehensive view of the possibilities for collaboration, we also conducted research at five sites that are actively pursuing collaboration. Each of these groups is a formal organization with participation from a variety of public and private agencies and other community sources. All five of the existing collaborative initiatives described in this section have significant experience working through the challenges of collaboration. They are striving to come together across agency boundaries, public/private distinctions, and differences in approach and philosophy to design comprehensive solutions to common problems. By telling their stories this section aims to provide concrete models of how the dilemmas of collaboration can be overcome in order to reap its rich rewards.

In recent years, "collaboration" has been one of the dominant buzz-words in the human services community. Everyone seems to agree that "inte-grated service delivery" and a "holistic, family-centered approach" are "the wave of the future." In the abstract, collaboration is an undeniably appealing model, one that variously promises to make the work of school and agency per-sonnel in dealing with at-risk families more coherent, to make services more humane and empowering from the client perspective, and maybe even to save money by achieving the Holy Grail of "efficiency." For all these weighty expec-tations, real-world experiences with collaboration are often frustrating or hard to pin down (Weiss, 1981). There is no easy blueprint for translating the vision of collaboration into a functioning organization. This chapter does not purport to provide such blueprints; by its very nature collaboration must emerge organical-ly from specific community needs. What the chapter does provide are some guideposts, some issues that five evolving collaboratives have faced. It is hoped that these guideposts will provide other emerging collaboratives with some direction and confidence on their own journeys.

Although all three phases of the research documented in this book are unified by the perspective that collaboration is a promising but elusive approach for delivering human services, the third phase differs in that it tells the story of deliberate and self-conscious efforts to collaborate. The people interviewed have moved beyond talking about collaboration to practicing it in a formal way; they therefore present more fully developed and realistic perspectives on the risks and rewards of collaboration. It is hoped that the chapter will prove useful to readers in two main ways: (a) by providing concrete models of collaboration, including membership, organizational structure, programs, mandates, staffing and funding; and (b) by offering "tricks of the trade," advice and perspectives from people who have already been through some of the challenges that newer collaboratives are just starting to encounter.

This section consists of five short chapters, each narrating the history of a different collaborative effort. The collaboratives we studied presented a wide range of models and approaches, each with its own mix of direct service, coordination/infrastructure, and policy development. Each evolved a definition of collaboration specific to the needs and resources of its community. The five groups we studied, in the order they are presented in the book, are:

- *Caldwell County Communities in Schools (CIS)*, an implementation of the national CIS model focused on broad-based community involvement and mentoring to support at-risk students in school;
- *Cleveland County Communities in Schools,* which provides core CIS services supplemented by intensive family development in school-based Family Resource Centers;

- *Cumberland County Coalition for Awareness, Resources and Education of Substances (CARES)*, a community action group aimed at coordinating and supporting substance abuse prevention-service providers with information, resources, and training;
- *UPLIFT, INC.*, a comprehensive family support system offering family empowerment through direct services, community development, and policy advocacy;
- *Wake County Children's Initiative,* a "floating think tank" that brings agencies together to create policy for children's services which transcend traditional agency boundaries.

Because we try to stay true to the unique stories of each group, each chapter follows the flow of the specific organization's development rather than conforming to a uniform outline. However, in each narrative we highlight common elements such as the history and rationale of the project, its current structure and activities, challenges they have faced, and future directions. The one structural device that is consistent across chapters is the "Lessons Learned" section at the end. These lessons summarize the perspectives of interviewees about the collaborative process and should be of particular interest to readers who are seeking practical advice.

Following the five chapters is a section drawing "Common Themes" from all the sites. Although each group we studied has a different take on what it means to collaborate and what makes it work, there are certain issues that they all must face. By summarizing these issues here we hope to provide a rough roadmap of the collaborative process.

9

Targeting Services to At-Risk Students— Caldwell County Communities in Schools

Catherine Awsumb
Kathy Hytten

Caldwell is a rural but highly industrialized county with a legacy of plentiful, low-paying, unskilled jobs, leading to a chronically high dropout rate and stubborn family problems. Collaboration in Caldwell first began to develop in an alarmed reaction to a state report placing Caldwell County in the top three counties in the state of North Carolina in the rate of teenage pregnancies, child abuse and neglect, high school dropouts, and juvenile crime. The County Commission realized that a concerted effort was needed to address county problems and joined forces with the Chamber of Commerce, who were particularly concerned with the economic ramifications of such statistics. The result was a Children's Advocacy Council composed of social service agency heads, school personnel, business people, and county officials.

The Council scoured the country looking for service delivery models that would bring together county resources to address the deep-seated problems which the state report had made painfully evident. After investigating various approaches, Council members were attracted to the Communities in Schools (CIS) model because "it addressed all of our issues," whereas other programs tended to focus on specific problems in isolation. The CIS model was also appealing because the strategy was to coordinate existing resources to focus on a target population and because it emphasized a broad sense of ownership both of problems and solutions.

After settling on the CIS model, the Council went to work adapting the program to the specific needs of Caldwell. Their first priorities were to put together a broadly representative CIS board to provide strategic direction and to search for an executive director to run the program on a day-to-day basis. According to those involved, the composition of the board was crucial. Because it includes "all of the movers and shakers in the county," the commitment and momentum behind CIS were evident from the start. The search for the right executive director was similarly critical. Board members emphasize that after interviewing more than 90 applicants they finally found someone with a "recognizable name in the community," "high community visibility," and "close ties to a number of different community agencies"—the characteristics they felt were necessary to drive the organization forward—not just one.

The new Director's first step was to visit the four functioning CIS programs in the state to select the best pieces of each to incorporate into the Caldwell program. From the experience of other counties she learned that because the school is the locus of integrated service delivery in the CIS model, the program cannot work without "open and flexible school system." Therefore, one of the keys to successful implementation was that the schools were involved in the planning process from the very beginning rather than seeing CIS as something imposed on them. The widely held perception of social crisis in the county was a major spur to collaboration among the original planners. In this atmosphere the schools were relatively willing to try any potentially beneficial programs, even if they challenged traditional assumptions about the roles of agencies. No one wanted to waste time or resources on turf battles or political infighting.

In addition to fostering an inclusive planning process, the Director spent much of her time in the program's early months making presentations to community groups to build a broad base of support and tangible resources. Her legwork paid off; since its initiation the program has been supported by a healthy mix of monetary grants and in-kind donations from the county government, a host of public and private agencies, the private sector, and the United Way. Various public and private agencies have pitched in by supplying office space, supporting repositioned workers, and providing tutors and instructors for CIS classrooms.

The hub of coordinated service delivery in the CIS model is the special CIS classroom at each school site. Each CIS classroom is staffed by a Site Director/Teacher and a Dropout Prevention Counselor, positions funded by the participating school, and by repositioned workers from the Department of Social Services and the Health Department, who are funded by their respective agencies. Participating students attend a daily CIS class, where the Site Director and community volunteers cover topics ranging from academic survival skills to self-esteem building. The repositioned workers from DSS and the Health

Department work directly with students in the classroom and make home visits to families to assure that each child and family receives the services that are available in the county. Additionally, each child in the program is assigned a tutor/mentor, usually from the private sector, who acts as a partner, helper, friend, liaison, advocate, and role model.

One day a week is set aside as Tutor/Mentor Day, where trained volunteers from the community come to the school and work with their assigned student. Additionally, one day a week is usually Speaker Day, where community resource volunteers come to the CIS classrooms to share their expertise. The list of agencies and volunteers who have taught in the CIS classroom is exhaustive, including Mental Health, the fire department, the recreation department, cooperative extension, the police department, and various other business and community groups.

The tutor/mentor component of the Caldwell County CIS is one of the most successful aspects of the program. The majority of the tutor/mentors are employees of local businesses, chosen by their employer and released 1 hour per week to work with their CIS student. To date, 250 community volunteers have been trained as tutor/mentors to work one-on-one with an at-risk child. Interviewees stated that much of the success of the tutor/mentor program depends on training the tutor/mentors, rather than just throwing them together with a child unprepared. All tutor/mentors take part in a 6-hour training course, in which the program and expectations are detailed and strategies for working with students are explored. Along with visiting the child once a week at the school and helping with school work, tutor/mentors develop personal relationships with their students, doing such things as taking them to tour their workplace or out to lunch, and attending tutor/mentor activities and community functions with their students. According to one of the school principals, the tutor/mentors do an invaluable service of showing kids that there is hope for the future and "reconnecting them to the community that they live in."

An additional benefit of the tutor/mentor program, according to a number of the program staff and board members, is that businesses and community members have become more involved and invested in the schools. According to one of the business executives on the CIS board, the "beauty of the CIS program is the exposure of the private sector in the schools." This exposure gives the community members a "good sense of what is going on in the schools," "greater understanding" of school efforts and programs, and more empathy with school staff. This direct exposure fosters the belief that the whole community needs to be involved in the "organized nurturance" of children, particularly those deemed at-risk. A principal at a CIS school speculated that, instead of just being asked for money, those in the private sector enjoyed being part of a program where individual impact is felt and where energy and effort are both valued and solicited.

In discussing collaboration, one of the school principals emphasized that "some group needs to be a bridge between agencies and schools," and that this group works most effectively "if housed on the school grounds." Agency representatives from DSS and the Health Department agreed that CIS "brings the agency to the child." They suggested that accessing services through the schools means that "children are less likely to fall through the cracks." Whereas the CIS program targets a select group of kids, having agencies involved in the schools has had a much broader impact. Relationships between schools and social service agencies have been enhanced in general, as the CIS partnership has strengthened everyday working relationships between schools and the agencies, benefiting all students.

LESSONS LEARNED

Collaboration Cannot Be Mandated

Community-wide partnerships and collaborative efforts only work when people and agencies are fully invested in them and have been involved in their creation and development. The CIS program in Caldwell County has sustained its momentum because it was not something that citizens were mandated to create. On the contrary, citizens saw a need and systematically attempted to address it on their own terms. Interviewees in Caldwell expressed the belief that requiring county agencies to collaborate on service delivery will not be meaningful or effective if the seeds of cooperation and communication have not been sown organically, and the agencies are not ready, willing, and able to work together. Local control and local ownership of collaborative arrangements is essential. The consensus sentiment is that "only Caldwell County knows what is good for Caldwell," what is possible and what can work. The most useful role that can be played by the state is creating legislation "enabling" collaboration to occur by easing regulations which create boundaries between agencies. On the other hand, "mandating" that collaborations occur will be ineffective and possibly counterproductive.

Concentrate Services on a Targeted Population

If collaborative programs are to be successful, a specific population needs to be "targeted." CIS staff feel that concentrating on a target population was an important aspect of having a tightly defined mission "as opposed to being all over the map." Interviewees believe that the CIS program is successful because the staff are able to work intensively with a select number of students. One of the board members suggested that although choosing a select group leaves CIS "vulnerable to being discriminatory," it is crucial to "organize and concentrate services in order to achieve success." The philosophy of targeting a specific population stems from the belief that services need to be given to this group personally and intensively, and not "watered down" in the effort to serve all students.

Involve Schools Early and Often in the Development of School-based Initiatives

A defensive or inflexible school system is potentially a huge barrier to the success of any program serving school-age children, especially if services are to be delivered at the school site. There needs to be a high level of trust between the program and the entire school staff that is nurtured over time in order for the program to function smoothly. This means involving school staff and "making teachers feel a part" of the program. Caldwell CIS invested time and energy up front in negotiating implementation and achieving ownership as to the program's mission among school staff.

Collaborative Boards Need Independence to Function

Because the Caldwell CIS program is controlled by a powerful, independent board made up of representatives from county agencies, the schools, and the private sector, the CIS program is viewed as a community program addressing community problems. Because no one group or agency is "in control," the program had not been viewed as an "exclusive effort," but as something in which everyone can get involved. The board members and staff suggested it was extremely important that the CIS program especially not be viewed as a "school program," as business and community support would be less strong, and the potential to view the effort as another in a long line of passing school reforms would be too great. Involving the schools, as well as all other community agencies, has fostered a sense of "community ownership" while improving the level of cooperation and trust among schools, businesses, and social services in general. Smooth functioning of the CIS program is also facilitated because the board is independent, and the resources are community generated, thereby allowing more control of program operation and less outside constraint and manipulation. A representative of one of the social service agencies offered that CIS is "the most effective program in operation in Caldwell County and the reason is because it is not locked up in the government." The community owns the program and thus is able to coordinate service delivery on their own terms, a piece of the CIS program deemed essential by all people and agencies involved.

10

Creating Opportunities for Families: Cleveland County Communities in Schools and Opportunities for Families

Catherine Awsumb
Kathy Hytten

As was the case in Caldwell County, the decision to develop a Communities in Schools (CIS) program in Cleveland County followed from community members taking a long hard look at the county's social and economic indicators and their implications for the future. The specific impetus for collaboration was the Cleveland Challenge, a strategic economic development planning process that was spearheaded by the county manager and included concerned private citizens, representatives from private and public social service agencies, and business leaders.

Under the auspices of the Cleveland Challenge, community members undertook extensive research and analysis about the state of the county, including a survey of the community and analysis of statistical data. As a result of this analysis the group decided to focus on three core areas: education, infrastructure, and social issues. Of these, education seemed the most important strategic economic concern for Cleveland County. Statistics painted a distressing picture of a community facing educational impoverishment, leading the group to believe that the entire community was weakened by inadequate education and that their collective future depended on building up educational resources.

Having established education as the key to the community's future, the task force began seeking models that would involve the whole community in

189

educational improvement, while also addressing what they saw as closely related issues of weak economic infrastructure and entrenched social problems. CIS, with its model of integrated services targeted to at-risk students, seemed to fit best with Cleveland's belief that educational, economic, and social issues must be looked at as parts of an integrated whole. The task force particularly liked the fact that CIS addressed the fragmentation of the various agencies which provided services to children and families.

The group decided to focus their efforts on elementary-age children because they felt they could have the greatest impact working with younger children and their families. A variety of sources showed commitment to the process by putting tangible resources behind their verbal support. The schools made space available at the selected elementary school sites for a Family Resource Center and allocated funds for Family Resource Specialists. The county appropriated $117,000 to operate the CIS program during the first year, while a United Way Venture Grant provided the initial funds to hire an executive director to oversee the program. Various other in-kind services were also provided to the CIS program, including commitments of Mental Health, Health Department, and DSS staff time at the Family Resource Centers.

At the same time that they were working to get CIS in place, members of the interagency group searched for a way to strengthen the student-focused CIS concept by reinforcing it with resources that addressed the self-sufficiency of the family as a whole. They decided to enter a grant competition from the Z. Smith Reynolds Foundation's Opportunities for Families Fund (OFF). Those involved in the grant-writing process worked from the assumption that no one agency or group could meet all the needs of children and families. To ensure coordination from the earliest stages, the OFF proposal was carefully studied by over 40 people in the county (including school and agency personnel, parents, key nonprofit sector players, community leaders, and members of county coalitions), before being submitted. The purpose of this intensive review was, according to the OFF grant application, "to assure open communication among all stakeholders in the county, to refine the proposal, and to continue to build ownership of the initiative."

The painstaking development of the proposal paid off. Cleveland County was one of the five counties in the state awarded a five-year, $1 million OFF grant. This grant allowed Cleveland County to "accelerate and stabilize implementation of the CIS project," which had already garnered initial funds and support from the community and to expand the focus to supporting whole families. The guiding notion during the planning for CIS and OFF was that the whole family needed to be the focus of services and that existing support systems for families should be tapped into, or created where they didn't exist. The vision of the planners, as articulated by the executive director, was that the "family should be a player" in the efforts to improve their own quality of life; that is, CIS should "do things with families, not to them."

Although CIS and OFF are functionally integrated at the school sites, they have somewhat different mandates. The core services of CIS are focused on supporting educational growth, and the CIS-funded Family Resource Specialists work primarily with students. Core CIS services include:

- assuring regular school attendance,
- providing assistance with basic skills development,
- increasing parent involvement,
- providing support for homework,
- supporting the development of self-control and positive behaviors,
- promoting positive relationships, and
- helping children come to school each day ready to learn.

CIS children receive academic tutoring at least once a week and receive personal support and guidance through their one-on-one relationship with staff members. Many of the CIS children are involved in an afternoon homework club. The CIS staff also works to get them involved with various local clubs and sports teams in order to promote personal and social growth. Sometimes making the difference can be as basic as providing transportation to meetings and practices. The CIS staff also observe children in their classrooms and provide support to classroom teachers and help in referring children for educational assessments.

The mandate of OFF is to address the needs of the entire family. The two OFF-funded Family Advocates at each site school provide intensive family development (case management) and holistic support to a smaller number of families than CIS serves, with the comprehensive goals of stabilizing living conditions and building family capacity for self-sufficiency. Often, the Family Advocates act as a liaison between the family and social services agencies, gathering information about available services, helping the family with paperwork, and transporting and accompanying the family to agencies so they can access services.

Along with core CIS educational services and programs, and the intensive family development with OFF families, the Family Resource Centers also provide walk-in resources to all community members. The CIS programs are also involved in community outreach activities, including an on-site health fair and a booth at the county information fair. The Family Resource Centers also cooperate with and support the Cleveland County Community College's Adult Education programs, which are offered at each of the three school sites. Ultimately, according to staff members, the Family Resource Centers "address factors beyond the classroom which impact on the child's ability to be a successful learner," identify and develop "resources and support to meet a wide range of economic, physical and emotional needs," and coordinate the involvement of the entire community in assuring "that all families, regardless of circumstances, have the opportunity for a bright future."

Two primary things CIS/OFF has provided for the citizens of Cleveland are knowledge and personal support. Prior to the implementation of the program, many parents were, suggested one staff member, "information poor" and lacking a "personal contact or link" to help them access support services. Staff members state that the personal relationships the program allows them to develop with families make all the difference. Says one, "CIS is not about programs (although many are provided or accessed through CIS) but relationships—the personal element being the most powerful aspect of the program." Because CIS/OFF staff work in an unofficial capacity (that is, they are not school or public agency representatives), they have been able to work in a neutral position as go-betweens. One staff member suggested that CIS has been able to act as a "catalyst" to get agencies to work together. From the perspective of the staff, collaboration has been easier because they are a new organization without "turf" to protect. In discussing CIS, a representative from DSS suggested that "it has been a wonderful resource for us," as "CIS people help to be a neutral advocate between DSS and clients."

CIS/OFF staff identified several barriers to continuing collaboration. Although the relationship between CIS/OFF programs and the schools they operate at has generally been positive, the staff hope to became more systematically integrated into the life of the schools. They realize that developing this relationship takes time and nurturing and open lines of communication. Although most teachers welcome the support services CIS/OFF provides, some school faculty were slow to develop faith in another school-based reform, asking, in effect, "How long do you plan to stay?" One Family Resource Specialist suggested that the biggest barrier in developing this relationship is differing philosophies. Her perspective is that although CIS defines its mission with children very broadly, schools have traditionally been more focused on academic development. She also indicated that some school staff view CIS as separate from the schools and have expressed concerns that CIS staff might "take the child's side" over the school's. CIS staff also mentioned that further role negotiation is needed with school social workers and counselors. Because their tasks often overlap with those of CIS, conflict is possible and a mutually reinforcing vision is critical.

One of the most important outcomes of CIS has been developing awareness of the need for increased collaboration in all social services. Significant involvement of social service agencies throughout the Cleveland Challenge and the CIS and OFF planning and implementation processes laid the groundwork for further successful agency collaboration beyond the formal bounds of the CIS/OFF program. For example, the county is currently working with a software development firm to design a "multiagency, computer-based case coordination system." The goal is to reduce repetitive paperwork between agencies and assist social services staff in collaborating between agencies. Integrating paperwork would address one of the most frequently heard complaints about service fragmentation, simplifying the process for both workers and families. This is just one example of the way in which collaboration can become a self-reinforcing process, with contacts, shared goals, and trust all developing in tandem.

LESSONS LEARNED

Dynamic, Persuasive, and Progressive-minded Leadership is Essential

Although successful collaboration requires that broad ownership be developed, a strong leader can be important in generating momentum and articulating a vision which others can embrace and develop. According to a member of the Cleveland Challenge, the county manager was able to set the tone among the agencies that "we are all serving the same families and that we need to do things differently and lay aside some of the boundaries between agencies." The fact that the county manager was in a powerful community position but was not a representative of the schools or any one social service agency was also critical in his ability to build consensus from all quarters.

Establish Neutral Turf

Schools and agency heads realized early in the process that if they were going to take a truly integrated approach to human services delivery across agency lines, they would have to think hard about issues of autonomy and control. Most agreed that it is important to have an independent body, like CIS, pulling agencies and resources together, and that it would be a mistake to "give" something like CIS to the schools or one of the existing agencies to run. The tendency for bias and turf issues to develop would be too great without a neutral control mechanism. Task force members also felt that community support would be weak if control were given to a traditional agency. In Cleveland County, repositioning staff workers in an outside agency like CIS has helped develop a sense of common turf among schools and agencies, thereby facilitating enhanced collaboration. It has also decreased the stigma associated with social service agencies from the perspective of families. Ultimately, control by an independent body has helped ensure community ownership, parity among players, and strong community voice and support, all necessary for collaboration to function successfully.

Involve School Staff in School-based Service Delivery

In order to integrate school-based collaborative initiatives smoothly into the school setting, lines of communication need to be kept open between collaborative planners and the school staff. In discussing the issue of school-based programs, one CIS staff member offered the perspective that "we need a commitment to help support teachers and make them aware of the larger picture." One of the Cleveland Challenge task force members suggested that if they had the planning to do over, they would have had more regular meetings with school and agency staff to help more clearly define roles and draw boundaries. Although the schools in Cleveland were generally receptive to the implementation of CIS, relationships and trust took time to nurture, and it would have been helpful if the entire school staffs, not just administrative personnel, were more involved in the process throughout. One future goal of CIS is to become more systematically involved in the schools by involving school staff in goal setting, widely publicizing goals and strategies among the staff, and working in conjunction with school staff development activities.

Communicate Realistic Expectations

When some frustrations arose in Cleveland County because the process seemed to move too slowly, planners realized the "need to educate the community," that this was going to be a long-term process involving systematic goal setting. By being open and widely disseminating goals, planners hope to avoid unrealistic expectations. If the program were oversold and citizens expected all of the county's problems to go away once CIS was in place, it could become more difficult to build success in the real world. Throughout the planning and implementation stages, those involved learned that communication lines must be kept open, that taking time to build relationships and trust is essential, and that a successful collaborative initiative requires long-range, systematic planning and not crisis-oriented, Band-Aid solutions.

11

Synchronizing Substance Abuse Prevention: Cumberland County CARES

Catherine Awsumb

Cumberland County CARES (Coalition for Awareness, Resources, and Education of Substances) is a broad-based community coalition that serves as a "hub" for substance abuse prevention services in Cumberland County. Social service agencies in Cumberland have historically faced a unique complex of problems stemming from the combination of a major urban center, a massive military installation, and the county's location along I-95, the major drug trafficking route from Florida to New York. CARES defines its mission as "using research-based strategies to enable existing prevention agencies to synchronize their program objectives, work toward common goals, and create focused, cohesive programs initiated at the grass-roots level." Members of the coalition emphasize the growing pains they have recently experienced and the difficulty of staying true to their vision through the vicissitudes of changing structure, funding, and bureaucracy during a period of explosive organizational growth. In particular, the history of CARES demonstrates how difficult it can be to make the transition from volunteer activism to formal organization.

CARES began to take shape when the Cumberland County Schools launched a prevention program funded by the Drug-Free Schools and Communities Act. This federal program included an explicit mandate to foster community involvement and coordinate services. To comply with this mandate, the director of the school-based program convened meetings with personnel from the military, law enforcement, the Department of Mental Health, and a private hospital. Although these were the first seeds of meaningful collaboration on substance abuse prevention in the county, several participants agreed that "it took us a long time to get momentum." One participant recalls that at that stage "the schools were just sharing out information, reporting to the community what they were doing. The commission was just advisory." In retrospect, however, members agree that this body was a first step in that at least people working on the same problem were beginning to exchange information and perspectives if not truly to collaborate.

It was a private grant competition by the Robert Woods Johnston Foundation that proved the catalyst for true collaboration as opposed to surface coordination. When multiple agencies in the county independently sent letters to the Foundation detailing the drug problem in Cumberland County and expressing interest in the grant competition, the Foundation urged them to pool their resources and write a single grant application representing the entire community. This was a fairly obvious demonstration of the fragmentation of prevention services in Cumberland County, and it suddenly became clear that what was needed was not one more program in the patchwork but a long hard look at how all the pieces fit together. What prevention resources were available in the county and what populations had access to them? Were there gaps in services? Duplications or overlap? No one body had the data to answer these questions. Thrown together by the grant application process, multiple agencies began to see that a lack of coordination, public awareness, and program evaluation hampered all prevention programs from serving the community as effectively as they might; the grant-writing group began to envision themselves as an organization that could provide those services.

Although the group was disappointed not to be one of the grant recipients, the momentum that the process had generated was such that the coalition continued working together. A current executive committee member recalls that "we just decided to keep moving. It all came together around the grant. That didn't work but we did." Another member says that despite their nonexistent budget, "since we had a nice finished product, the action plan/proposal, we decided to implement as much of the strategy as possible without the funding." Continuing to operate on an all-volunteer basis, the coalition began to search for other sources of funding to pursue their vision of a comprehensive drug prevention strategy for the county. Their perseverance paid off a year later when the coalition was awarded state and federal grants totaling over $1 million.

With full funding to actualize their vision of coordinated substance abuse prevention, CARES today is an organization representing almost 60 agencies, businesses, and community groups and has a full-time staff of three. CARES continues to define itself as primarily a coordinating body rather than as an advocacy group or provider of direct services. Leaders describe CARES with words like "hub," "clearinghouse," and "network," organized around the idea that although there were many worthy prevention efforts in the county, they all suffered from a lack of supportive infrastructure. Currently, in the words of their proposal:

> many local programs compete for participants, funding, prestige, and juris-
> diction. Evaluation methods and record keeping procedures tend to be omit-
> ted and program language or terminology may vary from program to pro-
> gram and present significant barriers to cooperative and collaborative
> efforts.

CARES aims to be the missing infrastructure, providing a systematic approach to research, program evaluation, public awareness, and strategic planning that no one agency or community group could achieve independently.

CARES is currently organized into a broad general membership (that meets quarterly) and five working committees. According to one participant, the current committee structure emerged from "brainstorming on needs during the grant-writing process. We started listing out our objectives and then grouping them and the committee structure just fell into place." Another member empha-sizes that the organic nature of this planning process was vital to the coherence and ongoing momentum of the committee structure: "Maybe the problem was so clear-cut that we all saw it the same way or maybe we were just lucky, but it turned out our objectives were very closely aligned." This was important because "the committees really owned those goals." Therefore, although the transition from an informal, volunteer coalition to a staffed organization with a substantial budget has caused some dislocation, the committees have preserved the core of the original vision intact.

The working committees and their major tasks are:

> *The Research and Evaluation Committee*, whose first accomplish-
> ment has been the compilation of a "Substance Abuse Resource and
> Referral Guidebook." This document details all prevention services
> offered in the county "in terms of services offered, target popula-
> tions, staffing, hours, eligibility, gaps, fees, referral process, special
> services to high-risk populations, and organizational philosophy."
> *The Prevention Services Committee*, which will work with the data
> compiled by the Research and Evaluation Committee to develop
> annual program initiatives based on the identification of unmet
> needs, underserved populations, and prevention priorities.
> *The Public Relations Committee*, which is now focused on building
> awareness of CARES itself and is also charged with planning blan-
> ket campaigns based on the annual initiatives.
> *The Government Committee*, which provides a consistent and factual
> message about the drug abuse problem to every elected body in the

county, including county commissioners, aldermen, and the school
board. By establishing this liaison CARES hopes to stay in touch
with all relevant legislation, programs, and policies as they evolve.
The Continuation Funding Committee, which focuses on identifying
and securing alternate funding resources. A particular priority is to
persuade funding sources, especially the county government, to
make CARES funding a stable line-item in their budgets.

CARES leaders agree that although the general membership is hearteningly
broad, ranging from DSS to the Army to the PTA to the Dupont Corporation,
"the real work gets done in the committees." Several interviewees expressed
concern about generating broader participation in the committees. As one current leader put it, "Having a representative of a community group is not enough.
We need individuals willing to commit to leadership roles. The real work of
CARES is in the committees and that takes time. What I'm not seeing yet is the
individual part." Another committee chair laments that "people will show up to
meetings but they won't commit to leadership." The current leadership core is
aware that they are approaching burnout, and achieving community participation that is as deep as it is broad is one of their major goals.

CARES has three full-time staff members: a project director, an educational specialist ,and a project secretary. This staff enables the coalition to carry
out the day-to-day logistical tasks of its clearinghouse role in a way that was
impossible when CARES was just a group of committed volunteers meeting as
often as they got a chance. The role of the staff is to help service providers
effectively utilize and share "resources such as volunteers, funding, information, training, facilities, media coverage, and public support." As one staffer
points out, "Prevention as a field is still in its infancy so people are still experi-
menting with what works. They all want to help the same population in different ways. It can be confusing to the communities they work with to have a different person with a different philosophy coming in every day." Additionally,
"many may not have access to state-of-the-art ideas."

As CARES currently exists it is only a semiautonomous organization.
According to the terms of the federal grant, the county Mental Health
Department is the "lead agency," with responsibility for the fiscal and personnel
management of the grant. This forced some renegotiation of roles in what had
been essentially a loose, "flat" organization. Although the role of the lead
agency does not impinge on the executive committee's decision-making autonomy, it does impose some bureaucratic constraints in the way of timetables,
paperwork, and the like. Defining lines of authority and responsibility has been
an ongoing and sometimes frustrating task for CARES since winning the grant.
Several members said they wished they had thought out the implications of the
lead agency structure more clearly in advance. The excitement of having funding to realize their vision has been tempered by the need to adjust to the restrictions and conditions imposed by that funding. The transition from activism to

bureaucracy is an important organizational development issue that must be faced by any coalition which hopes to achieve substantial integration between community organizations and government agencies and dollars.

Regarding their organizational development, CARES has two major priorities for the future. These complementary objectives are (a) a reorientation of the organization from top-down, agency-based decision making to more community involvement and (b) the establishment of organizational autonomy, specifically through filing for 5013C nonprofit status. The emphasis on community development and grass-roots involvement is being pushed by CARES' federal funding but is also essentially a return to CARES' roots. They caution, however, that it is not easy to shift management models in midstream. Initially the new emphasis caused "dislocation" and "frustration," because while preaching the paradigm shift "the government gave us a philosophy but no samples or models. We struggled to define what this meant, given our particulars." One member recommends to coalitions just starting out, "from the very earliest stages, bring in the people you are trying to serve and put them in decision-making positions, even if they don't know what they are doing. You need to get community role models in from the start." CARES members hope that one of the tangible benefits of community development is that it will generate a new wave of enthusiasm and commitment and take some of the burden from key members who have been committee workhorses for years. "In the beginning," one of the original group recalls, "we were pure grass roots. We put in hundreds of volunteer man hours preparing that grant. The paradigm shift is really just saying to us to shift back away from the agency/bureaucratic focus that dominated" while they were establishing systems to manage the grant.

Complementing the "new paradigm" is the coalition's application for autonomous nonprofit status. Although the two issues are not inextricably linked, it is easy to see how the removal of even the appearance of decision-making control by the "lead agency" will tend to emphasize grass-roots activism rather than bureaucratic management. The coalition will have to stand on its own, which is both exciting and intimidating. As one member notes, "There is a safety and security in bureaucracy which some will find it hard to abandon." Questions of fiscal and legal responsibility, which have been taken care of by the Mental Health Department, will now fall squarely on the coalition itself. This process can be tortuous; at a recent executive committee meeting, for example, the accountant who is handling the 5013C paperwork asked whose name would be signed on the legal documents. An uncomfortable silence followed; no one seemed eager to assume that responsibility. The coalition is currently undertaking a feasibility study dealing with the transition to autonomy and they hope to "flesh out in advance all the legalities and structural things we might get hung up on." Mixed with apprehension about increased responsibility is hope and excitement that autonomy will renew some of the early activist spirit of the coalition and shake off some of the bureaucratic encumbrances which have frustrated many members.

LESSONS LEARNED

"Funding is a double-edged Sword"

Many CARES members advised future coalitions to be prepared for grants to take on a life of their own. Feelings of burnout and frustration were often attributed to the inevitable change in the nature of an organization that comes from the responsibilities of managing a grant. One leader commented, "The grant gave us encouragement but it also slowed us down in that we spend a lot of time managing the grant. We are buried under grant administration and have lost a sense of momentum." Another member said with a sigh that "A million dollars equals a million reports. Good things happen with money but it slows you down. It creates bureaucracy and artificial parameters on progress." In retrospect, many members saw their unfunded days as a sort of halcyon period of activism and commitment. "It seemed so simple in the beginning—we talked more about issues and prevention. Now we talk about structure and by-laws and reports." This is certainly an accurate description of a recent executive committee meeting, which was conducted in a highly formal manner and was almost entirely devoted to motions on administrative matters. The paradox is that funding gives such coalitions the power to realize their visions but may mean that the day-to-day work becomes less activist and more bureaucratic.

Be Ready For the Honeymoon to End

Because grants do take on a life of their own and structure and bureaucracy are the inevitable companions of organizational growth, CARES members cautioned that coalitions must be ready for the culture shock. During the grant-writing period, one coalition member recalls, "We had tremendous motivation. We were trying to get a million dollars to make something happen! The process drove itself and had its own power. Once we got it some of the excitement dissipated." One member urges, "When the honeymoon is over you still have to believe. It is hard when disillusionment sets in but you have to go out there and do the painstaking, sometimes boring work." Another member, reflecting on changes in the 2 years since CARES received its grant, says that her advice to other coalitions would be to remember that, "There is a rough period of being inundated by bureaucracy. It feels abnormal but it is just growing pains. Persevere!"

Keep Focused on Your Core Mission

Jumping through the various bureaucratic hoops that come with a federal grant can be painful. For CARES, the most important success factor in surviving the end of the honeymoon has been a clear consensus as to its mission. Although it is easy to get consumed in the everyday issues of structure and administration, coalitions can keep the fire alive if they have a strong sense of purpose and keep pushing that notion to the foreground. The sometimes frustrating development of CARES demonstrates the importance of remembering that the vision is the meaning of the coalition and that changes in structure or organization are only incidental. A coalition is an idea, not a particular structure. One CARES member stresses the importance for coalitions of "fleshing out the commonalties first and keeping them on the table" during periods when the organization is at risk of getting bogged down in "administrivia."

Understand the Paradox of Continuity

The survival of CARES largely depends on the commitment of core members who have nurtured the enthusiasm of the activist, grant-writing period through the more structured work of committee leadership. This continuity has enabled the organization to stay true to its original mission. Continuity also has downsides, however. The same closeness that can sustain commitment and see an organization through tough and uncertain times can also be "clubbiness" that prevents hard choices from being made. One CARES member warns that "there needs to be a time to talk straight out. People get so close working together that when that time comes, hidden agendas may be the only way to express their frustrations. The closeness makes it hard to make midcourse corrections." Continuity also creates a risk of burnout; it is vital for coalitions to seek sources of "fresh blood and new enthusiasm."

Be Honest About the Risks and Benefits of Autonomy

For many members of CARES, their semiautonomous position under the "lead agency" structure of mental health is a necessary evil. One member reasons that "it adds bureaucracy and more reports which we all find frustrating but it is important to have a system to funnel money through. I don't think we would have gotten the money in the first place without a responsible structure." Personnel and financial management systems were frequently cited as responsibilities better undertaken by an agency with established practices. As coalitions mature, the benefits of autonomy begin to outweigh the risks, but the level of commitment required to shoulder the responsibilities of a legal organization should not be underestimated. Both before aligning themselves with an agency and before going out on their own, coalitions need to specify lines of authority and responsibility in detail. Role-playing future management issues might be one way to do this.

Find the Right Mix of Coordination, Advocacy, and Service

"Coalition" and "collaboration" can be interpreted in widely different ways. Before a group representing diverse agencies and community interests begins a common attack on a common problem, they would be well advised to articulate their definition of collaboration carefully. Groups like this may see themselves in a purely coordinating role, providing technical support and services to direct services providers. On the other hand, they may want to advocate specific policies or programs, or even provide those programs themselves. There is no reason why all these activities cannot coexist, but the balance needs to be specified early to avoid future tensions about the direction of the organization. In particular, if the group advocates policy or provides services they may bump into the missions of participating organizations, and the nature of this overlap will need to be negotiated. Because of the way they were brought together by the grant process, the members of CARES had a clear focus on coordinating, empowering, and supporting existing service providers. However, several members of the leadership would like to see CARES move toward more direct advocacy in the future, using their research as a framework to set specific priorities. The very existence of the Government Committee indicates a wish to influence policy. The line between coordination and advocacy is a fine but important one and coalition members need to explore their common understanding of how they wish to draw it in defining their mission.

12

Building Communities: UPLIFT, Inc.

Catherine Awsumb
Jean Patterson

Greensboro-based UPLIFT, Inc. is a private, nonprofit organization that works to improve services to children and their families on a number of levels. Their vision of collaboration includes providing direct services to children and families, community building, and developing policies and interagency agreements that foster more integrated family services. UPLIFT believes that they are able to articulate their vision of integrated services in a more comprehensive way than collaboratives which focus on direct service *or* coordination *or* advocacy. UPLIFT strives to do it all. UPLIFT places significant emphasis on empowering families to become less dependent on conventional service systems. They see formal service delivery systems as inadvertently fragmenting and disempowering families through the autonomous imposition of their services and professional expertise. UPLIFT believes that families who learn to negotiate the service delivery system on their own and to access information increase their ability to control their own lives.

Like many successful collaboratives, UPLIFT has flourished in part because of the drive of a strong leader with a clear vision of a better way to meet the needs of families and children in poverty. UPLIFT was founded by Robin Britt, former Congressman and recently appointed Secretary of the North Carolina Department of Human Resources. During his stint in Congress, Britt had several experiences in the area of human services that had a strong impact on him and provided some of the seed ideas which later blossomed into UPLIFT. Britt began his crusade by making speeches to various civic groups about how to combat poverty through empowering families, but decided that speeches were not enough. He realized that people "needed something they could look at," a concrete example of a better model for service delivery. The Z. Smith Reynolds Foundation awarded Britt a planning grant that enabled him to establish an office, research programs, and potential sites, and seek ongoing financial support. Major government grant awards in recent years have had significant impact on UPLIFT, Inc. as an organization, raising questions about how they will retain their activist, community orientation as they expand. After all, UPLIFT was founded on the belief that large, entrenched bureaucracies are not well-suited to the human scale of human services. The executive director emphasizes that, "There is no way in the world that a bureaucratic and hierarchical organization can meet the needs of families."

Of UPLIFT's three components—service delivery, community building, and policy development—direct service delivery was the initial focus and remains the cornerstone. The first service delivery project was the Child Development Center for 4-year-olds, which opened in November 1988 at Ray Warren Homes, one of Greensboro's poorest and most drug-infested housing projects. It provides an enriched early childhood program with strong parental involvement and is designed to prepare at-risk children for kindergarten.

The Center's director recalls several initial stumbling blocks. In the first year of operation participation at the Center was not limited to residents of Ray Warren Homes and lack of transportation resulted in a high absentee rate among off-site families. The following year the Center decided to focus exclusively on the Warren Homes, building a strong base in the surrounding community. A more significant problem was the general hesitancy and lack of trust among all of the families they hoped to assist. This was particularly frustrating, as the program emphasized parental involvement and empowerment as crucial elements in strengthening the learning process. Parents would have older children drop off younger children at the Center to avoid participating in the program themselves. According to a staff member, "It is valuable time to see the parents twice a day; regular attendance and participation are important for building trust." Staff members understand that poor families may have valid fears and frustrations after dealing with the social services bureaucracy and that overcoming these requires empathy and patience. UPLIFT had to show how it was different, how its philosophy would translate into a better experience for the families. Apparently, it has been successful in building trust; participation has grown year by year and the Child Development Center now has a waiting list.

The next step was to supplement the Child Development Center with a Family Resource Center. According to the director, this second phase took longer to develop because the concept was so new and there was no blueprint: "We learned from the parents what kind of services we should have there." The current mix of services includes maternal and child health care, community building, "brokering" services, and intensive family development. Bringing these services on site and under the UPLIFT model brings significant differences from the family perspective. For example, with their maternal and child health program the Family Resource Center simplified and consolidated what had been two separate programs at the Health Department, one for expectant mothers and babies up to 3 months in age and a separate program covering children from 3 months to 3 years. UPLIFT staff believe the change goes beyond the technical difference of enabling mothers to remain in one consistent program. They stress that the entire philosophy of service delivery is different. One staffer said that although the Health Department is moving toward a more integrative approach to family needs, some of their staff "are more technically oriented; social support is not what they understand. We're not always in synch." Providing health services under the UPLIFT umbrella enables a more comprehensive approach to the needs of the family.

One of the more nontraditional efforts of the Family Resource Center is the focus on community building. Community building is viewed by UPLIFT as an ongoing effort to work with families to develop community ownership of the programs and to build informal support networks among client families. The goal is to give families the tools and skills to define and manage their own needs, rather than just being "serviced" by agencies. For example, UPLIFT helped the Ray Warren residents to organize a transportation program. Lack of transportation had previously been a major barrier to many residents participating in programs, receiving services, or just going about the business of everyday life. Robin Britt negotiated with GATE, Greensboro's transportation service, to donate a van. The residents are now responsible for operating the program and planning the schedule to rotate van driving duties among themselves.

The Family Resource Center also provides childcare to Ray Warren residents who are attending Center programs or have appointments at the Maternal and Child Health Clinic. In keeping with the UPLIFT philosophy, a Ray Warren resident is employed as Childcare Coordinator. Because of her involvement with UPLIFT, she has taken childcare classes at the local community college and plans to pursue further education as a childcare assistant. Additionally, she has brought in other members of the Ray Warren community to assist her. According to the director of the center, when the residents are involved, they feel they have more control and feel good about their community.

Another of the core activities of the Family Resource Center is "brokering" services, defined as linking families with other service providers in the community. As a staff member puts it, "I make contact with the agencies—the services are already there—I serve as liaison; bringing it on site, if available." When asked how she established relationships with the various service agencies, this staff member responded, "It was a learning experience from what families told me they needed." Staff act as advocates for families, identifying barriers and relating success stories to encourage service providers to help.

Family Development, another of the Resource Center's more ground-breaking tactics, is described as moving beyond traditional services by providing an intensive, long-term commitment to families around general issues rather than specific and limited-term services. The Family Development Specialist works with up to 15 families at a time and serves as the liaison between families and other agencies. Because of the paperwork and transportation involved in accessing services, families would often become discouraged. Families would be unable to receive financial supplements because they were unable to complete the required paperwork; some of them were unable to read and did not want anyone to know. The Family Development Specialist assists with any part of application process as requested by the families. The Family Development Specialist meets with the family and other agencies on a monthly basis to discuss needs, barriers, what is working, what is not working, and what goals they need to establish. The meetings are held at the Family Resource Center, where the families feel more comfortable and less intimidated because they are on their own turf.

The value of UPLIFT's carefully nurtured neutral role in the community is demonstrated by the cool reception the on-site social worker initially received. Because she had previously worked for DSS, when she first started working at UPLIFT, Ray Warren residents would see her car and not come to the Family Resource Center because they associated her with DSS. Although she remains technically employed by DSS, she is referred to as an UPLIFT Social Worker, which has helped the Ray Warren residents accept and trust her. She mentioned that DSS and UPLIFT are working on overcoming technical barriers; for example, linking their computers so she is able to access DSS files from her computer at UPLIFT. She feels that an intimate knowledge of both organizational cultures helps her negotiate some of the barriers:

> My job on-site here has fewer constraints and works on a more personal level. Of course, DSS has their guidelines and that doesn't change, but I have a good understanding of DSS and how they operate. I haven't had any problems with conflicting rules and regulations because I understand both and know what to do.

LESSONS LEARNED

Take Time to Build a Foundation and a Reputation

Before attempting to collaborate formally with other agencies, UPLIFT established a strong foundation within the community. Everyone agrees that

UPLIFT's solid reputation has paved the way for interagency collaboration where little common ground existed before. A staffer commented that when recruiting agencies to participate, "a lot depended on our personal relationships. UPLIFT has a good reputation—not just Robin—but the program. People think 'This is where the action is; let's get on board; we want to be part of the winning team.'" UPLIFT's reputation extends beyond agencies and service providers to the trust it has earned from the families it serves. As a staff member commented:

> Before we wrote grants involving other agencies, we established a reputation in the community. It's just been in the past couple of years that we have brought people from other agencies on-site. Even though they're from other agencies, the families associate them with UPLIFT. It probably would have not worked as well if we had brought them in from the very beginning.

Generate Agency Ownership in a Nonthreatening Framework

UPLIFT works at fostering broad ownership and commitment, as they have learned that agencies are more likely to collaborate if invested in the initiative. A staff member notes, "You have to establish a win-win situation. You have to have something for the agencies; they have to feel ownership. They developed the interagency team, so they have ownership. Why would an agency want to collaborate if they're not getting anything out of it?" All of the participating agencies are represented on the UPLIFT Advisory Board, which provides an additional feeling of ownership and keeps them involved in strategic planning. As a further spur to team building, DSS and UPLIFT conducted joint interviews when hiring the DSS/UPLIFT Social Worker position. A staffer recalls, "We did a lot of team building right from the beginning. The DSS Director and DSS Supervisor came to the site to see exactly where and what their worker would be doing." As a result of their own experience, UPLIFT recommends that collaborating agencies who plan to share staff conduct joint interviews and together decide whom to hire.

Put it in Writing

Although they stress that true collaboration must be based on personal trust, UPLIFT has established written agreements with every agency with whom they will either be contracting or collaborating for services. Each agreement is individualized and documented on a form determined by the agency. A staffer noted, "They're more apt to sign if it comes from them, is in a format they're familiar with. The written agreements cover all of the services to be provided; the intent is to cooperate in getting services to the family."

Don't Sweep Philosophical Differences Under the Rug

Many of the agencies with whom UPLIFT collaborates approach service delivery from a more traditional perspective, with beliefs and values that sometimes clash with UPLIFT's philosophy and mission. These philosophical differences do not appear to hinder UPLIFT's collaborative efforts significantly, although a staff member did comment that some agencies do not believe that UPLIFT families will eventually achieve independence from agency services. Although staff clearly and persistently articulate UPLIFT's vision and mission, there is agreement that, to effect change, they must be responsive to and respectful of agency differences. An UPLIFT staffer cited openness and trust as essential for keeping interagency bridges operational: "We don't have all the answers—you need to be open to others' views and opinions. We can learn from each other." Another staff member said that, "Respect of the organization is paramount." Still another staffer felt that the key was "regular meetings with agencies—not allowing anything to fall through the cracks. Address problems immediately, don't let them go." The executive director is also adamant about the need for keeping an open mind and an ongoing dialogue regarding collaboration: "You need to know what you're getting into. Be clear about outcomes and roles. Keep open lines of communication and talk about the philosophy of how you work with families. Most of all, open your minds—be open to something different."

Be Knowledgeable About How Other Agencies Do Their Jobs

In addition to being clear about philosophical differences among agencies, UPLIFT staff also think it is important to achieve mutual understanding of the nitty-gritty of each agency's processes and operations at all levels of the organization. A staffer advises, "Talk to agency heads. Get a feel for other agencies by allowing yourself to go through their processes." This worker also sees a need to acknowledge that there is often a dichotomy between agency administration and client contact workers: "If agencies are going to work together, they must understand what's going on at the administration level as well as the line level." Gaining understanding also means a willingness to be flexible with relatively minor operational differences rather than allowing those differences to escalate into major problems. As an example, one staff member noted, "Some agencies have their quirks and we work with that. Family and Children Services has a 37 1/2-hour work week, so their person works 37 1/2 hours." UPLIFT personnel have found that being respectful of and flexible about these small procedural differences makes for a smoother relationship when it comes to negotiating large philosophical differences.

13

The Floating Think Tank: Wake County Children's Initiative

Catherine Awsumb
Brian McCadden

As have many urban areas with thriving and diverse economies, Wake County has suffered growing pains over the past decade. One of the most pressing issues facing the county is that budget allocations for the county's social service agencies have not matched the growth rate of social needs. Seeking a response to this situation, the Wake County Board of Commissioners held a planning retreat. As they discussed ways to get more "bang for the buck" in social service expenditures, they were drawn to the idea of increasing interaction and cooperation among agencies. The group agreed that Wake County's human service agencies had a tendency to go their separate ways due mainly to the sheer size of the departments involved and the noncoordination of organizational and service delivery plans. The same clients were often involved with multiple agencies, but current structures meant that each agency acted in isolation, frequently duplicating efforts and reinventing the wheel when it came to a particular client or, worse, acting at cross-purposes. There had to be a better way.

The Commissioners passed a resolution to promote more effective case management procedures among Wake's human service agencies. At this early stage, the problem was defined as lack of an efficient procedure for agencies to pass cases back and forth amongst themselves. The primary motivation for developing collaboration was to save money. After an extensive process of assessment and strategic planning, the county convened a steering committee for collaboration that includes the heads of the county's human service agencies and is led by the Assistant County Manager. The research, including interviews with over 100 administrators and line workers from public and private social service agencies, as well as service recipients, documented what most people had suspected: Wake already had clusters of informal interagency relationships that revolved around client issues rather than departmental structures. The steering committee decided to build from the organic, issue-specific collaboration that already existed rather than trying to design collaboration in the abstract and out of thin air. The first "cluster issue" on which they focused was the needs of children. The Children's Initiative was born.

As the steering committee decided to focus on children as the first "cluster issue" of their collaborative work it seemed natural that schools play a major role in the policy planning. The Assistant County Manager convened a 2-day meeting on children's issues, inviting the Wake County School Superintendent and roughly 50 school administration staff and human service agency personnel. Participants recall that during the planning process new understandings about the complex interrelationship of social problems developed on the part of both the schools and the human service agencies. Agency personnel began to realize that social service problems don't end at the schoolhouse door and that agencies had a role to play in addressing many of the problems which impact learning. For their part, the school personnel began to see their mission as more than simply imparting knowledge—they were also acting as human service delivery agents. Because the needs of children resist neat compartmentalization, so should the agencies that serve them.

During this planning meeting the current committee structure of the Children's Initiative was established. One subcommittee would work on developing the full spectrum of children's programs and services in the county and decide which were applicable to the mission of the Initiative. A second subcommittee would work on a highlighted program, that is, a single program on which all agencies could work together with the reasonable expectation of achieving some much-needed initial success. A third subcommittee would identify target populations for future highlighted programs. This structure enabled the Children's Initiative to maintain a "big picture" view of children's needs while simultaneously implementing a tangible model of collaboration in one particular area. These three subcommittees worked together for 3 to 6 months, planning strategy and adding members as the need arose to include more agencies. They tried to let their structure evolve from their tasks rather than vice versa. In the course of their work they also began to see the need for a full-time staff person to coordinate and facilitate their work. This person, it was decided, must not be hampered by other duties specific to a particular position at a particular agency.

As the Children's Initiative took shape, two critical issues regarding the organizational culture of participating agencies emerged: the need to be focused on results over process and the need to break out of status quo thinking about agency missions. The steering committee found that because these issues are tightly connected, change in one demands change in the other. The committee defined being results-oriented as measuring the actual outcomes of service delivery to children and their families, instead of measuring statistics about numbers of families served, number of shots administered, or numbers of people passing through intake. A focus on results over process, however, calls the entire structure of discrete agencies with independently defined missions and separate funding streams into question. It was impossible to create a results-oriented culture in the individual agencies without making it glaringly obvious that their results were highly interdependent. This perspective constituted a major breakthrough for the steering committee. If the Children's Initiative hoped to accomplish meaningful collaboration, agencies could no longer think of themselves as operating in a vacuum.

Steering Committee members believe that the focus of changing agency culture will need to be on midlevel administrators. The members of the Initiative, all top administration and agency heads, are already believers in collaboration, whereas line workers already collaborate informally across agencies on an as-needed basis. Midlevel administration is believed to be the one area that is dominated by linear thinkers, who primarily conceptualize human services delivery in terms of the discrete programs that their agencies target at discrete problems. Members of the initiative stress that this attitude is a function of the job. Rather than condemning individual job holders for their "backward" attitudes, the Initiative wants to rethink the jobs themselves. As one steering committee member said:

> We are fighting history here. People are not accustomed to operating in this way. The departmental [linear] view can be represented as a sense of responsibility for a set of services, many of which are handed down governmentally from above. This structure breeds a "that's the way it is" mentality which is not conducive to change. This is what we have to address in our planning.

The Children's Initiative is planning joint training sessions and specialized staff development as part of their cultural reorientation strategy.

The Initiative's approach to their first highlighted program, substance abuse services, illustrates their strategy for rethinking agency missions. The issue of substance abuse had been receiving considerable attention in Wake County before the existence of the Children's Initiative, but each agency had devised its own approach to the problem. Public Health focused on prevention, Mental Health dealt mostly in treatment, and Social Services tries to keep abusive families together through mediation. These diverse approaches to the common problem of substance abuse flowed naturally from the discrete missions of each agency. Through the Initiative these agencies, as well as the schools, juvenile justice, and other groups, sat down to plan a way to deal with substance abuse that would involve all agencies in a united effort. For this to succeed, each agency had to modify its priorities to focus on the overall *problem* rather than their particular *programs.*

The most striking example of this new unified front is that the schools and Mental Health recently teamed up before the North Carolina General Assembly to argue against drawing budgetary distinctions between prevention/education and treatment. They contended that these distinctions were more symbolic than real and had the detrimental effect of tying up potential funding sources. They argued for a community-centered, cooperative plan instead, and succeeded in getting the Adolescent Substance Abuse Plan legislated by the General Assembly. This was a big victory for the Children's Initiative: a concrete model for breaking down arbitrary barriers to focus on people, not programs. Assembly members were taken aback by the cooperation and teamwork displayed by the Initiative; several committee members speculated that this was the main reason the plan got approved. Their ability to form consensus around a specific action-oriented proposal gave the group credibility in the county and the state. Their future policy-development efforts will build on this foundation of demonstrated success.

The Wake County Children's Initiative has been designed as a policy center. It is not a physical entity, but more of a floating think tank, designing policies that are carried out by the appropriate member agencies. The monthly meetings are really what constitute the Initiative. Its budget consists of the salary of its Director, the one-full time member of the Initiative. The Initiative hopes to increase its directly allocated funds so that member agencies can implement policies with dedicated funds rather than scraping money together from their individual budgets. Achieving this budgetary autonomy, however, is proving a tough sell in a period of governmental fiscal austerity. Because the Children's Initiative is not a physical entity and most of those who work with it hold primary duties in individual agencies, the money that currently goes toward implementing their strategy comes from existing agency resources, shared among the agencies according to the "cluster issue" needs. In tight economic times convincing the county government to shift money from established agencies to a deliberately less tangible "initiative" is difficult. Members of the Children's Initiative hope that their success with collaboration on substance abuse issues will increase confidence among budgetary authorities about the value of their floating think tank approach.

LESSONS LEARNED

The Virtuous Cycle of Collaboration

One of the main difficulties in generating collaboration is in the challenge it poses to people's traditions and routines. The monthly meetings the Initiative members attend have been acclaimed by all as tremendously important in breaking down those routines. Participants emphasize that the critical factor is not any particular organizational element of the meetings but the simple "serendipity" of getting people together regularly to talk. The general feeling of steering committee members can be summed up by this statement: "Just by being together things get done, things that weren't planned on." Instead of a vicious cycle where agency fragmentation leads to unnecessary burdens that make personnel too occupied by their own crises to work together, a virtuous and self-reinforcing cycle of collaborative strategizing and action has developed.

One member told an illuminating story about his experience with collaboration in another state. He called his counterpart in a nearby city and asked if they might meet to compare notes on how they each did their jobs. In the course of the conversation it emerged that whereas his counterpart collaborated most on a day-to-day basis with the Public Health Department, his own primary interagency contact tended to be the Mental Health Department. As they explored this discrepancy, it turned out that his counterpart's agency was housed in the same building as Public Health, whereas his own agency was housed with Mental Health. The moral this steering committee member drew was that simple sharing of time and space breeds, in itself, collaboration; the monthly meetings of the Children's Initiative create this same effect in Wake County.

From Tool to Philosophy

Like it or not, sometimes people need a push to begin collaborating. One way to get the ball rolling is to have a mandate for collaboration from above, where budgets are set. One Initiative member put it in this way: "There is no motivator like enlightened self-interest." Current economic and political trends indicate that budgetary imperatives will be an ever-more important spur for collaboration. For the agency personnel involved in the Initiative, however, collaboration has become much more than a way to be more "efficient." The more they practice it the more they come to believe that it is an overall better model of human services for everyone involved. Collaboration has moved from being a tool to being a guiding philosophy.

Breaking Out of the Specialist Mentality

A member of the Children's Initiative noted that in human services, "The move towards professionalism has been from generalist to specialist. Now we need to get the specialists together to get depth and breadth—that's what collaboration is about." However, a group of specialists will all bring their own priorities, assumptions, and language to the table. This group stresses the importance of hashing out these differences early and articulating the group's common goals and beliefs. This requires each participant to step back from his or her own specialized training and standard operating procedures, beginning with client problems rather than preconceived solutions.

Realistic First Steps: The Importance of Early Success for Building Momentum

One problem for many collaboratives is selecting a feasible first project. An Initiative member suggests that "it is wise to start with something small instead of starting out trying to change everything. Get some pilots going to have some empirical data to go on, something to show when you're out looking for new money and support. Tackle a problem you think you can solve first to build some confidence." The idea of choosing a manageable first target was important for the members of the Initiative because they did not want to risk having their efforts falter early by choosing something too big to be accomplished by a fledgling method. The steering committee members stressed the importance of building confidence to sustain the momentum for collaboration. This is especially true because the struggle to form new collaborative structures and change agency cultures is a long one that could easily fizzle out without some attainable milestones. Their success in completing and implementing the substance abuse program has given them both the confidence to continue in the face of adversity, and the credibility within the county to allow for the easier implementation of future programs and policies.

Avoiding the Bureaucracy Trap Through Bottom-up Strategy Development

By using cluster issues as their focal point, the Initiative is moving in a bottom-up fashion. Other counties have begun collaborative efforts by trying to create one superagency, that is, by reorganizing their agencies under one authority structure to deliver services as a whole instead of in parts. The members of the Children's Initiative wanted to steer away from this model because they thought it would distract them from the task of filling people's needs and possibly bog them down in political infighting and jockeying for position. Talk of interagency collaboration sometimes sends up a red flag for wary agency personnel because they fear that it will develop into just another layer of bureaucracy. By focusing on cluster issues and letting those drive the strategy, the Children's Initiative has avoided that trap and moved directly toward integrated service delivery.

Some Obstacles to Watch Out For

Members of the Children's Initiative cited the current state of categorical funding, irrelevant regulation, and nonuniform automation as potential stumbling blocks for developing collaboratives. They wrestled with all three issues as they got off the ground and will continue to address them in the future. Budgets can be tricky for collaboratives because human service agency funding is very structured. Members note that most funding is marked for certain departmental "pots," especially federal funds. As one member said, "There is not much general use money out there." A key success factor for collaboratives is selling funding sources on the virtues of a more integrated approach and making tangible demonstrations of the effectiveness of working together. Like funding, regulations tend to be fragmented and agency specific. Differing eligibility criteria or confidentiality policies leave little room for the development of innovative, client-centered solutions. Overcoming this obstacle requires "a commitment from the very top to relax regulations in the name of client needs." Lack of automation is a third manifestation of agency fragmentation that must be overcome. From the client point of view, having to go from agency to agency filling out the same information on different forms is one of the most serious drawbacks of the current delivery structure. Agency automation systems are presently designed in vertical configurations, presenting collaboratives with the critical challenge of designing better ways to share information. Although the lack of systems integration is sometimes justified by appeal to confidentiality regulations, some members of the Children's Initiative feel that the plea of confidentiality can be a cop out: "If a client authorizes you to help them, you can contact whoever you need to in order to help them."

The Importance of Dedicated Personnel

Despite their insistence that "you find time for what is important," members of the Initiative felt it was important to have someone whose sole responsibility is to the collaborative effort. When committee members get caught up in the day-to-day business of their own agencies, a dedicated staff person can maintain continuity, focus, and momentum. Members of the Initiative also pointed out that a staff person can play the key role of "facilitator," someone with no vested interests in particular agencies and who can help members to debate on neutral ground. One Initiative member described the ideal person for such a job as "a leader, an advocate, a red tape cutter."

Public Enemy #1: The Past

Members of the Initiative felt that one of the worst mistakes a collaborative could make would be "building the same old boat out of new wood." This group recognized from the outset that substantive collaboration would never happen without cultural change. As noted earlier, a battle has to be waged against the status quo and traditional ways of doing things have to be questioned in terms of current client needs. This means moving beyond fine-tuning efforts such as "efficient case management" to question the root assumptions behind why things are done a certain way. Often, policies and processes just build up over time because no one has had an opportunity to step back and question them. Members of the Initiative felt that this process of stepping back and questioning assumptions was one of the most rewarding aspects of collaboration and would continue to inform their work in a host of ways.

PART III CONCLUSION: Common Themes from Best Efforts

Catherine Awsumb

The five collaborative initiatives whose stories are told in this part vary in the ways they understand and practice collaboration. Because each developed from the particular needs and resources of a community, each has found its own approach. All, however, are united in their commitment to integration as a better model for human services delivery. Whatever the particular contours of the models they evolved, they all emphasize that successful collaboration requires broad ownership and participation in the community. This implies a willingness to take risks in redefining traditional agency boundaries and roles. They also share a belief in empowering the recipients of services and making them full partners in collaboration. In addition to these philosophical commonalties, the five groups studies had certain common milestones and themes in their development that may be useful to other collaborative initiatives as they evolve.

THE IRONIC ROLE OF MANDATES

Mandates from above played a somewhat ironic role in the development of these collaborations. Although there was unanimous agreement that "collaboration

217

can't be mandated," in fact mandates in several situations provided the initial push towards collaboration. Necessity *is* sometimes the mother of invention, and sometimes people only begin to work together in the face of an obvious crisis or a budgetary imperative. However, although a mandate may be what first gets diverse service providers around a table, it is not enough to sustain momentum. For genuine collaboration to occur, ownership and support must be generated from below, from the people who will have to take the risks and do the everyday work. Often what a mandate does is give people the opportunity to define their common ground. Once this consensus has been reached collaboration takes on a life of its own, often far exceeding the scope of the original mandate.

DEFINE AND UNDERSTAND DIFFERENCES AND SIMILARITIES UP FRONT

All of these groups stressed the importance of early, open, and ongoing communication among group members. There is a danger in being overly polite and trying to steer clear of conflict; gaps in understanding or philosophy that are not explored early on will come back to haunt the group later. As the group strives to come together they should be brutally honest about what they have in common and what they do not, establishing clear boundaries for collaboration. One of the areas in which it is most crucial to be explicit is the definition of the "problem" that the group is trying to address. Who is the target population and what are their most pressing needs? Using safe, vague language that encompasses everyone's view is insufficient; when it is time for action differences will reassert themselves. All of these groups found plenty of common ground from which to work, but they also emphasized that it is important to recognize differences where they exist rather than sweeping them under the rug. Frank conversation is also important as the group tries to nail down the specifics of how collaboration is to be practiced. Will the group focus on direct service delivery, coordination and infrastructure, or policy development? Talking about the right mix early keeps everyone on track.

ESTABLISH NEUTRAL TURF

All of these groups felt strongly that neutrality was crucial to their success. Although it may sometimes be necessary to formally empower an existing agency for purposes of grant administration or other funding flows, decision-making autonomy is a must. An autonomous structure creates a safe environment where agencies may practice innovative strategies without fear of losing in political or turf battles. If the collaborative is perceived to be under the inequitable control of one agency or group, participants will play defensively and collaboration will stall. Autonomy may also make the collaborative more attractive and inviting to the community at large and particularly to service recipients. Traditional agencies come with a great deal of baggage and may be less able to get things done under their own banners, whatever their good intentions. Neutral turf allows ownership to be established from the ground up. All of these groups felt that freeing funds to flow directly to collaboratives rather than through agency channels was a crucial next step in providing an environment where collaboration can flourish.

COLLABORATION IS A VISION, NOT AN ORGANIZATION

The evolution of these collaboratives brings home the importance of focusing on a core vision and on not getting too attached to the particular structures used to implement it. All of them went through many permutations of membership, organizational structure, and service mix, evolving in response to issues and opportunities. By holding to a commonly defined problem and a vision of integrated services, they were able to go through these changes without losing focus. It also helps to keep this in mind as the organization grows and the day-to-day realities of "how?" threaten to make people lose sight of the "why?" As long as people maintain their faith in the "why?" the specifics of "how?" can evolve without disturbing the core.

INVOLVE THE WHOLE COMMUNITY, INCLUDING THE POPULATION YOU WANT TO SERVE

All of these groups demonstrated the rewards of taking collaboration beyond the level of interagency collaboration to genuine community collaboration. Although there are clear benefits to traditional public agencies working together, the rewards multiply geometrically when nonprofits, community groups, businesses, and services recipients get in on the action. Broad and diverse participation tends to generate new perspectives on problems and solutions and create a sense of ownership and pride that emerge infrequently from formal bureaucratic structures. Involving service recipients in all phases of planning and implementation has the added benefit of empowering them to name their own problems and take responsibility for solutions.

A FINAL WORD: PATIENCE!

Nearly every participant in every collaborative studied volunteered that patience and perseverance are required to make collaboration work. Collaboration is sometimes sold as the "Holy Grail" of human services delivery and thereby burdened by unrealistic expectations. As exciting as the vision may be, however, it takes trial and error to make it work in practice. The transition from a period of activism and enthusiasm to one of increasing structure can be frustrating, but the collaboratives studied indicate that it is part of the normal organizational growth process. By constantly returning to the roots of their shared beliefs, collaboratives can maintain momentum. One useful strategy is to set achievable early hurdles rather than setting out to save the world. By building collaboration around a specific problem and/or population, groups can create tangible success stories that will make a solid core for enlarging and expanding their vision.

14

Looking Forward: Lessons for Future Practice

George W. Noblit
Penny L. Richards
Amee Adkins
Catherine Awsumb

At the end of each part, we have offered concluding lessons to be learned. Each of these are useful for people when considering interagency collaboration in terms of current practice, client experiences, and best efforts at collaboration. However, these studies taken together suggest another set of lessons. In some sense, these lessons are sobering reminders of how much we are asking when we say we want to promote interagency collaboration. The reality is that interagency collaboration is rarer than we think, harder than we think, and more promising than we think. This means that people who wish to embark on this path may find it useful to use these cross-study lessons as initial discussion points that will set the stage for more strategic planning. However, we think the following lessons also should lead some to abandon efforts that are unlikely to be productive. Both are worthy goals that may be served by considering what follows.

LESSON 1: INTERAGENCY COLLABORATION IS SPORADICALLY PRACTICED

Clearly, some counties engage in more collaboration than others, but none of the counties studied have been able to design and implement a full system of collaboration. Rather, collaboration happens when there are mandates and a willingness to go beyond the minimum possible, and where there have been some successful initiatives in the past. It is important to note that even in these cases, mandates tend to be directed toward a specific target population; thus mandates limit collaboration even as they encourage it.

LESSON 2: THE MOST EFFECTIVE FORMS OF COLLABORATION ARE INFORMAL

In each county, informal networking worked best to bring services together for a particular client. It has many advantages, including being unofficial (and thus allowing for hypothetical and explorative conversations), requiring no paperwork, and being time effective. On the other hand, recognized limitations of informal networking include high personnel turnover and legal restrictions (confidentiality requirements were often mentioned). Informal networking was easiest when people had worked in other agencies and understood their logics, limitations and possibilities. Although formal mechanisms are important to restructuring service delivery to be more integrated, it is important that these informal networks not be disrupted in the process. These networks can be protected by:

- creating incentives to combat turnover of personnel and to promote cross-agency internships and training;
- informal cross-agency gatherings;
- better use of technology (electronic mail, voice mail, phone options, common computer systems across agencies);
- creating a confidentiality procedure that still allows access for personnel from other agencies; and
- designing cross-agency directories of personnel, and other publications, that update all (not just administrators) as to changes in personnel and procedures.

The goal should be to bring front-line workers (including private agencies) together to work on actual cases and issues of common concern, while avoiding excessive time and paperwork demands. Such issues might include: transportation, parental involvement, uniform agency requirements, information exchange, streamlining paperwork, personnel retention, and local economic, cultural, and political conditions.

LESSON 3: THE BEST INFORMAL COLLABORATORS ARE CLIENT ADVOCATES

The best informal collaborators seem to share some personal characteristics, such as being:

- persistent, resourceful, and creative (in assembling services and avoiding tangles);
- trustworthy and willing to trust;
- proactive in seeking services that address future problems;
- willing to work with others, regardless of their professional status or authority;
- committed to make new contacts and maintain existing contacts; and
- client-oriented—getting what the client needs, not what the agency normally provides.

Some practical conditions help agency workers foster advocacy for clients:

- time to explore options and consult with experts;
- access to appropriate technologies, up-to-date information about agencies procedures and services; and
- experience in other agencies, particularly service in a broad range of community organizations that provide both knowledge and contacts about services, local residence over a long period of time, and friendships across agencies.

Clearly, not all of these characteristics and conditions can be controlled by agencies. There are some things agencies can do, however:

- set up incentive systems to retain staff;
- request that staff live in local communities;
- reward persistence, trustworthiness, and resourcefulness in service delivery to clients;
- provide appropriate technologies, up-to-date information, and training;
- design cross-agency learning and apprentice experiences; and
- seek ways to ease current time constraints for staff.

LESSON 4: MORE IS NOT NECESSARILY BETTER: MORE POTENTIAL COMBINATIONS OF PROGRAMS AND RESOURCES DO NOT IMPROVE COLLABORATION

Increasing the number of service combinations may actually inhibit increased collaboration. A caseworker with too many options will likely resort to some smaller set of referrals with which she is familiar and in which she has confidence. Considerable time and effort can be spent considering alternatives further burdening already overworked service providers.

LESSON 5: INTERAGENCY COLLABORATION IS A "TWO-TIERED" SYSTEM

Formal collaboration is often limited to meetings of top administrators who design ways for the agencies to better serve clients. Informal collaboration typically is practiced by front-line service providers. Ironically, it appears that the two tiers often do not communicate with each other and at times seem to work at cross purposes. As noted previously, informal collaboration results in more direct and timely benefits to clients. Formal structures that promote collaboration and integration of services, therefore, are more likely to be effective when they are designed with the input of front-line service providers.

LESSON 6: INFORMAL COLLABORATION IS USEFUL ON A CASE-BY-CASE BASIS, BUT IT IS NOT SUFFICIENT TO ADDRESS THE INTERRELATED NEEDS OF CLIENTS ON AN ONGOING BASIS

Informal collaboration can be a great boon to clients, but, by definition, it is practiced only sporadically, leaving clients vulnerable to falling through the cracks between agencies. The interrelated needs of children and families require a more consistent and systematic approach to collaboration. Informal collaboration often works covertly against established agency logics; formal collaboration requires that agency structures and logics be challenged directly and redesigned. Formal collaboration allows social services professionals to work flexibly to serve client needs without having to negotiate current agency boundaries on a case by case basis as they do now. The patterns and practices that emerge organically through informal collaboration may serve as useful suggestions of the direction in which to move, but only by remaking the social services system to reflect the needs of clients will these needs be met consistently.

LESSON 7: FORMAL COLLABORATION REQUIRES DECISION-MAKING AUTHORITY AND AUTONOMY

One of the dissatisfactions expressed about many current collaborative efforts is that they are purely advisory and avoid discussion of specific cases. If collaboration remains at an advisory level, it can be seen as a distraction from caseloads rather than as a more effective way to address them. Interviewees felt it was crucial that such groups be empowered to take action rather than having each member go back and clear decisions through existing agency channels. In addition to having decision-making authority, formal collaborative groups need autonomy. The effort must not be perceived to be under the control of any one existing agency or issues of turf protection will arise; equal power relationships are crucial among such groups. Establishing autonomy allows participants to start with a clean slate, free from the inherited assumptions of existing structures and able to question and justify practices anew from the perspective of client needs. Interviewees also indicated that having full-time staff is an important component of organizational autonomy. Dedicated personnel are free from conflicting obligations to individual agencies and can thus serve as neutral arbiters and keep other group members focused on a common vision.

LESSON 8: THE SPURS, REINS, GREASE, AND GRAVEL FOR INTERAGENCY COLLABORATION ARE NOT GENERALIZABLE FROM ONE COMMUNITY TO ANOTHER

As previously noted, what worked to foster or inhibit collaboration in one county might not work the same way in another. Further, what at one time in one county improves collaboration might constrain it at another. In short, any lists such, even those we have offered here, should be used as a loose framework to prompt consideration. Local agency representatives might find the list useful to foster discussion in the planning process. In thinking about how services need to be restructured, the central question must always be, "What is in the best interest of the client in order to produce positive results?" This question poses some serious threats to the status quo and to traditional categorical service delivery.

LESSON 9: AGENCIES EVERYWHERE HAVE SOME SIMILAR PROBLEMS

According to the results of this study, Mental Health, Juvenile Services, and Social Services, in particular, have a stigma associated with them. For this reason, clients as well as other agencies were reluctant to collaborate. Social Services departments were seen as beleaguered on many fronts: poor facilities, large and difficult caseloads, high turnover rates, legal restrictions and high levels of stress. Although in some counties Mental Health agencies were seen as having improved its work with other agencies, clients were, at times, reluctant to apply for their services. Juvenile Services is largely viewed as a last resort. The justice system most often was considered for clients to be a "one-way street" to increased identity with a life of crime and prison. By seeming to prefer to take care of their own problems in house rather than referring to other agencies, schools are most often viewed by other agencies as being closed systems. To make matters worse, the teacher, assumed by other agencies and by clients to be a key player, is inaccessible by phone and cannot attend meetings during the regular workday. Health agencies, often not thought of as social service agencies, are frequently left out of collaborative efforts.

LESSON 10: COLLABORATION MEANS DIFFERENT THINGS TO DIFFERENT PEOPLE

In words and deeds, collaboration means many things. For some, communication and information sharing is an adequate definition. For others, cooperation among separate agencies is sufficient so that each agency can do what it normally does more efficiently. True collaboration is harder to find. Agency workers rarely ask, "What will it take to make the client self-sufficient?" or "How can agency services work together to make client self-sufficiency possible?" Although the literature teaches us there is no one best way to collaborate, developing some shared understandings about how collaborative service delivery will be defined by local agencies is an essential starting point.

LESSON 11: SERVICES AGENCIES ARE OVERLOADED, LEAVING LITTLE TIME FOR COLLABORATION

Contrary to current political rhetoric, service agencies have high caseloads and scarce resources. If collaboration is to become institutionalized it will have to redefine the work of service providers so that the current workload is reduced and time is created for collaboration.

LESSON 12: TECHNOLOGY HELPS COLLABORATION

The most important technology of collaboration is the telephone. The absence of telephones in classrooms is one reason why teachers are often left out of the problem-solving process. Computers, electronic mail, voice mail and fax machines also help. However, it is also true that each agency has its own computer and software system; therefore, sharing information electronically is not easy. A key issue for the State of North Carolina is the development of a technological infrastructure for human services.

LESSON 13: LAW AND REGULATIONS ARE INTERFERING WITH COLLABORATION

According to the agency workers interviewed, some laws, regulations and mandates require collaboration whereas others forbid it. Probably the stickiest area is confidentiality. Collaboration for most agencies is constrained because of confidentiality restrictions. Those agencies that have found creative ways to share client information when necessary are not sure that their strategies would survive legal scrutiny. Moreover, agencies sometimes find it useful to have the threat of legal sanction in order to get parents to cooperate with coordinated service delivery. The barriers related to confidentiality were so pervasive as to be a key issue to address formally statewide.

LESSON 14: KEY SERVICE AGENCIES HAVE DIFFERENT LOGICS OF DECISION MAKING

The five agencies each make decisions internally by rather different processes. In most agencies, determining eligibility and the nature of the services needed is a large part of the decisions. Schools, for example, have limited eligibility concerns, and the primary service is teaching classes of children. DSS, on the other hand, must determine eligibility before services can be provided and then has a number of different services that it can offer. Further, each agency has different time considerations. DSS is generally seen as cumbersome and slow, and schools generally offer only selected programs during the summer. These factors have implications for interagency collaboration. Health, for example, checks with DSS immediately to confirm eligibility for Medicaid, whereas schools tend to handle most problems in house. DSS is perceived as "slow" because caseworkers are not involved until after eligibility has been determined, and so on. Cross-agency experience, therefore, is a valuable commodity because of the knowledge and understanding of how other agencies work.

LESSON 15: COLLABORATION AMONG AGENCIES DOES NOT NECESSARILY STRIKE THE CLIENT AS DESIRABLE

Clients say they want and need services but do not want to ask for help or become dependent on services of agencies that have a stigma attached to them. Clients have a number of concerns that mitigate their support of interagency collaboration:

- their sense of control of their own lives is eroded by increased violations of privacy;
- their understanding of what they have committed to in seeking services is uncertain;
- a perception of exclusion emerges—"I want to be at that meeting if they are talking about me";

- collaboration as currently practiced increases the paperwork and visits to agencies rather than reducing them.

LESSON 16: CLIENTS WANT COLLABORATION TO WORK FOR THEM

Clients have little interest in collaboration for the sake of organizational streamlining or caseworker relief. What may seem to be a great improvement for agencies may be a jarring change and/or an intrusive new policy to current clients. It may impede the delivery of usual services without resulting in appreciably improved service in the client's view.

LESSON 17: AGENCY SERVICE ELIGIBILITY DETERMINATION PROCESSES MAY CONTRIBUTE TO STIGMA AND FEAR ON THE PART OF CLIENTS TOWARDS THE AGENCIES THAT SERVE THEM

Some clients are reluctant to seek assistance because they fear their needs being made public, as is the case with Food Stamps. Others are reluctant to seek assistance because the complex and time-consuming application process is more trouble that the resulting assistance is worth. Still others are reluctant to seek services because they fear losing control over decision making or becoming helplessly dependent on public assistance. Many clients say "the system" makes it easier to continue receiving public assistance than it does to become self-sufficient.

LESSON 18: CLIENT CONTACT WORKERS NEED INCREASED DECISION-MAKING AUTHORITY IN ORDER TO MOST EFFECTIVELY HELP CHILDREN AND FAMILIES IN A TIMELY MANNER

As noted earlier, the most effective collaboration was seen in the informal networks of front-line service providers; however, the different agency decision-making logics make it difficult to use these informal networks systematically. In schools, the usual interagency contact person is administrative or middle management (principal, guidance counselor, etc.) whereas in DSS it is a caseworker. In health departments, physicians have the ultimate decision-making authority. In Juvenile Services, much depends on what the judge decides. This mix creates uncertainty for those engaging in collaborative problem solving. The collaboration of front line service providers requires those in authority over them to delegate more of the decision-making among service providers. The differences in rules and regulations, and agency strengths and needs, also mean that each community needs to design the processes that work best for all involved. Again, note that it is up to teachers to be a vital part of the interagency collaboration process.

LESSON 19: WITHIN-AGENCY COLLABORATION DETERMINES SERVICES MORE THAN BETWEEN-AGENCY COLLABORATION

For most of these children, the key step in receiving services involved the single agency setting its staff to cooperate and consider what could best be done for the child and family. Interagency collaboration was less likely to be initiated. The children's chances depend on how well single agencies can meet their needs.

LESSON 20: THE CHILD WILL RECEIVE THE SERVICES THE AGENCIES NORMALLY PROVIDE RATHER THAN THE SERVICES HE OR SHE NEEDS

With or without interagency collaboration, it is clear that the services provided are based on what the agencies are designed to provide. There was no systematic attempt to determine what clients actually needed to resolve their needs; rather, every agency was providing the services it was in the business to provide. In other words, agencies tend to follow the doctrines "business as usual" and "one size fits all."

LESSON 21: DIAGNOSIS IS MORE IMPORTANT THAN TREATMENT

There is a lack of balance in the resources spent diagnosing versus treating or preventing problems for children and families. Diagnosis is an important part of treatment, but many times it seemed to be an end in itself rather than a means to an end. Agencies are structured to offer categorical rather than individual services and to design piecemeal rather than comprehensive solutions.

LESSON 22: THE SERVICES THE CHILD RECEIVES ARE UNLIKELY TO REDUCE DEPENDENCY ON PUBLIC AGENCIES

Because the services delivered are determined by the agencies' logics rather than the child's needs, it is unlikely that the child's problems will be resolved.

LESSON 23: COLLABORATION CANNOT BE MANDATED, BUT STATE POLICY CAN PLAY A ROLE IN ITS DEVELOPMENT

Interviewees in social service agencies are wary of any collaborative policy that is dictated from above. There is a concern that state-mandated collaboration could turn into another layer of bureaucracy, regulation, and paperwork standing between social services professionals and their clients. Because the whole idea of collaboration is to begin with client needs rather than agency structures, it is vital that collaboration be allowed to evolve around the specific needs of a community.

However, the research did uncover two ways in which the state can facilitate the development of collaboration at the local level. First, states can study client case flows, such as those presented in this book, to uncover ways in which regulations on such matters as eligibility and confidentiality can present artificial barriers to meeting the needs of clients. Agency personnel suggest that the original intention of such regulations has been obscured and they have calcified into unnecessarily rigid obstacles which do not reflect the interrelated nature of client problems. By providing for more flexibility and discretion in such matters, states would allow more space in which collaboration could flourish. Second, the experiences of many of the counties in this book demonstrate the value of simply getting personnel from different agencies into the same room on a regular basis. In this sense, state-mandated collaborative efforts can nudge people out of their regular agency routines and give them a chance to confront issues from other perspectives. Such meetings can provide the "face time" that can jump start the process of collaboration by allowing relationships to develop. It is crucial, however, that such groups include not just administrative staff but also client contact workers, those likeliest to understand interrelated client needs in detail.

LESSON 24: INTERAGENCY COLLABORATION IS TOO OFTEN SEEN AS AN UNBRIDLED GOOD BY POLITICIANS, POLICYMAKERS, AND SERVICE PROVIDERS, AND THUS CANNOT BE CRITICALLY EXAMINED

The last lesson is in some ways the most important. Interagency collaboration is an apple-pie-and-motherhood type of concept in our current dialogues. Although we consider it a valuable idea, we think the concept itself should be interrogated as part of the planning process. As the counties, clients, and existing collaboratives all testify, there are compelling reasons why it is not a good idea for some contexts and clients. Making decisions about where and when it is appropriate is vitally important as we move ahead.

Epilogue: Moving Forward—Interagency Collaboration in Context in North Carolina

Dee Brewer

According to the 1994 Kids Count Data Book, the Center for the Study of Social Policy and the Annie E. Casey Foundation reported that the United States slipped backward in 6 of 10 measures of child well-being during the period of 1985 to 1991. The six measures include percent of low-birth weight babies, percent of births to single teens, juvenile violent crime arrest rate, percent graduating from high school on time, teen violent death rate, and percent of children in single-parent families. The status of these indicators varies from state to state and from community to community. However, on the whole, they paint a portrait of families and children in trouble and in need.

The physical, social, and economic conditions in the child's community are interrelated, and they have tremendous impact on each young person's life chances and opportunities for success. Components in the network of human services, whether locally, state or federally initiated and whether compensatory, rehabilitative, or preventative, are intended to shape that impact in a positive direction—one that increases promises for success for the individual, the local community, and the society at large. Testimony to the failures of the current system of social services presents itself in various forms: the decline in quality of life indexes, the continuing sprawl of the bureaucracies within that system, and the skepticism in the public discourse about whether "welfare works." On the national level, there is increasing discussion in Congress, the Administration, and the mass media about the need to revamp public services, as well as to "take a hard line" on welfare mothers. This volume has introduced a body of research which, hopefully, suggests to its readers that simply cutting back the programs or "taking the hard line" are not the only alternatives for improving the quality of service from public agencies. Instead, it offers some perspectives on redefining the provision of service, in ways that are driven by client needs rather than bureaucratic structures.

Within North Carolina, we face similar issues: declining quality of life among the poor and rising public skepticism about the effectiveness of social services. State leaders have demonstrated considerable interest in the potential for interagency collaboration, the focus of this text, to respond to these issues. The following is an outline of the policy context in North Carolina regarding human services, the state's attempts to refine them, and the role collaboration plays in that refinement.

THE CONTEXT OF NORTH CAROLINA'S POLICIES FOR FAMILIES AND CHILDREN

North Carolina, like many other states, has many families in need. According to the 1994 Children's Index published by the North Carolina Child Advocacy Institute, North Carolina is still among the 10 worst states in the nation for children and families to live. Although we are making progress in some areas, the state still fares worse than the national average in the percent of low-birthweight babies, infant mortality rate, child death rate, percent of births to single teens, percent of students graduating high school on time, percent of teen violent deaths, and percent of children in single-parent families.

Increasingly, disadvantage has shifted from the oldest people to the youngest. Those children living in mother-only households have become the most deprived of all. More preschool and school age children live in poverty in this state than do adults. Whereas the overall rate of poverty is 16%, for preschool children it is almost 23% and for school-age children it is 19%. Poverty is also concentrated among minorities and those with little education. Along with poverty comes a range of other problems such as substandard housing, poor health, child abuse, and teen pregnancy. These problems can have a powerful impact on a young person's ability to perform and their motivation to stay in school.

Another major family policy issue in our state is accessible, affordable child care. In 1990, more than 60% of all of North Carolina's children under 6 had either both parents or their sole parent in the labor force. Two-thirds of the state's women whose youngest child is under 6 are in the work force. Further, 80% of women with school-age children are working. Consequently, many children need some form of childcare. State leaders in the legislature and the human services departments acknowledge all of these issues as crucial to the well-being of the state and all of its constituents. Although they do not agree on a single agenda to address these problems, they have forged a number of initiatives that begin to focus resources and energy on improving the life chances of North Carolina's children and making them, as Governor Jim Hunt puts it, "safe, healthy, and ready to learn."

North Carolina is pursuing four avenues of family-centered policy that integrate complementary areas of services for the public. These include: (a) the Smart Start initiative, (b) the JOBS program and welfare reform, (c) family support and educational initiatives such as family resource centers and after-school programs, and (d) a unified support model for high-risk families and children, modeled after *Facing the Future: A Blueprint for Kansas Children and Families.*

Smart Start was proposed by Governor Hunt and enacted by the 1993 North Carolina General Assembly. It is designed to provide every child in North Carolina who needs it with affordable childcare, early childhood education, and other crucial services. The overriding goal of the program is to prepare children from birth to 5 years old to succeed in school. Two emphases of the Smart Start initiative are increased collaboration among community services and organizations and locally defined agendas for meeting each community's health, education, and childcare needs. Fiscal year 1993-1994 appropriations were $29 million for demonstrations in 12 of the state's 100 counties, with that number expected to double for fiscal year 1994-1995.

The Job Opportunities and Basic Skills (JOBS) Training Program is a federally mandated initiative to assure that AFDC recipients obtain the necessary training, education, supportive services, and employment they need to avoid long-term welfare dependency. The JOBS Program is administered by local departments of social services in 73 of the state's 100 counties, potentially reaching 95% of the state's adult AFDC recipients. State and federal expenditures for fiscal year 1993-1994 for JOBS were approximately $22 million.

The 1994 Special Session of the General Assembly in North Carolina also made a significant investment in family support for fiscal year 1994-1995. Loosely grouped under the banner of School Success or school-related initiatives, the General Assembly funded the Support Our Students (SOS) after-school programs for kindergarten through the ninth grade ($5 million), family resource centers for families and children from birth to elementary age (just over $2 million), the Governor's One-on-One mentoring program ($1.15 million), Intervention/Prevention Grants for local school districts to enhance educational outcomes and coordinate services ($12 million), local programs to assist children at risk of school failure ($18.2 million, some of which may be used to hire additional school counselors and other student support personnel), and family preservation ($500,000).

The fourth component of the state's emerging family-centered policy is a unified family support model. The Division of Social Services in the North Carolina Department of Human Resources formed a private-university partnership in the Spring of 1993, with the support of a grant from the W.K. Kellogg Foundation. From that partnership has emerged Families for Kids, an initiative to reduce inappropriate placement of children. The elements of this model reflect a continuum of services, dependent on needs, that includes family support and family preservation services, child welfare services (including child protective services, foster care, adoption, reunification, and independent living services), and services that link families to employment, health, and housing services.

To move toward a unified family support model, in 1991 the North Carolina General Assembly passed the Family Preservation Services (FPS) program, now codified as the Family Preservation Act. Funding, however, was limited to little more than $0.5 million in fiscal year 1992-1993. The Family Preservation and Support Provisions of the Federal Omnibus Budget Reconciliation Act of 1993 established a capped entitlement program as Part 2 of Title IV-B of the Social Security Act. Through this act, North Carolina will receive a little more than $1 million in fiscal year 1994-1995 and approximately $17.4 million over the 5 years of the Act. The planning associated with the Kellogg Families for Kids initiative and the linkages established with one aspect of Title IV-B, "Family Preservation and Family Support Services," will go a long way toward strengthening families, slowing and rolling back the trend toward out-of-home care, and increasing successful family reunification, adoption, and strong, stable foster care placements.

These four initiatives share the assumption that no single agency, no one category of services, can adequately respond to the needs of children and families in North Carolina. Rather than continuing to allocate more funds to projects that address discrete parts of the problem, all four represent a move in the direction of integrating government support services toward concerted actions, meant to address the "big picture" families in need face.

CONVENTIONAL VERSUS INTEGRATED APPROACHES TO SERVING CHILDREN AND FAMILIES

One reaction to public dissatisfaction with current norms of administering human services is to streamline them by tightening eligibility standards and imposing arbitrary limits on the amount of time for which clients may receive services. Another reaction, and one that we find compelling given this study, is to reassess the means of the administration of services. Here we are speaking of another way to "trim the fat;" namely, by increasing the efficiency of human services delivery without necessarily altering the definitions of client eligibility. To illustrate this approach, we begin with an assessment of conventional standards for service delivery and then compare that with opportunities from an integrated approach.

According to the document *What It Takes: Structuring Interagency Partnerships to Connect Children and Families with Comprehensive Service* (Melaville & Blank, 1991, p. 9), our current human services system has several critical flaws:

> *First, services are crisis-oriented.* They are designed to address problems that have already occurred rather than to offer supports of various kinds to prevent difficulties from developing in the first place.
>
> *Second, the current social welfare system divides the problems of children and families into rigid and distinct categories that fail to reflect interrelated causes and solutions.* Services designed to correspond to discrete problems, commonly referred to as categorical problems, are administered by literally dozens of agencies. Each has its own particular focus, source of funding, guidelines, and accountability requirements. Even though a child and his or her family may need a mix of health, education, child welfare, or other services, separate and often conflicting eligibility standards and rules governing the expenditure of funds work against comprehensive service delivery. Services are provided within, rather than across, service categories.
>
> *Third, the current system is unable to meet the needs of children and families due to a lack of functional communication among the various public and private agencies that comprise it.* Agencies with pronounced dissimilarities in professional orientation and institutional mandates seldom see each other as allies. Operating like ships passing in the night, agencies have little opportunity to draw on services available throughout the community that might complement one another.
>
> *Fourth, the current system falls short because of the inability of specialized agencies to easily craft comprehensive solutions to complex problems.* Existing staff typically represent only a narrow slice of the professional talent and expertise needed to plan, finance, and implement the multiple services characteristic of successful interventions.

We know that the change which is needed to address these problems is not a new set of programs routinely applied without seeing how it fits the needs of people. There is no "one-size-fits-all" solution. Communities need the flexibility and imagination to take a little from here and a little from there and create their own responses to their own needs.

We have learned something about the fundamental concepts and practices of service delivery and service orientation that facilitate the flexibility and imagination mentioned earlier. Following is a schema that arranges these concepts and practices in continua that can guide communities and service providers as they move themselves from a traditional to an integrated orientation toward service delivery.

Traditional Service Delivery	Integrated Service Delivery
Follow agency procedures	Help families solve problems
Turf-building	Partnerships
Separate agencies	Multi-disciplinary centers
Separate agency buildings	Flexible service sites
Single agency vision and mission	Shared service vision and mission
Single agency goals	Cross-agency goals
Competitive funding	Shared resources
Single agency accountability	Cross-agency accountability
Evaluation = number of clients	Evaluation = results for families
Accountability to funding source	Accountability to community
Agency workers	Cross-agency team service providers
Narrow eligibility requirements	Flexible regulations
Separate applications & eligibility	Single application & eligibility
Separate data bases	Shared data base
Rigid confidentiality rules	Individualized privacy agreements
Office hours 8 am to 5 pm	Flexible hours based on customer need
Client sent to different agencies	One-stop shopping, single broker
Quick-fix solutions	Continuous improvement
Crisis-driven	Prevention-focused
Foster dependency	Foster self-sufficiency
Depersonalized	Personalized
Standardized menu of services	Customized services tailored to needs
Service delivery plans	Family goals for self sufficiency
"That's not my job"	"Whatever it takes"

COOPERATION, COORDINATION OR COLLABORATION?

A review of the literature yields few established definitions of collaboration. In fact, many people use terms like collaboration, cooperation, and coordination interchangeably. Some, however, are coming to view collaboration on a continuum of "working together" to deliver services. The continuum can be thought of as having two dimensions. One dimension looks at "working together" based on the degree of "separateness" or "connectedness" of agencies in terms of vision, goals, power, resources and responsibilities. The other dimension looks at "working together" based on the degree of participation and effort of agencies toward common solutions for shared clients.

As indicated in Figure E1, cooperation represents a low degree of joint participation and effort and a high degree of separateness among agencies and schools. Coordination requires a moderate degree of participation and effort and less separateness. Collaboration represents a high degree of participation, effort,

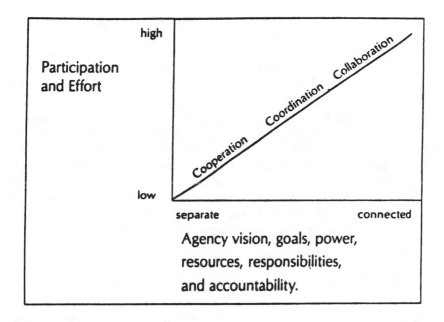

Figure E1. The collaboration continuum: Cooperation, coordination, collaboration

and connectedness. Achieving this degree of connectedness implies the sharing of goals and intended results, power, resources, and responsibilities among the partner organizations and with clients.

The ultimate goal is to bring needed services together for the benefit of clients. Achieving this goal requires a shift in thinking and in practice, from agency-based services, which begin with the agency, to needs-based services, which begin with the client. Families become critical partners in service and empowerment.

COLLABORATION: A VEHICLE FOR SYSTEMS CHANGE

If we operate from the philosophy that "It takes an entire village to raise a child," we begin to think about building community and cultural competence to strengthen the support for families. From this view, "working together" would include a broader scope of partners beyond schools and human service agencies, such as police, parks and recreation, and other community-oriented professions. Working with the entire community demands new competencies and new programs that cut across agencies, services, and professions in an attempt to reorganize them around the needs of children and families. It is difficult, if not impossible, to be both family-centered and community-based in the current categorical system. To focus on the full needs of families and communities is inconsistent with categorical funding, which only addresses needs for which funding is available and for which clients are eligible. Problems for which there is no funding or for which the client does not meet eligibility requirements will likely remain unattended.

Collaboration is viewed by many as a vehicle for systems change. Because there is no "one-size-fits-all" solution, some communities are using the principles of collaboration to strengthen connectedness within the community in terms of shared vision, goals, power, resources, and responsibilities to improve the well-being of children. Although program structures and administrative arrangements facilitate such collaboration, it is also a matter of attitudes, skills, and knowledge of the individual practitioners that determine how effectively services will be delivered and to what degree self-sufficiency is fostered.

SCHOOLS ARE VITAL COMMUNITY FOCAL POINTS

In North Carolina, there is increasing coherence in the state level policy framework to bring increased opportunities for communities to start early with families and to build some important safety nets and supports for the educational success of young people. The support for this shift receives alternative billing—sometimes as long-term "crime prevention," other times as "economic capacity building," and still other times as "a return to traditional family values." Often at the same time that these long-term social interests are linked to the immediate goal of the well-being of children and families, state leaders insert a medium-range goal, improved educational outcomes. Their thinking ties all three of these community interests into a comprehensive plan for improving the quality of life in the state.

Some communities are already creating new kinds of arrangements in order to bring together community resources to ensure that children can grow up to be responsible, productive and fully participating members of society. As primary institutions in the community, the schools offer several key opportunities to coordinate and integrate services. This does not necessarily mean that the schools need to organize or operate all the services to be delivered, but the physical facility or the cooperation of the school administration are critical elements to integration and coordination efforts. Across the nation, many communities see schools as vital focal points for service integration because schools are where the children are. In addition to the reforms in the classroom, links are being established between schools and other human services. These links are not meant to replace the traditional roles of families or teachers, but to provide vital support to both.

Full service schools, as some are called, are seen as a cost-effective way to serve the community. Instead of spending money to build or maintain a separate facility, resources go directly to programs and services. Agencies and schools coordinating services with other community resources focused on youth (e.g., YMCA, parks and recreation) provides a means to leverage resources to avoid duplication and service gaps. For schools, making other human services easy to access can relieve some of the time pressures teachers face in their attempts to serve as teacher, guidance counselor, social worker, and nurse, allowing them more time to plan and prepare lessons. Offering family support and educational services can also build the capacity of families to prevent future problems and increase family self-sufficiency, making educational dollars that much more meaningful.

SHOULD SERVICES FOR CHILDREN AND FAMILIES BE LOCATED AT A SCHOOL?

The practical guide entitled *Together We Can* (Melaville & Blank, 1993) was developed jointly by the U.S. Department of Education and the U.S. Department of Health and Human Services to assist local communities in the process of creating a coordinated education and human service delivery system. The guide offers a set of criteria for deciding whether to locate comprehensive services directly at a school. The authors caution that the decision depends on factors unique to each community and to each school. They suggest that the following collection of factors be discussed by everyone involved in the planning:

> *Trust:* Do families in the neighborhood trust the school? Has the school involved parents in making decisions, planning programs and meetings based on their needs, and learning about their children? Do groups from the community already use the school for community meetings and classes? Do parents come to school staff for help in meeting their daily needs? If parents do not voluntarily come to the school already, they may be reluctant to use additional services located at the school.
> *Access to Services for Children During School Hours:* Teachers and other school staff often become aware of problems while children are at school. Services located at a school allow immediate access to support and special services and can forge a critical connection between the child, family, and school. Referring the child and family to services away from the school site often means the child and family never receive the needed services.
> *Connection Between School and Other Staff:* When services are located at a school, there is ample opportunity for school and service

agency staff to communicate about the needs of children and families. The communication may take the form of shared staff development, a joint consultation process involving school and service agency staff, or a quick conversation during recess. This communication is essential if school staff are to develop a broader perspective of the needs of children and to participate actively in a system of integrated services for children and families.

Availability of Space: Some neighborhoods have plenty of school space and may even have whole school buildings that are not being used for instruction. Other schools may not have any room at all. Sometimes portable classrooms can be placed on a school site and used for integrated service programs. Careful and realistic planning is needed to balance staff needs for integrated services with the amount of space available.

Accessibility: Access to services is complicated, especially for families who must walk or rely on public transportation. To be accessible, schools and other sites for services must be well lighted, close to public transportation, and located in areas considered safe by all groups in the community. Some school buildings may not be available after regular working hours. Hence, they would not be accessible to parents who are away from home during the day.

Where the Children Are: In some neighborhoods, almost all children attend the local public school. In others, many children go to schools outside the district because of integration or choice programs, or they attend private or parochial schools. Some schools also enroll a large number of students who do not live in the neighborhood. The issue is whether services will be available and accessible to children and families who need them.

Regulations: Schools and other agencies are sometimes subject to baffling and conflicting facilities regulations. In California, for example, schools are subject to a much stricter set of seismic safety standards than other buildings. Only buildings meeting these standards may be used by children during school hours. Medical facilities are subject to another set of regulations to be eligible for federal and state funds to reimburse the cost of services. There may be other important regulations in your area. A thorough check of applicable regulations is an important part of deciding where to locate services.

In the best scenario there are strong connections between schools and families, increasing the likelihood that families will actually use the new services in the school building when they are needed. In some communities, schools may not be the most convenient sites for bringing services together for families. Alternately, families, for various reasons, may not feel all that closely connected to community schools; indeed, they may feel alienated from them. In many communities in North Carolina, busing and school consolidation for the purposes of desegregation interrupt the tradition of neighborhood schools, which, in turn, displaces schools as a community center.

In short, it makes sense to bring services together where the families live who will use the services. Although in many communities schools may offer the best answer, in their absence, care should be taken to identify a location that is convenient and comfortable. Regardless of the site in question, the most critical factor in determining whether or not families use needed services is that they do not feel stigmatized or embarrassed. If a more distant site offers a more warm and welcoming atmosphere for families, that site offers a better chance of working for families than a convenient location that no one will use.

ABOUT SCHOOLS: WHAT'S NEEDED?

Our research identified certain areas of concern that are common to all five agencies involved in the local communities: Schools, Mental Health, Social Services, Health Services and Juvenile Services. Careful study of the summaries reveals some areas that may be of particular interest to schools. Although the mission statements of many schools are based on the belief that all children can learn well, complicated problems make it more difficult to reach many young people. Hopefully, shedding light on some of the perceived breakdowns will lead to better understanding of the nature of the problems and ultimately to more lasting solutions. The following list presents some of the more critical "needs" that schools must acknowledge if they are to be more fully integrated into the service delivery system.

1. *Increased access to teachers and student support personnel in schools.* The teacher is highly valued by all agencies and by parents both in understanding the nature and scope of a young person's needs and in being part of the day-to-day working for progress toward solutions. In fact, when other agencies do not gain easy access to teachers in order to give and receive information about shared clients, they believe this barrier to limit the degree of achievable success with the client. Agency workers and parents also view student support personnel as valuable contributors of information and as important links between the home, the school and other agencies working with the family. Addressing this need requires the following changes:

> *Time in daily schedule for teachers to work with other agencies concerning shared clients:* Teachers often do not have released time in their daily schedules to meet with parents or workers from other agencies. Further, teachers are generally not routinely available after school hours or during summers. Teachers feel torn during the little planning time they may have during the school day to address the primary expectation in their job to teach school.

Teachers viewed as front-line workers, "in the loop" with other caseworkers: Other agencies view teachers as the "front-line workers" comparable to their case workers. However, in the organization of schools, teachers often have limited involvement in cases. Teachers make initial referrals, but principals or other school staff manage the case after the initial referral. This is frustrating to workers from other agencies, because they view teachers as being vital to the case—giving and receiving information and guidance regarding what is in the best interest of the young person. Likewise, teachers often express the sense of being left "out of the loop," saying they are usually not involved in decisions about what happens to children after making the initial referral for assistance.

Increased involvement of student support personnel: In addition to teachers, workers from other agencies report that student support staff, including social workers, nurses, guidance counselors, and school psychologists, have limited involvement in cases because many of them are itinerant, serving several schools, or working part-time while covering an entire school district.

2. *Technology to foster accessibility and timely communication.* Accurate and timely information is a must when different agencies are working with the same client families. Technologies can, when properly applied, enhance a school's collaborative capability. These technologies include the telephone, computers, copiers, fax machines, electronic mail (e-mail), voice mail, and audio/video equipment. Technology cannot by itself cause collaboration, and thoughtless application might in fact hinder such attempts. However, appropriate technologies can vastly improve the chances of collaboration, whereas their absence can seriously hinder the work of those who serve children and families.

3. *Communication among providers about a child's life, both in and out of school.* The need for timely, effective communication is often just as much a barrier within schools as it is between schools and other human service agencies. Increased use of technology within and between schools, as well as with families, can greatly enhance service delivery to children. The stronger the family in supporting the child's needs at home, the better chance the child has of taking advantage of learning opportunities at school. Student support personnel often have access to specific and extensive evaluations of a student's educational, social, and health needs as well as family and school history that can provide valuable and necessary information to teachers and to other human service agencies as they work with families to design effective solutions. Teachers work with children on a daily basis and have important insights about children based on daily interactions and observations of students' work. Further, teachers and other school personnel are often able to meet children's learning needs more effectively when they understand more about what may be happening in

the child's life outside of school. Without all the pieces to the puzzle, a child's behavior can be misunderstood and misinterpreted, leading to serious consequences for the child, both in and out of school.

4. *A view of schools as open systems.* In general, the findings across the research indicate that our public schools are seen as closed systems as they relate to clients and other service agencies. Part of this perception stems from clients and other agencies viewing schools as handling problems with students internally through existing educational programs established within the school system. A large part of the perception may stem from barriers related to lack of time to meet with other agencies and lack of timely, effective communication about shared clients. Here are a few other related issues:

> *The view that schools tend only to address educational problems, not "root causes":* As the issue is further defined, the concern is that the educational needs of students but not the "root causes" of students' problems are addressed. From the point of view of families and other agency workers, many times schools do not have all the information about family circumstances that may be contributing to children's learning needs. Hunger, homelessness, family violence, parent unemployment and financial concerns can all be invisible to teachers who teach 30 to 150 students a day. However, without additional support children may experience difficulty in learning, achievement, motivation, and self-confidence.
>
> *Practices for schools to follow through with referrals of families to other agencies:* When problems are recognized, agencies and parents report that school personnel tend to make referrals informally or to rely on parents themselves to make their own connections with other agencies. This tendency often results in a breakdown for families when they do not follow through or when they are met with complicated agency requirements and language they do not understand. Unfortunately, when things get too complicated, many parents give up before getting needed assistance.

MOVING FORWARD: SCHOOLS THAT ARE "OF" THE COMMUNITY, NOT MERELY "IN" IT

Schools' responsibility to children is not met simply by providing a program that works pretty well with most children. It is met when the school, the home, and the community surround the child with the support needed for success. Connectedness in schools and communities helps prevent young people from feeling and being anonymous. Quite often, educational problems are merely symptoms of more complex or pervasive problems, often involving conditions in the child's family. From research and from daily life experiences the lessons are the same: Dealing with any problem separate from its more fundamental cause is short-sighted, leaving many needs unattended and possibly worsening over time.

Students and teachers are, for the most part, confined to the four walls of a classroom every day, isolated from others, lacking basic equipment like telephones, computers, and other forms of technology that enable and foster communication. The isolation of educators from other community agencies needs attention. For students, connections to the world outside the school can create powerful learning experiences. In addition, before-and after-school programs and year-round programs can create opportunities connecting learning to the "real world." These experiences can be for student enrichment, "catching up," or for learning programs designed on a smaller and more personal scale.

Even when school personnel address educational problems from a broader framework, needed services are not immediately available from any agency's standard menu of services. From the case studies in these six counties we found that problems leading to chronic conditions such as delinquency, poverty, alcohol and drug abuse, teen pregnancy, child abuse, inadequate housing and unemployment often go unattended because of the narrow range of services and limited resources available in most communities. When services are available, lack of transportation, childcare, and telephones are nearly always mentioned as serious barriers to service delivery.

Fulfillment of our commitment to children requires collaborative arrangements because the needs are too complicated and interrelated for schools, community agencies, or families alone to solve. We must be willing to address the roles of schools, community agencies, and parents, as well as turf and quality of care issues. We must address long-term financing so that we can see the ways to accomplish broad and permanent implementation of collaborative arrangements, instead of scattered pockets of hope. In some communities in North Carolina and around the nation, however, necessary conditions are being created to successfully implement collaborative service delivery among agencies. These communities invariably foster creativity and some risktaking, driven by a determination to offer more lasting solutions and a better quality of life for members of the community. It is common in these communities for individual citizens, not just agencies, to perform support functions and to serve as important links in the gaps that agencies do not fill. Ultimately what hinders or fosters collaboration is perception: perceptions about other agencies, perceptions about the right way to do things, and perceptions about the priority of client needs. Perceptions can be changed through experience and dialogue to increase understanding.

THERE ARE NO BOUNDARIES; WE MADE THEM UP

A young man recently delivered a powerful message to us when he said, "I wish you would look at me as someone who can do great things instead of someone you are preventing from becoming a delinquent." Creation of solutions that work must begin with putting the human face with the data and putting teachers together with other service providers. We must begin with the person in need and not the category of service. To assess and categorize people for their weaknesses is not helpful to them. We must begin to look for strengths.

Lisbeth Schorr (1988), director of the Harvard University Project on Effective Services, argues in her book, *Within Our Reach*, for breaking the cycle of disadvantage, saying that we know what needs to be done and we know how to do it. Her reviews of research led her to the following conclusions:

> Programs that succeed in helping the children and families in the shadows are intensive, comprehensive, and flexible. They also share an extra dimension, more difficult to capture: Their climate is created by skilled, committed professionals who establish respectful and trusting relationships and respond to the individual needs of those they serve. The nature of their services, the terms on which they are offered, the relationships with families, the essence of the programs themselves—all take their shape from the needs of those they serve rather than from the precepts, demands, and boundaries set by professionalism and bureaucracies. (p. 259)

We must be willing to say some uncomfortable things in order to identify and solve these complex problems. To get to core solutions that are lasting, we must tell the truth about where we are. Rarely are we encouraged to learn from our mistakes because we feel we must deny we have ever failed.

We must take great care to understand the nature of the problems and we must not be satisfied to aim our solutions at the symptoms. The rush to action can add to the problem if we do not understand the multi-facetedness and interrelatedness of the problems. However, we can no longer afford the programmatic solutions where we label the symptom, create a category for it, and think our work is done when the "fix" is in place. Fragmented, separately organized, physically scattered, and confusing services create serious barriers for school-age children, as do different eligibility rules and lack of communication between professionals.

We must be willing to wrestle with new definitions of leadership to distinguish it from authority so that leadership can be cultivated in all areas. Our services and our organizational structures must be redesigned to reflect that caring does not always equal money and poverty does not always equal ignorance or lack of ability. It is likely that not all leadership will be "shirt and tie," and not all leaders will be "well educated." We must make a place for our clients when the problems are defined in order to get beyond the "symptoms" and understand the true nature and extent of the problems so that solutions will work in their lives. It is imperative to recognize that regardless of how long or short a time the clients receive needed services, nearly all express a strong desire for self-sufficiency.

Most important, we must give things the *time* they need. Developing self-sufficiency within our organizations and our customers requires new ways of thinking and new ways of working together. It is most of all about developing trust and nurturing relationships. Those things require patience and commitment to be real about our solutions and to see situations through, all the way, until they work—and not to quit when things get tough.

References

Agranoff, R. (1985). Services integration is still alive: Local intergovernmental bodies. *New England Journal of Human Services, 5*(2), 16-25.

Beatrice, D.F. (1990). Interagency collaboration: A practitioner's guide to a strategy for effective social policy. *Administration in Social Work, 14*(4), 45-59.

Benson, J. K. (1975). The interorganizational network as a political economy. *Administrative Science Quarterly, 20,* 229-245.

Berger, P., & Luckmann, T. (1967). *The social construction of reality.* Garden City, NY: Anchor.

Berliner, A.K. (1979). Integrating child care services: Overcoming structural obstacles to collaboration of institutional and community agency staffs. *Journal of Sociology and Social Welfare, 6*(3), 400-409.

Brown, R.H. (1977). *A poetic for sociology.* Cambridge, England: Cambridge University Press.

Bruner, C. (1991). *Thinking collaboratively: Ten questions and answers to help policy makers improve children's services.* Washington, DC: Education and Human Services Consortium.

Children's Index. (1994). Raleigh: The North Carolina Child Advocacy Institute.

Daniels, M.S., & Bosch, S.J. (1978). School health planning: A case for interagency collaboration. *Social Work in Health Care, 3*(4), 457-467.

Edelman, P.B., & Radin, B.A. (1991). *Serving children and families effectively: How the past can help chart the future.* Washington, DC: Education and Human Services Consortium.

Douglas, J. (1976). *Investigative social research.* Newbury Park, CA: Sage.

Flaherty, E.W., Barry, E., & Swift, M. (1978). Use of an unobtrusive measure for the evaluation of interagency coordination. *Evaluation Quarterly, 2*(2), 261-273.

Flynn, C.C., & Harbin, G.L. (1987). Evaluating interagency coordination efforts using a multidimensional, interactional, developmental paradigm. *Remedial and Special Education (RASE), 8*(3), 35-44.

Gans, S.P., & Horton, G.T. (1975). *Integration of human services: The state and municipal levels.* New York: Praeger.

Glaser, B. , & Strauss, A. (1967). *The discovery of grounded theory.* Chicago: Aldine.

Goldman, H.H. (1982). Integrating health and mental health services: Historical obstacles and opportunities. *American Journal of Psychiatry, 139*(5), 616-620.

Guthrie, G.P., & Guthrie, L.F. (1991). Streamlining interagency collaboration for youth at risk. *Educational Leadership, 49*(1), 17-22.

Heintz, K. (1976). State organizations for human services. *Evaluation, 3,* 106-10.

Hooyman, N.R. (1976). The practice implications of interorganizational theory for services integration. *Journal of Sociology and Social Welfare, 3*(5), 558-564.

Iles, P., & Auluck, R. (1990). Team building, inter-agency team development and social work practice. *British Journal of Social Work, 20*(2), 151-164.

Kids Count Data Book. (1994). Washington, DC: Annie E. Casey Foundation and the Center for the Study of Social Policy.

Knott, J., & Miller, G. (1987). *Reforming bureaucracy: The politics of institutional choice.* Englewood Cliffs, NJ: Prentice-Hall.

Leideman, S., Reveal, E., Rosewater, A., Stephens, S.A., & Wolf, W.C. (1991). *The Children's Initiative: Making the system work. A design document for the Pew Charitable Trusts.* Bala Cynwyd, PA: Center for Assessment and Policy Development.

Lewis, K.A., Schwartz, G.M., & Ianacone, R.N. (1988). Service coordination between correctional and public school systems for handicapped juvenile offenders. *Exceptional Children, 55*(1), 66-70.

Lipsky, M. (1980). *Street-level bureaucracy.* New York: Russell Sage.

Lynch, E.C., Mercury, M.G., DiCola, J.M., & Widley, R. (1988). The function of a central referral system in interagency identification, eligibility, and service delivery: A case study. *Topics in Early Childhood Special Education, 8*(3), 86-97.

Martin, P.Y., Chakerian, R., Imershein, A.W., & Frumkin, M.L. (1983). The concept of "integrated" services reconsidered. *Social Science Quarterly, 64,* 747-763.

McGrath, M. (1988). Inter-agency collaboration in the All-Wales strategy: Initial comments on a vanguard area. *Social Policy and Administration, 22*(1), 53-67.

McNeely, R. L., Feyerherm, W.H., & Johnson, R.E. (1986). Services integration and job satisfaction reactions in a comprehensive human resource agency. *Adminstration in Social Work, 10*(1), 39-53.

Melaville, A.I., & Blank, M.J. (1991). *What it takes: Structuring interagency partnerships to connect children and families with comprehensive services.* Washington, DC: Education and Human Services Consortium.

Melaville, A.I., & Blank, M.J. (1993). *Together we can: A guide for crafting a profamily system of education and human services.* Washington, DC: U.S. Department of Education and U.S. Department of Health and Human Services.

Merriam, S.B. (1988). *Case study research in education: A qualitative approach.* San Francisco: Jossey-Bass Publishers.

Mittenthal, S.D. (1976). A system approach to human services integration. *Evaluation, 3*(1-2), 142-148.

Noblit, G., & Hare, D. (1988). *Meta-ethnography.* Newbury Park, CA: Sage.

Nordyke, N.S. (1982). Improving services for young, handicapped children through local, interagency collaboration. *Topics in Early Childhood Special Education, 2*(1), 63-72.

Patton, M.Q. (1990). *Qualitative research and evaluation methods.* Newbury Park, CA: Sage.

Roberts-DeGennaro, M. (1988). A study of youth services networks from a political-economy perspective. *Journal of Social Service Research, 11*(4), 61-73.

Schorr, L.B. (1988) *Within our reach: Breaking the cycle of disadvantage.* New York: Anchor.

Vander-Schie, A. R., Wagenfeld, M.O., & Worgess, B.L. (1987). Reorganizing human services at the local level: The Kalamazoo County experience. *New England Journal of Human Services, 7*(1), 29-33.

Weick, K. (1976). Educational organizations are loosely coupled systems. *Administrative Science Quarterly, 21*, 1-19.

Weiss, J.A. (1981). Substance vs. symbol in adminstrative reform: The case of human services coordination. *Policy Analysis, 7*, 21-45.

Wells, K., & Freer, R. (1994). Reading between the lines: The case for qualitative research in intensive family preservation services. *Children and Youth Services Review, 16*, 399-415.

Wimpfheimer, R., Bloom, M., & Kramer, M. (1990). Interagency collaboration: Some working principles. *Adminstration in Social Work, 14*(4), 89-102.

Yin, R.K. (1989). *Case study research: Design and methods.* Newbury Park, CA: Sage.

Zald, M.N. (1969). The structure of society and social service integration. *Social Science Quarterly, 50*(4), 557-567.

Author Index

Subject Index